Framed Visions

Social History, Popular Culture, and Politics in Germany
Geoff Eley, Series Editor

Framed Visions

Popular Culture, Americanization,
and the Contemporary German
and Austrian Imagination

GERD GEMÜNDEN

Ann Arbor

THE UNIVERSITY OF MICHIGAN PRESS

2001   2000   1999   1998   4   3   2   1

A CIP catalog record for this book is available from the British Library.

Library of Congress Cataloging-in-Publication Data

Gemünden, Gerd, 1959–
     Framed visions : popular culture, Americanization, and the
  contemporary German and Austrian imagination / Gerd Gemünden.
     p.   cm. — (Social history, popular culture, and politics in
  Germany)
     Includes bibliographical references and index.
     ISBN 0-472-10947-2 (acid-free paper)
     ISBN 0-472-08560-3 (pbk. : acid-free paper)
     1. Popular culture—Germany—American influences.   2. Popular
  culture—Austria—American influences.   I. Title.   II. Series.
  NX550.A1   G385   1999
  700'.943'0904—ddc21   98-25521
                                                                  CIP

Contents

Acknowledgments

As Theodor W. Adorno once remarked, "It is scarcely an exaggeration to say that a contemporary consciousness that has not appreciated the American experience, even in opposition, has something reactionary about it." Though Adorno did not know Frank Zappa, he may well have been thinking about him when he made this out-of-character statement because it captures Zappa's obstinate, oppositional, and irreducible music. If I had to name one single person who inspired me to write this book it would be Zappa whose lyrics made me fluent in English in all its lowly variations and whose music saved my life.

My fascination and obsession with things American thus began long before I ever set foot in this country; now that I've been an academic for many years here, it has become time to understand what 'Americanization' means. *Framed Visions* is the result of this effort and of many fortuitous encounters over the years with Zappa fans here and abroad (Kenn and Carol—stay in touch!).

It is also the result of the interest and support of friends, colleagues, the filmmakers and writers, and various institutions. A grant from the American Council of Learned Societies gave me time for research. Dartmouth College has also been generous in providing time off from teaching as well as financial and logistic support to pursue my research interests, including funding for conferences and guest speakers.

At the University of Michigan Press, editor Susan Whitlock has been a pleasure to work with.

Wim Wenders, Monika Treut, and Herbert Achternbusch took time out of their busy schedules and hectic lives to answer my questions.

Michael Töteberg opened the vaults of his Wenders archive; Patsy Carter and Marianne Hraibi at Baker Library managed to trace materials from even the skimpiest of reference; Jan-Christopher Horak at the Munich Film Museum screened hard-to-see Achternbusch films for me; Tim Gemünden and Martin Spitta had their fingers on the recording buttons of their VCRs when it mattered.

David Bathrick, Bruce Duncan, Michael Ermarth, Werner Hoffmeister,

Andreas Huyssen, Jeff Peck, Ulli Rainer, Heide Schlüpmann, Marc Weiner, and Rolf Wiggershaus commented on individual chapters of this study, as did the members of the 1996 Dartmouth Humanities Institute on Cultural Memory, organized by Jonathan Crewe and Leo Spitzer. I also profited from the anonymous (and not-so-anonymous) readers who read the manuscript, or parts of it, for various journals, my tenure review, and the Press.

Several friends and colleagues read the manuscript in its entirety: Eric Rentschler helped me strengthen my argument and gain a better sense of coherence; Karla Schultz challenged me to modify my "straw-target-use" of Adorno; Al LaValley offered many suggestions for nuancing my description of Hollywood, drawing my attention to unknown and exciting materials; Susanne Zantop provided critical insight and rigorous editing with an enthusiasm most people reserve for their own work; Alice Kuzniar showed me how to be a fan and an intellectual at the same time.

With Susanne and 1/2 Zantop, Al LaValley, Irene Kacandes, Leo Spitzer and Marianne Hirsch, Carol Bardenstein, and Diana Taylor and Eric Manheimer I've been fortunate to have friends with whom to share my fascination for the intersection of European and American literature and film. The pride they take in their work has helped me gain a sense of what it means to be an academic in the United States. Their friendship and support also helped me survive the challenges of New England rural life.

Finally, there is my family (on both sides of the Atlantic) who made my work both possible and meaningful: my parents, Änne and Karl Gemünden; my brothers and sister, cuñados y cuñadas, nephews and nieces; my sons Lou and Sean; and Silvia, always my first reader, in more sense than one. From her, I learned not only about literary transculturation but also about the transcultivation of life. To her I dedicate this book.

Portions of this book have appeared previously. They have all been revised for inclusion in this book.

Chapter 2 appeared as "The Depth of the Surface, or, What Rolf Dieter Brinkmann Learned from Andy Warhol," *German Quarterly* 68.3 (1995): 235–50. Reprinted by permission of *German Quarterly.*

Chapter 4 appeared as "Re-Fusing Brecht: The Cultural Politics of Rainer Werner Fassbinder's German Hollywood," *New German Critique* 63 (1994): 55–77. Reprinted by permission of *New German Critique.*

Chapter 6 appeared as "Travelling Subjects, Moving Images: Peter Handke's America," *Seminar* 26.1 (1995): 32–49. Reprinted by permission of *Seminar.*

Chapter 7 appeared as "Oedi-pal Travels: Gender in the Cinema of Wim Wenders" in *The Cinema of Wim Wenders: Image, Narrative, and the Postmodern Condition,* ed. Roger Cook and Gerd Gemünden (Detroit: Wayne State UP, 1997) 205–21. Reprinted by permission of Wayne State University Press.

CHAPTER 1

Framed Visions: An Introduction

This book is a study about the relationship of two cultures—that of the United States and of (West) Germany and Austria—as manifested in the films, novels, plays, and poems of the generation of German and Austrian intellectuals born between 1938 and 1946 (with the notable exception of Monika Treut, who was born in 1954), whose sense of personal and national identity was shaped in complex and contradictory ways by both the popular culture of the United States, with which they grew up in the 1950s and early 1960s, and a critique of that culture in the works of the Frankfurt School, which exerted its greatest political influence as they came of age in the late 1960s.[1] The forms of cultural transfer described in this book have to do with the appropriation and transformation of images *of* and *from* America by German and Austrian writers and filmmakers. In a more general sense this book is also a study about the relationship between one set of texts and images and another. Let me begin, therefore, with the description of an American painting and an analysis of what certain German language poets, novelists, film directors, and screenwriters saw in it.

"Nighthawks": Fathoming the Sensibilities of the 1970s

> If you could say it in words, there'd be no reason to paint.
> —*Edward Hopper*

Edward Hopper's famous painting "Nighthawks" (1942) is a nocturnal scene of three solitary figures sitting in an all-night diner. Jo Hopper described the canvas at length in her husband's notebook:

---

1. Let me point out that for the sake of my argument I largely disregard the historic and cultural differences between the two nations. This lack of differentiation is legitimized because, in the context of my study, the similarities between postwar West Germany and Austria clearly outweigh the differences. The two Austrian writers I consider here in detail, Peter Handke and Elfriede Jelinek, spent much of the 1970s and 1980s living in Germany and actively engaging in German cultural politics, while Bavarians such as Achternbusch and Fassbinder have often felt much closer to Austria than to many parts of Germany.

Night and brilliant interior of a cheap restaurant. Bright items: Cherry wood counter and tops of surrounding stools; lights on metal tanks at rear right; brilliant streak of jade green tiles ¾ across canvas—at base of glass of curving window and counter. Light walls, dull yellow ochre door into the kitchen right. Very good looking blond boy in white (coat, cap) inside; nighthawk (beak) in dark suit, steel gray hat, black band, blue shirt (clean) holding cigarette. Other figure dark sinister back—at left. Light sidewalk outside pale greenish. Darkish old red brick houses opposite. Sign across top of restaurant, dark—Phillies 5¢ cigar, picture of cigar. Outside of shop dark green. Note bit of bright ceiling inside shop against dark of outside street at edge of stretch of top of window.[2]

As Jo Hopper's description makes clear, the powerful effect the painting has on the viewer is created by its use of contrast—the brightly illuminated interior is set off against a darkened exterior space. Within the restaurant a harsh, direct light shines down on the four characters, further enhanced by its reflection in the polished surface of the counter, the tile, and the towering metal containers in the back. The nonexpressive faces of the four people bespeak their isolation: the bar man gazes past the two men at a dark wall outside; the man smoking a cigarette seems absorbed in his thoughts, while the woman next to him eats a sandwich in silence. Significantly, their hands, though close together, do not touch. The third man turns his back to the viewer, and his face remains invisible, just as the other guest's face is obscured by the shadow of his wide-rimmed hat. Although bathed in light, the guests retain their anonymity. Outside, the light emanating from the diner forms a rectangular pattern on the wall of the house across the street, thus repeating the contrast of dark and light of the interior space. Small triangles of well-lit spaces alternate with dark windows and doorways. The precise geometric formations of the illuminated spaces contribute to a sense of abstraction that also pervades the relations of the four characters. They seem to be arranged, immobile, static. The composition creates the feeling of a sinister and nightmarish place, a place of stagnation and immense isolation but also of latent violence and threat of action. Looking from the dark into the light, the viewer assumes the position of a voyeur who clandestinely observes a drama yet to unfold.

Going beyond the mere act of observation, Wolf Wondratschek animates "Nighthawks" in a homage to Hopper's painting:

Nighthawks
After Edward Hopper's Painting

It is night
and the city is deserted.

---

2. Quoted in Gail Levin, "Edward Hopper's 'Nighthawks,'" *Arts Magazine* 55.9 (1981): 154.

The lucky ones are at home,
or more likely
there are none left.

In Hopper's painting, four people remain
the usual cast, so-to-speak:
the man behind the counter, two men and a woman.
Art lovers, you can stone me
but I know this situation pretty well.

Two men and one woman
as if this were mere chance.
You admire the painting's composition
but what grabs me is the erotic pleasure
of complete emptiness.

They don't say a word, and why should they?
Both of them smoking, but there is no smoke.
I bet she wrote him a letter.
Whatever it said, he's no longer the man
who'd read her letters twice.

The radio is broken.
The air conditioner hums.
I hear a police siren wail.
Two blocks away in a doorway, a junkie groans
and sticks a needle in his vein.
That's how the part you don't see looks.

The other man is by himself
remembering a woman,
she wore a red dress, too.
That was ages ago.
He likes knowing women like this still exist
but he's no longer interested.

What might have been
between them, back then?
I bet he wanted her.
I bet she said no.

No wonder, art lovers,
that this man is turning his back on you.[3]

---

3. Nighthawks
    nach Edward Hoppers Bild

    Es ist Nacht
    und die Stadt ist leer.
    Die Glücklichen sind zu Hause
    oder, noch wahrscheinlicher,
    es gibt keine mehr.

    Auf Hopper's Bild sind vier Menschen übriggeblieben,
    sozusagen die Standardbesetzung:
    der Mann hinterm Tresen, zwei Männer und eine Frau.
    Kunstfreunde, Ihr könnt mich steinigen,
    aber diese Situation kenne ich ziemlich genau.

    Zwei Männer und eine Frau,
    als ob das ein Zufall wäre—
    Ihr bewundert den Bildaufbau,
    mich packt das Lustgefühl einer vollkommenen Leere.
    Geredet wird nichts, was auch?
    Beide rauchen sie, aber nirgendwo Rauch.
    Ich wette, sie hat ihm einen Brief geschrieben.
    Was auch immer drin stand, er ist nicht mehr der Mann,
    ihre Briefe zweimal zu lesen.

    Das Radio ist kaputt.
    Die Air-condition dröhnt.
    Ich höre das Heulen einer Polizeisirene.
    Zwei Ecken weiter steht im Hauseingang ein Fixer,
    stöhnt und sticht sich eine Nadel in die Vene.
    So sieht das aus, was man nicht sieht.

    Der andere Mann ist allein
    und erinnert sich an eine Frau,
    auch eine in einem roten Kleid.
    Es ist eine Ewigkeit her.
    Es gefällt ihm, daß es solche Frauen noch gibt,
    aber es interessiert ihn nicht mehr.

    Wie könnte es damals
    zwischen ihnen gewesen sein?
    Ich wette, er wollte sie haben.
    Sie sagte, ich wette "Nein".
    Kein Wunder, Kunstfreunde,
    daß dieser Mann euch den Rücken zudreht.
    (Wolf Wondratschek, *Die Gedichte* [Zurich: Diogenes, 1992] 450f.)

The subtitle, "after [*nach*] Edward Hopper's painting," invokes the source of Wondratschek's poem and also names the mode of adaptation: the story that the poem extracts from the painting is fashioned both *according to* and *after* Hopper's work, using it as inspiration for a verbalized image that is to be continued or brought to an end in the poet's imagination. The creative tension between mere description of the painter's work and fictitious rewriting by the poet is established in the first stanza, in which the first two verses evoking the emptiness of an urban night are quickly supplemented by the more interpretive thought that the lucky ones, if there are any left, are all at home. The poem then proceeds to trace the course of events that has brought together the people in the diner, the "Übriggebliebenen," or last ones. The ensuing fictional account provides the background story of the three customers. It opens with the dramatic conflict at a climax before a lengthy flashback fills in the developments that lead to it. Assuming that the triangular situation of two men and a woman is no accident, the lyric "I" fantasizes about what brought them to the diner and what their respective histories might be. The man and the woman sitting next to each other are seen as an estranged couple; she has written him a Dear John letter, and he is a broken man who no longer has the energy to read her letters twice. The flamboyant woman in red makes the second man reminisce about a woman he once knew ages ago, and even though this woman turned him down he is pleased to see that such women still exist. The lyric "I"'s knowledge of the characters and their respective lives is underscored several times by the phrase "I bet," suggesting that the familiarity with their situation is based on the "I"'s own experiences. The term *standard cast* describing the quartet of the man behind the counter and his three customers indicates, however, that this is less of a personal experience than one of reading of fiction or visits to the playhouse and the movie theater. The three are seen as types, not individuals, an interpretation that finds further proof in the aforementioned tendency toward abstraction in the painting.

Whereas Wondratschek's poem "Nighthawks" dramatizes the question of what has happened to lead to the situation depicted in the painting, the filmmaker Wim Wenders and the writer Peter Handke have been inspired by Hopper's paintings (including "Nighthawks") to pursue the question: what will happen next in this image? Handke has described his fascination with Hopper's paintings by saying that in them he found "the home of the hero of a yet to be written story."[4] In a similar vein Wenders has explained that Hopper's paintings suggest the beginning of a story: "There is this famous painting of a New York street with a barber shop in the middle . . . The painting is at the Whitney Museum in New York. I often went there. Every time I thought, next time I'll get there the painting will have changed: perhaps somebody will be just crossing the street. It is a painting where you expect a

---

4. Peter Handke, *Die Lehre der Sainte-Victore* (Frankfurt am Main: Suhrkamp, 1984) 17.

certain movement; something will change, for instance the light. It is a painting on hold [*in Wartestellung*]."[5] The proximity of Hopper's paintings to narrative noted by Wenders and Handke—respectively, a painter turned filmmaker and a writer frequently involved in filmmaking—evokes the feeling of still photographs from films. Like stills, Hopper's paintings suggest movement not only because they momentarily arrest the action, but they also capture the very movement of observing the unfolding drama. This freeze-frame-like quality characterizes much of Handke's prose as well as the poetry of Rolf Dieter Brinkmann, whose collected poems significantly bear the title *Standphotos* (still photographs).

If for Handke and Wenders Hopper's paintings provide the site where stories can begin, it needs to be added that it is a particular kind of story that they associate with them. Talking about Hopper's "Gas" (1940), Wenders said: "A car is about to drive up to the gas station with someone behind the wheel who has a gun shot wound in his stomach."[6] The proximity of Hopper's paintings to narrative means for Wenders, as well as for Handke and Wondratschek, the proximity to a story of crime, suspense, or urban melodrama. This relation is also explored by five screenwriters, Jürgen Egger, Günter Schütter, Christof Schlingensief, Matthias Selig, and Sherry Hormann, whose short scripts (written for a special issue of *Der Spiegel* commemorating the hundred-year history of film) rewrite "Nighthawks"—significantly described by the editors as "the most famous bar scene [*sic!*] in the world."[7] The scripts sometimes parody the conventions of detective thrillers or film noir—in Schlingensief's outrageous version the latent violence of Hopper's nocturnal scene turns into a chainsaw massacre that claims the lives of the most prominent German film critics and producers—but they all convincingly suggest that their plot is already prefigured in Hopper's painting.

The association between a thriller and "Nighthawks" is not surprising, for, as one critic pointed out, it is very likely that the painting itself was inspired by a story whose main ingredient is crime and suspense: Ernest Hemingway's "The Killers."[8] Hopper was familiar with Hemingway's short story—he complimented the editor of *Scribner's* for its publication—and the setting and the mood of Hopper's paintings offer striking resemblances to the story, which is also set in a diner at dusk and begins like this: "Outside it was getting dark. The street-light came on outside the window. The two men at the counter read the menu. From the other end of the counter Nick Adams watched them." Like the guests in "Nighthawks," the two killers in Hemingway's story "sat leaning forwards, their elbows on the counter."[9] The quali-

---

5. Wim Wenders, *The Act of Seeing: Texte und Gespräche* (Frankfurt am Main: Verlag der Autoren, 1992) 171.
6. Ibid.
7. *Spiegel Spezial* 12 (1994): 125.
8. Cf. Levin 156f.
9. Ernest Hemingway, *The Complete Short Stories* (New York: Scribner, 1987) 215f.

ties of Hemingway's story that Hopper praised in his letter to the editor such as the complete lack of "concessions to popular prejudices, the side stepping of truth, and the ingenious mechanism of trick ending"[10] are also visible in his own painting, which celebrates the harsh reality of urban America. As in "The Killers," violence is impending but never actually takes place. As Gail Levin has pointed out, the fact that Hopper preferred the title "Nighthawks" over the more innocuous "Nightowls" shows further that he was interested in portraying not just people up and moving about late at night but precisely their predatory activity.[11]

Wondratschek, Handke, and Wenders share a fascination with how Hopper's art foregrounds the tension between drama and still-life, between narrative and image, and between the visual and the verbal in general. As the respective chapters on Handke and Wenders show in more detail, this tension lies at the center of their aesthetics but also of that of most other authors discussed in this study; it can perhaps be singled out as one of the most pervasive and imaginative aesthetic concerns in contemporary German literature and film. What further unites these authors is the fact that the images in which they are interested generally come from the United States and that they are mostly associated with contemporary popular culture such as Hollywood film, film noir, B-pictures, but also Pop art, comics, advertisement, pornography, and everything else that makes up the iconographic quality of today's American mythology.

In this respect the discussion of Edward Hopper seems somewhat out of place. Hopper, after all, was born in 1882 and died in 1967, that is, before most artists of the generation under discussion had emerged with their first work. In fact, Handke, Wenders, and Wondratschek were not even born when "Nighthawks" was painted. Furthermore, Hopper was openly hostile toward his contemporaries such as the Expressionists, Cubists, and Abstract Expressionists and other movements representing the spirit of modernism, and his work showed little of the avant-gardism that first fascinated young Austrians and Germans. Nor was his work part of the youth culture of American and British rock music, experiments with drugs, and flower child culture that heavily influenced the Austrian and West German formation of an alternative culture, or *Subkultur,* in the late 1960s. If Hopper is situated here in the larger context of the European reception of postwar American popular culture, this has to be seen in terms of what Ernst Bloch called *Ungleichzeitigkeiten* (nonsynchronisms)[12]—in this case, a mode of appropriation that combines elements from different temporal and spatial contexts and which is characteristic not only of Hopper's reception by the aforementioned artists but generally describes the kind of cultural transfer analyzed in this study.

---

10. Quoted in Levin 156.
11. Ibid.
12. Cf. Ernst Bloch, "Non-Synchronism and the Obligation to Its Dialectics," *New German Critique* 11 (1977): 22–38.

This nonsynchronism is constituted by the fact that, for Handke, Wenders, and Wondratschek, Hopper's work formed part of Pop art's backlash against the elitism and esoteric quality of high modernism and of a general trend toward infusing high art with elements of popular culture. (The fascination with Pop art that exemplifies these modes of reception is discussed in detail in chaps. 2 and 3.) In this context Hopper's portrayals of cityscapes and the everyday suddenly showed great affinities to Pop art's return to realism. Like Pop, Hopper's canvases of restaurants, gas stations, movie theaters, and hotel lobbies demonstrated an interest in the iconography of contemporary America. Pop art and Hopper's shared concern with popular culture is per- haps best expressed in Gottfried Helnwein's painting "Boulevard of Broken Dreams" (now widely reproduced as a poster and on T-shirts), a parody of "Nighthawks" in which Hopper's four strangers have been replaced by James Dean, Humphrey Bogart, Marilyn Monroe, and Elvis Presley as bar boy— Hopper's urban realism of angst and alienation meets Pop art's fetishization of the star. Alongside Pop art's defense of the trivial and the banal, Hopper's paintings were suddenly understood in Germany as part of a counter-, or anti-, art that challenged dominant modes of reception of art and even the definition of what art ought to be. This interpretation of Hopper is especially obvious in Wondratschek's poem. Here, the "I" sets himself off from the art lovers who contemplate Hopper's paintings for purely aesthetic reasons. For the "I" their formalist interest in the "composition" (*Bildaufbau*) deprives art of its immediacy and energy; as the concluding verses of the poem suggest, the man who turns his back to the viewer does so perhaps not only because of a frustrated love affair but because he is disgusted with the aestheticizing approach of contemporary art criticism. For Wondratschek's "I" Hopper's painting is primarily a defense of the vitality of art, and the real hawks threat- ening to kill their prey may well be the museumgoers eager to devour indis- criminately any kind of artistic representation.[13]

For Wondratschek, in contrast, the value of art is a different one. Con- sider what the "I" experiences when looking at Hopper's painting: "I am seized by the erotic pleasure / of complete emptiness." This erotic pleasure of the complete vacuum refers to the subject of the painting: to the estranged relations of the guests in the diner, to the abandoned dark streets of urban America, to the alienation ruling contemporary life, to the elimination of meaning and the celebration of nihilism. But it also describes the viewer's mode of experience. For it is indicative that the pleasure of the abyss can only be a pleasure afforded to the spectator, to a voyeur who watches while remaining unobserved. It is in this context, then, that the parallel to cinema becomes most obvious: being a spectator in the movie theater affords the

---

13. Wondratschek's image of junkies in dark entries offers a striking example of how the West German 1970s intrude into and dehistoricize the American 1940s. And, of course, there was no air conditioning in restaurants at that time.

spectator the same kind of protection of being seated in the dark and watching a drama unfold as the viewer of Hopper's painting.

Hopper's affinity to film is appealing to Wondratschek, Handke, and Wenders not only because it foregrounds their own interest in the tension between spatial and temporal arts but also because it contributes to the blurring between high art and mass medium. As is well-known, Hopper himself was an avid consumer of popular culture and a regular moviegoer, and at certain stages in his career he even drew movie posters.[14] As "Nighthawks" indicates, he was well aware of the functions of stage design and lighting and the cinematic devices of framing and editing. The format of the painting (33¼ × 60 in.) deliberately imitates that of wide-screen film projection. As Erika Doss has shown, gangster films of the early 1930s including *Little Caesar* (1930), *Public Enemy* (1931), and *Scarface* (1932), with their awareness of urban culture and social constrictions, are reflected in many of his works. "Nighthawks" in particular resembles the look of these movies and their characters—from the stiffly cut, cubical suits and the rigidly angular hats of the male customers that resemble the style and tenacious square poses of James Cagney and Edward G. Robinson to the "typical Hollywood gangster women [who] were sleazy and blowzy, like Jean Harlow in *Public Enemy*. They dressed in loud, tightly fitting clothes, enameled their nails, dyed their hair, and chain-smoked cigarettes, like the red-haired floozy pictured in 'Nighthawks.'"[15] Like these films, Hopper was interested in creating certain types that would be easily recognized by the viewer. As he explained, his painting was "suggested by a restaurant on Greenwich Avenue where two streets meet. 'Nighthawks' seems to be the way I think of a night street. I simplified the scene and made the restaurant bigger."[16] It is this simplification that allowed Hopper to paint a diner whose iconographic qualities capture the transformation of an entire country from the 1930s to the 1940s.

But, more than being an imitator of these images, Hopper should be seen as anticipating and inspiring later film directors and filmmaking techniques. The early etching "Night Shadows" (1921), for example, contains motifs such as the strange high-angle, dark shadows cast by a roof and lamp post and the lonely man in a deserted street that would become the trademark of film noir of the late 1940s and 1950s. Many directors of these hard-boiled narratives of solitary detective work, ill-fated romance, aimless travel, or psychological suspense found inspiration in Hopper's urban landscapes. For them his

---

14. For Hopper's relation to theater and film, see Gail Levin, "Edward Hopper: The Influence of Theater and Film," *Arts Magazine* 55 (1980): 123–27; Erika L. Doss, "Edward Hopper, 'Nighthawks,' and Film Noir," *Post Script* 2.2 (1983): 14–36; Marc Holthoff, "Die Hopper-Methode: Vom 'narrativen' zum 'abstrakten' Realismus," *Edward Hopper 1882–1967* (Frankfurt am Main: Schirn Kunsthalle, 1993) 19–27.

15. Doss 24. The fact that John Dillenger was turned in by the woman in red provides another association with a gangster scene.

16. Katherine Kuh, *The Artist's Voice: Talks with Seventeen Artists* (New York: Harper, 1972) 134.

sceneries became scenarios. Direct influences where paintings were used for certain sets or shots may be traced from "House by the Railroad" (1925) to Hitchcock's *Psycho* (1960) and Terrence Malick's *Days of Heaven* (1978), from "Nighthawks" and "New York Movie" (1939) to Herbert Ross' *Pennies from Heaven* (1981), and from "Approaching the City" (1946) to Wenders's own *Alice in the Cities* (1973).[17] Wenders has cited the paintings of Hopper as models for his thriller *The American Friend* (1970);[18] here his presence is felt both in the look of individual shots as well as the overall ambiance of the film, and even in the plot, which revolves around a supposedly dead painter forging his own works. A shot in *Reverse Angle* (1982) shows "Morning in a City" (1944); and his first feature film, *Summer in the City*—which, according to Wenders, took its title from a song by the Lovin' Spoonful—may well be an illustration of Hopper's painting by that name (1949), since the film turns around the impossibility of relationships, especially between men and women, in urban West Berlin. In Wenders's recent film, *The End of Violence* (1997), Hopper's *Nighthawks* has been reconstructed as a movie set for an American thriller directed by a European *auteur*—the latest, and most self-reflexive quoting of Hopper in what has been a life-long fascination with the American painter.

Hopper's tendency to paint objects, people, and buildings with the "eye of the camera" is a further important link to his proximity to cinema. Often his paintings depict angles only imaginable from a mounted camera ("Night Windows" [1928]; "Office in a Small City" [1953]) or the glimpse of a passerby, as in "Nighthawks" or "New York Office" (1962), that evokes the feeling of a traveling shot or a dolly shot. His fascination with trains and railroads, which he shares with Wenders, can be explained in this cinematic context, for looking out of a train compartment creates the same sensation of the rolling-by of framed images as a visit to the movie theater. Like going to a movie, traveling on a train endlessly rehearses the clashing of masses and anonymity, of spurious encounters with people on the screen or behind the glass panel, of a solitary experience shared with many.

Hopper's most abstract paintings, such as "Rooms by the Sea" (1951)

---

17. Cf. also Peter Schjedahl, "Hopperesque," in *The Hydrogen Jukebox: Selected Writings of Peter Schjedahl 1978–1990*, ed. Malin Wilson (Berkeley, Los Angeles, and Oxford: U of California P, 1991) 293–99; and Celia McGee, "Hopper, Hopper, Everywhere," *New York Times*, 24 July 1994, 1 and 33. More recently, the Whitney Museum of American Art curated the exhibit "Edward Hopper and the American Imagination" (from June 22 to October 15, 1995). As an example of Hopper's influence on music, see—or listen to—Tom Waits's album *Nighthawks at the Diner* (Elektra / Asylum Records, 1975).

18. *Die Logik der Bilder: Essays und Gespräche*, ed. Michael Töteberg (Frankfurt am Main: Verlag der Autoren, 1988) 120. In a recent review Wenders called Hopper's paintings the model for many shots ("Vor-Bilder für viele Einstellungen") of *The American Friend*. Wenders here plays on the double meaning of *Einstellung*, which translates not only into "shot" but also "attitude," thus implying that Hopper's presence is felt both before and behind the camera ("Der Sonnenfleck wandert. Und die vierbändige Werkausgabe zeigt: Edward Hoppers Gemälde sind Einzelbilder des amerikanischen Traums," *Die Zeit*, April 5, 1996, 28).

Shades of noir in Edward Hopper's etching *Night Shadows* (1921)

and "Sun in an Empty Room" (1963), which focus exclusively on the composition of light and space, entertain obvious similarities to Wenders's short
films and their minimalist narratives but also to the so-called pillow shots of
Yasujiro Ozu (a director whom both Handke and Wenders but also Herbert
Achternbusch avidly admire). Like the paintings, these shots often depict
empty rooms, still-lives of urban settings, clothes drying in the breeze, or, as
in Handke's film *The Left-Handed Woman,* the withering of grass as a train
passes by. These shots have no function in the diegesis of the film but serve as
moments of contemplation and reflection—much as one stops to look at a
painting or a photograph. To emphasize the transitional aspect of this experience, both Hopper and Ozu gave many of their works names of seasons or
certain times of the day.

  Hopper's paintings are attractive for Wondratschek, Handke, and Wenders because his foregrounding of the tension between image and story, or
between the arrested image of a painting and the moving image of a film, is
related to their own interest in fusing high art and popular culture. His proximity to cinema and to Pop art makes him, at least in their eyes, an elective
affinity with an aesthetic agenda similar to their own. The sense of being
directly addressed by Hopper is especially prevalent in Wondratschek's poem

"The paintings of Edward Hopper are also beginnings of stories."—Wim Wenders

Detective Doc Block (Loren Dean) meets stuntwoman Cat (Traci Lind) on the Hopper-inspired set of the film within the film in *The End of Violence.* (Publicity still, Stiftung Deutsche Kinemathek Berlin.)

in which the "I"—which we may see as a thinly disguised stand-in for the author[19]—recognizes a situation he "knows pretty well." Significantly, the experience of the "I" when looking at Hopper's "Nighthawks" is one of "erotic pleasure." Wondratschek's emphasis on erotics echoes Susan Sontag's call for "an erotics of art" with which she wanted to replace the hermeneutics of suspicion as the dominant approach for understanding literary and artistic works. As she argued in her 1964 essay "Against Interpretation," the traditional task of interpretation was to resolve the discrepancy between the meaning of a work and the demands on the recipient, but in contemporary criticism interpretation has contributed to making art manageable and conformable, amounting "to the philistine refusal to leave the work of art alone."[20] Sontag continues that the answer of much of contemporary art,

---

19. Cf., for instance, Wondratschek's statement about going to a bar, which recalls the opening lines of the poem: "I've never gone to a bar just for pleasure. If I want pleasure I stay home or visit with friends. What forces me into a bar is despair—the despair of the entire earth" (*Menschen, Orte, Fäuste: Reportagen und Stories* [Zurich: Diogenes, 1987] 159).

20. Susan Sontag, "Against Interpretation," *Against Interpretation* (New York: Delta, 1966) 8.

including Pop art and the films of Raoul Walsh and Howard Hawks, to this interpretive practice has been to create works that do not rely on symbolism but, instead, present things as they are (or at least pretend to do so). The critic's main task thus is not to make sense out of something that would otherwise remain unintelligible but "to reveal the sensuous surface of art"[21]— precisely what Wondratschek's poem performs.

This tribute to the surface of things and to the imagistic and iconographic quality of life in general is ubiquitous in all works discussed in this study. Handke calls Hopper one of the painters "who led me away from mere opinions about the paintings and taught me how to consider them as examples and to respect them as works" in *Die Lehre der Sainte-Victoire,*[22] a book that, as so many of Handke's works, centers on the connection of visual experience and narrative.[23] Significantly, Hopper is situated here in a tradition that extends from Paul Cézanne to the "Master John Ford."[24] Wenders praises Hopper for his attention to details, which taught him that the film camera, too, "lets things appear as they are."[25] A recurring motif in Wenders's filmmaking and writing is the looking out of an open window or door. His review, "Van Morrison" (1970), combines a quote from the rock singer, "Open up the window / And let me breathe, let me breathe. / Looking down in the streets below, darling / I cried for you," with Wenders's drawing of a woman by a window, a variation of Hopper's "Morning in a City." The review praises Van Morrison's music for liberating his vision and creating a sense of what kind of experience the cinema could provide: "perception that doesn't always jump blindly at meanings and assertions, but rather lets your senses extend further and further."[26] This kind of liberation is clearly also associated with Hopper's art, whose recurrent depictions of open windows are understood by Wenders as metaphors for an unobstructed, authentic mode of perception. Again we notice that Hopper is read side by side with an exponent of popular culture, the rock singer Van Morrison. In the writings of Rolf Dieter Brinkmann the motif of the open door is also taken up. His poems reiterate the mistrust in verbal communication and favor the embracing of the surface of things advocated by Handke and Wenders. Though Brinkmann makes no mention of Edward Hopper, the sources for his interest in the open-door-motif resemble Wenders's and Handke's conflation of

21. Ibid. 13.

22. *Die Lehre der Sainte-Victoire* 25.

23. For a detailed analysis of the relation between narrative and painting in this text, see Ingeborg Hoesterey, *Verschlungene Schriftzeichen: Intertextualität von Literatur und Kunst in der Moderne/Postmoderne* (Frankfurt am Main: Athenäum, 1988) 101–29.

24. *Die Lehre der Sainte-Victoire* 42.

25. Wim Wenders, "Reverse Angle: NYC March '82" (director's original voiceover); reprinted in Roger Cook and Gerd Gemünden, eds., *The Cinema of Wim Wenders: Image, Narrative, and the Postmodern Condition* (Detroit: Wayne State UP, 1997) 42–44.

26. Wim Wenders, *Emotion Pictures: Essays und Filmkritiken* (Frankfurt am Main: Verlag der Autoven, 1986) 71.

Wim Wenders, *Morning Sun* (1970)

high and low as they range from William Blake's doors of perception and René Magritte's surrealism through Aldous Huxley's experience with drugs and the American rock band the Doors.

Common to Wenders, Wondratschek, and Handke (but also to Brinkmann and Achternbusch and to a lesser degree to Monika Treut) is an anti-intellectual and antitheoretical sensibility that favors experience over meaning and sensuality over sense. In polemic renunciation of the critical discourse then dominant that taught to be suspicious of appearances, these artists hold that the surface *can* be trusted. Since the reception of images is more sensual than intellectual, "the hunger for experience," a term Michael Rutschky coined to describe the 1970s, can best be satiated in the movie theater: "It became more and more obvious during the 1970s that what mattered in the cinema was to see, not to interpret. The hunger for experience is stilled by what the cinema makes visible, and not by the meaning suggested through the plot."[27] We may add that for Wenders, Handke, and Wondratschek, as well as for most other artists discussed in this book, the hunger for experience

27. Michael Rutschky, *Erfahrungshunger: Ein Essay über die siebziger Jahre* (Cologne: Kiepenheuer and Witsch, 1980) 214.

can also be satisfied by looking at paintings—especially when these paintings look like films.

Yet the antitheoretical stance of many contemporary German writers and filmmakers is not without conceptual coherence, just as their claim to realism relies on *particular* representations of reality. Hopper's paintings are embraced so wholeheartedly by these artists precisely because of their icono-graphic and mythical dimension. "Nighthawks" is a painting that depicts in very clear terms a familiar situation; it would be hard to be more direct about it—and yet the painting is enigmatic and challenges us to wonder about what has happened or will happen. In the words of J. A. Ward, it is "a realism of possibility, not probability."[28] Just as in the hard-boiled detective fiction of Dashiell Hammett and Raymond Chandler, which Wenders, Handke, and Wondratschek admired, simplicity and obviousness create a dramatic mys-tery. Reviewing an exhibit of Hopper's painting in West Germany in 1981, the critic Karl-Heinz Bohrer attempts to explain the overwhelming success of Hopper's art with German audiences by saying that "never before did the time seem so ripe for the emotional message and the mythological language of his classic paintings from 1927 and 1965."[29] Hopper's paintings stylize loneliness to such a proportion that they no longer merely reflect its social or political roots but turn loneliness into a myth. It is this mythological aspect of Hopper's art—so prevalent also in Hollywood cinema, hard-boiled detective fiction, and even Pop art, where it is playfully subverted—that appeals directly to a German sensibility eager to rewrite its own cultural traditions.

But why was the time so ripe? To address this question we have to situ-ate the list of negotiations, borrowings, and adaptations between Hopper and certain film directors and writers, the interpretations and interdependencies of their artistic sensibilities, in a larger historical and theoretical framework in order to contextualize this cultural transfer. Having established one of the main aesthetic concerns that informs the works analyzed in this study—the creative exploration of the tension between image and narrative as part of a larger development to infuse high art with elements of popular culture—I will now turn to a discussion of the historical determinants of this concern and then place it within the debate about the significance of popular culture in postmodern art and society.

Historicizing Imaginary America

> The need to forget 20 years created a hole, and people tried to cover this
> . . . in both senses . . . by assimilating American culture. . . We covered it
> with chewing gum. And Polaroid pictures.
>
> —*Wim Wenders*

---

28. J. A. Ward, *American Silences: The Realism of James Agee, Walker Evans, and Edward Hopper* (Baton Rouge and London: Louisiana State UP, 1986) 174.

29. "Die neue Kultfigur: Edward Hopper," *Frankfurter Allgemeine Zeitung,* March 30, 1981, 12.

The reception of Edward Hopper by German language writers and filmmakers addresses aspects of cultural transfer around which all analyses in this volume revolve: the Americanization of West Germany and Austria after World War II. Discussions of this topic by historians and social scientists have traditionally focused on how German and Austrian culture, society, politics, and economics have been shaped by the United States ever since the Allies first established their presence in that country.[30] Typically, these have been ideologically charged debates about the benefits and damages of the imposition of one culture over another. While supporters point to the spirit of freedom and democracy celebrated in American popular culture, to its promotion of progress and economic prosperity, to the celebration of the young and the new—thereby often making Americanization a synonym for modernization itself—detractors are critical of the "leveling-down" effect of popular culture, its tendency to homogenize, its negligible artistic and educational value, its commercial takeover of art. For them America is a country without history and therefore without culture. What these debates indicate more than anything else is that *Americanization* is a loaded term that designates much more than just the mapping of influence of one country over another. Discussing Americanization in Austria and West Germany, and also in the unified Germany, means taking issue with a variety of problems and open questions, including the value of Western democracy, capitalism, national identity, cultural autonomy, and so forth. My own discussion of Americanization attempts to disentangle at least some of this conundrum. It is confined to Austrian and (West) German literature and film after 1968 and thus concentrates on the two most important realms of cultural production in the period following the student protest movement. With the recent unification of Germany this period has come to an end, as the significance of Americanization has come under scrutiny in light of new emerging problems: the opening of Germany and Austria toward the East; the relocation of a unified Germany in a larger (West) European context; and renewed discussions about German national identity.

In contrast to most discussions of Americanization, I do not want this term to be understood as a foreign principle imposed from the outside. Indeed, it must be asked to what degree the discourse of cultural imperialism, so prevalent among intellectuals during the late 1960s and after, should not be considered a particular German invention—an invention intended to legitimize certain "anti-imperialist" strategies that, when closely analyzed, reflect

---

30. Cf. Reinhold Wagnleitner, *Coca-Colonization and the Cold War: The Cultural Mission of the United States in Austria after the Second World War,* trans. Diana M. Wolf (Chapel Hill: U of North Carolina P, 1994). Many of the points made by Wagnleitner about Austria apply in equal measure to West Germany, despite the different histories of the two countries. That is also why I do not differentiate between the two countries' responses to what Wagnleitner calls Coca-Colonization, as I pointed out earlier.

a blindness of German intellectuals toward the complexities of their own national history or even a voluntary displacement of that history. As the chapter on the writer and filmmaker Herbert Achternbusch shows, the discourse of colonization is always entangled in strategies to claim victim status and thus in a refusal to assume responsibility for a future national and cultural identity.

No matter how real or imaginary, it is certain that Americanization (or American cultural imperialism) is far from being a unified or unifying process. In Germany and Austria it has triggered a wide variety of responses, and my focus will be on how filmmakers, poets, novelists, and playwrights have appropriated U.S. culture in their own works—fusing and refusing, using and abusing, forming and transforming, it in order to create a hybrid and genuine form of artistic expression. My line of inquiry is informed by a number of scholars who have all insisted that an emphasis on the creativity of reception deflects monolithic accounts of one culture imposing on another. In her study on Latin American transculturation, Silvia Spitta has shown how Latin American cultures radically transformed, displaced, and subverted Spanish, and later U.S., cultural impositions. These re-semanticizations have produced a hallucinatory overlapping of different cultural codes and meanings that call for double and at times mutually exclusive readings of what is apparently a unitary sign or symbol.[31] Since many artists under discussion here perceive of themselves as "colonized" by the United States, this theory of colonization has obvious bearings when studying the presence of American culture in Germany and Austria, even if questions of cultural imperialism have to be seen in their specific historical context.[32] Focusing on the realm of reception and consumption of popular culture, Michel de Certeau has shown how consumers and users of culture can become something like "poachers." By employing an "art of practice" that consists of strategies and tactics through which they "do" or "make" something with the objects and messages they receive or consume, users are able to leave behind their status as passive recipients.[33]

This emphasis on the productivity of reception has also been advocated by Dick Hebdige, who, in *Subculture: The Meaning of Style* and *Hiding in the Light: On Images and Things,* explores how working-class youths in postwar England appropriated the wide variety of offerings of the British and American culture and consumer industries to piece together their own "personal"

31. Silvia Spitta, *Between Two Waters: Narratives of Transculturation in Latin America* (Houston: Rice UP, 1995).

32. For a helpful discussion of the complexities of the notion of cultural imperialism, see John Tomlinson, *Cultural Imperialism: A Critical Introduction* (Baltimore: John Hopkins UP, 1991).

33. Michel de Certeau, *The Practice of Everyday Life,* trans. Steven F. Rendall (Berkeley: U of California P, 1984).

style.[34] As Hebdige points out, American popular culture, including Hollywood cinema, pulp fiction, images from advertising and fashion, music, cult of the beautiful body, offers British youths "a rich iconography, a set of symbols, objects and artefacts which can be assembled and re-assembled by different groups in a literally limitless number of combinations. And the meaning of each selection is transformed as individual objects—jeans, rock records, Tony Curtis hair styles, bobby socks, etc.—are taken out of their original context and juxtaposed against other signs from other sources."[35] While the quest of the counter- or subculture to create new meaning is circumscribed by the original meanings of the found objects, it is possible to highlight contradictions and paradoxes of the culture industry. In contrast to Hebdige's emphasis on working-class youths, in *No Respect* Andrew Ross points to how the last generation of American intellectuals has shown a decidedly different approach to popular culture than previous ones. They no longer abide by the polarized view of popular culture as, on the one hand, aesthetically inferior to European taste or, on the other, useful to raise political consciousness but, rather, understand popular culture as a wide and contested field where the institutionalization and commercialization of knowledge does not necessarily seal the fate of political criticism.[36] Before turning to a more theoretical discussion of the "creativity of consumption" (Ross) that informs the various confrontations with American popular culture reflected in the literary and cinematic texts discussed here, we have to sketch how American mass media and popular culture have shaped the political, social, and psychological identity of the generation of Germans and Austrians under discussion.

America has always claimed a privileged space in the German imagination, both as a promising new habitat and a literary topos. From Goethe to Kafka and beyond there is hardly a major writer in the German language who did not at some time or other address this topic. As Goethe wrote in 1827: "America, you're better off than / Our continent, the old. / You have no castles which are fallen / No basalt to behold. / You're not disturbed within your inmost being / Right up till today's life / By useless remembering / And unrewarding strife."[37] Like Goethe's poem, most contributions to this subject

---

34. Dick Hebdige, *Subculture: The Meaning of Style* (1979; rpt., London and New York: Routledge, 1991); and *Hiding in the Light: On Images and Things* (London and New York: Routledge, 1988).

35. *Hiding in the Light* 74.

36. Andrew Ross, *No Respect: Intellectuals and Popular Culture* (London and New York: Routledge, 1989).

37. J. W. Goethe, "To America," trans. Stephen Spender, in *The Permanent Goethe,* ed. Thomas Mann (New York: Dial, 1948) 655. The original German reads: "Amerika, du hast es besser / Als unser Kontinent, das alte, / Hast keine verfallene Schlösser / Und keine Basalte. / Dich stört nicht im Innern / Zu lebendiger Zeit / Unnützes Erinnern / Und vergeblicher Streit" (*Sämtliche Werke,* vol. 2: *Gedichte, 1800–1832,* ed. Karl Eibl [Frankfurt am Main: Deutscher Klassiker Verlag, 1988] 739).

typically revolve around the promise of a better life. For most writers America stands for political, social, and religious freedom, economic prosperity, progress, democracy—or for the flip side of this optimism: disappointment, disillusion, despair. The titles of two nineteenth-century novels, Ernst Willkomm's *Die Europamüden* (1838) and Ferdinand Kürnberger's *Der Amerika-Müde* (1855), illustrate well the narrow confines and strict dichotomy of the topic for Germans.[38]

As we know, none of these authors ever set foot on the American continent. This cautions us not to consider their representations of the United States at face value. In fact, in most texts about this topic we learn more about the authors and their particular psychological, social, and historical disposition than about the object they "describe." For many America quite obviously serves as a counterimage to a specific state of things at home. But, even where the writings are based on personal experiences such as prolonged stays, extensive travels, or briefer more touristic visits, the United States often function as a catalyst that sets in motion the exploration not of a foreign country but of the visitors themselves. Most works considered in this study stress this imaginary role America fulfilled in the minds of their authors—a playground for the imagination and a site where the subject comes to understand itself through constant play and identifications with reflections of itself as an other.[39] Handke's novel *Short Letter, Long Farewell*, for instance, demonstrates how America serves as a specular medium for the protagonist, who is primarily concerned with his self-image and the pleasure of recognizing sights familiar from their reproductions. The films of Werner Herzog and Herbert Achternbusch also feature protagonists whose imported conflicts and preoccupations are intensified by an exotic-absurdist American West and Midwest. For Monika Treut's respective female protagonists America emerges as the space of a postpatriarchal sexual liberation denied at home. My concern in this study is not to judge the merit of these literary and filmic representations by their realism (although the pretentiousness with which certain European intellectuals pass themselves off as "America

---

38. The representation of America in German literature has been well explored. The following works provide comprehensive overviews and detailed analyses: Sigrid Bauschinger, Horst Denkler, and Wilfried Malsch, eds., *Amerika in der deutschen Literatur: Neue Welt—Nordamerika—USA* (Stuttgart: Reclam, 1975); Wolfgang Paulsen, ed., *Die USA und Deutschland: Wechselseitige Spiegelungen in der Literatur der Gegenwart* (Bern and Munich: Francke, 1976); Manfred Durzak, *Das Amerikabild in der deutschen Gegenwartsliteratur* (Stuttgart: Kohlhammer, 1979); Heinz D. Osterle, *Bilder von Amerika: Gespräche mit deutschen Schriftstellern* (Fulda: Fuldaer Verlagsanstalt, 1987); Heinz D. Osterle, ed., *Amerika! New Images in German Literature* (New York: Peter Lang, 1989); Hans Galinsky, *Amerikanisch-deutsche Sprach- und Literaturbeziehungen* (Frankfurt am Main: Athenäum, 1972); Alexander Ritter, ed., *Deutschlands literarisches Amerikabild* (Hildesheim: Olms, 1977); Alfred L. Cobbs, *The Image of America in Postwar German Literature: Reflections and Perceptions* (Bern: Peter Lang, 1982).

39. Cf. Eric Rentschler, "How American Is It? The U.S. as Image and Imaginary in German Film," *Persistence of Vision* 2 (1985): 5–18.

experts" after even the briefest of stays has been baffling).[40] Rather, I am interested in the historical and psychological ballast invested in these representations of America. Thus, my analysis follows Foucault's argument that discourses construct the object they describe. I thought it preferable therefore to use the term *America* rather than *United States,* even if this means applying the name for an entire continent to designate only one of its countries. *America* here has to be seen as an intertext—that is, as a common denominator for a variety of discourses and textual references dealing with the New World, North America, and the United States. This intertext *America* has to be understood as a complex signifier and contested textual construct that is subject to historical change. Most authors discussed in this study have foregrounded the constructedness of their object of inquiry. This awareness, I would claim, distinguishes them from many of their predecessors; it has its origin in their extraordinary sensitivity to the productive power of images, which in turn is connected to their (American) image-dominated postwar upbringing. Wim Wenders, for instance, has stressed that "AMERICA / always means two things: / a country, geographically, the USA, / and a concept of this country, its ideal."[41] And while touring the United States in 1977, Wolf Wondratschek said "I'm in the United States for the first time, but I've been to America many times."[42]

The statements by Wondratschek and Wenders point to the peculiarity of postwar Germany and Austria, when the influx of American culture and consumer goods reached heretofore unparalleled dimensions. America became something like second nature: foreign and exotic and, at the same time, thoroughly familiar and familial.[43] Yet, contrary to accounts that claim a decisive rupture between postwar Germany and preceding historical periods (also prominent with some of the authors under discussion here), it has to

---

40. A telling example of this kind of writing is Hans Christoph Buch, *Der Herbst des großen Kommunikators: Amerikanisches Journal* (1986), a cliché-ridden diary based on a two-month stay in New York City during the fall of 1984. Uwe Johnson (whom Buch unsuccesfully seeks to emulate in his diary) has described the temptation of superficial understanding in the following words: "During my first stay in America in 1961, I made the common mistake to not understand anything during the first week, to understand almost everything during the second week, and by the end of the third week I was sure I had America, or at least North America, in my pocket. That's the point in time when most people write their America book, or at least their America stories. I was fortunate enough to be allowed to stay on so I could get to the point where I didn't understand this country at all" (Uwe Johnson, "Einführung in die *Jahrestage,*" in *Johnsons Jahrestage,* ed. Michael Bengel [Frankfurt am Main: Suhrkamp, 1985] 15–27; here 17).

41. *Emotion Pictures* 142.

42. *Menschen, Orte, Fäuste* 270.

43. Detailed accounts of postwar influence of the United States in Germany are given in the following: Ralph Willett, *The Americanization of Germany, 1945–1949* (London and New York: Routledge, 1989); Kaspar Maase, *BRAVO Amerika: Erkundungen zur Jugendkultur der Bundesrepublik in den fünfziger Jahren* (Hamburg: Junius, 1992).

be stressed that the Americanization that began in the mid-1940s has important parallels in the early twentieth century and that, already then, the image of this country was tied to its self-representation in its popular culture. Already in the 1920s discussions about modernity, democracy, and technological progress but also about film and art were fought out with reference to the model of the United States. The fixed set of stereotypes that had determined Germany's image of America at least since the mid-nineteenth century (best exemplified in the novels by Willkomm and Kürnberger) was now rearticulated and contested as the traditional understanding of the role of art in society was challenged by the "spirit of America." American cinema, jazz, the Charleston, boxing, and spectator sports flooded Germany and were enthusiastically welcomed by Germans eager to put behind their recent military past. Particularly the movies celebrated ideas of consumption and material abundance, and Charlie Chaplin became the icon of a truly democratic and egalitarian culture.[44] As Anton Kaes has shown, it was especially the intellectuals who understood American mass culture "as a modern folk culture that grew out of the needs of large urban masses . . . the Berlin avant-garde saw American mass culture as a vehicle for the radical modernization and democratization of both German culture and life."[45] American mass culture was pitted against the traditional bourgeois notions of a German *Kulturnation;* Dada saw in it an ally to challenge the institutionalization of art that endowed art with an autonomy that rendered it politically irrelevant. The technological optimism of Brecht and Benjamin that hoped to enlist film in the revolutionary struggle would have been impossible without the presence of American film. (As I show in more detail in my chapter on Fassbinder, this enlisting of film in the service of a social and political agenda also informs the New German Cinema of the 1970s.) Yet by the mid-1920s a noticeable shift in the image of America took place. The avant-garde became disenchanted with the mass culture of jazz, sports, and cinema as its progressive potential became increasingly streamlined according to the laws of capitalist production. Instead, America now connoted technology and industrial rationalization. The American economy became a model for an ailing German industry. It was then that Julius Hirsch coined the term *Wirtschaftswunder* to describe how the United States was able to recover from a severe depression. The fact that we now use it to designate the miraculous postwar recovery of West Germany—which, in turn, was largely due to the U.S. Mar-

---

44. The fascination with Chaplin by writers during both the Weimar Republic and postwar years is documented in the literary anthology *Das Kino im Kopf,* ed. Hans Stempel and Martin Ripkens (Zurich: Arche, 1984) 173–204.

45. Anton Kaes, "Mass Culture and Modernity: Notes toward a Social History of Early American and German Cinema," in *America and the Germans: An Assessment of a Three-Hundred-Year History,* 2 vols., ed. Frank Trommler and Joseph McVeigh (Philadelphia: U of Pennsylvania P, 1985) 2:323. The following remarks retrace Kaes's analysis.

shall Plan—may be the best indicator of the continuities of Germany's perception of the United States from the 1920s to the 1950s and beyond.[46]

Contrary to common belief, the American influence in Germany did not end with the Nazi's rise to power. While Goebbels was eager to ban jazz and other "decadent extremes" of the "Jewish-Negro conspiracy," the positive, dynamic, and egalitarian image associated with America held sway. Coca-Cola, always a symbol for how successful the United States was in penetrating a foreign market and culture, flourished during the 1930s despite official disapproval, and Hollywood stars could be seen on German movie screens until the United States entered the war in 1941. Ufa (Universum-Film Aktiengesellschaft) films from the 1930s through the mid-1940s tried to imitate the stars, styles, and plots of Hollywood cinema, which was both its most important role model and its hardest rival for the domestic market.[47]

When after the war America established its presence in Germany again, first in the Allied Occupation Zone and then in the Federal Republic, the pattern of influence and cultural transfer that had dominated the 1920s and 1930s was taken up again—including the debates about the implications of imported or imposed notions of democracy, politics, and culture. Yet, as Frank Trommler has pointed out, in contrast to earlier periods, postwar American involvement in German affairs was much more comprehensive and political dominance absolute. "With the onset of the Cold War between the United States and the Soviet Union, a new political identification process was set in motion, which pointed beyond national borders and pitted the so-called West, including the western part of Germany, against the so-called East, including the eastern part of Germany."[48] The eagerness to put a difficult past behind (similar to the situation after World War I), particularly much of the inhuman dealings with the East during the war, paved the way for Adenauer's broad commitment to Westernization. The reconstruction of capitalism went hand in hand with American cultural imperialism. American reeducation taught Germans the values of democracy, but even more decisive was the influence of American popular culture in shaping an eagerness to identify with the United States. For, while the Americans had not really gained a say in how to reform the German school system, they did succeed in imposing an American model for the rebuilding and restructuring of crucial institutions of mass communication, the radio, and the press. It was through these channels

---

46. Cf. Trommler, "The Rise and Fall of Americanism in Germany," *America and the Germans* 335.

47. For a detailed account of the marketing of Coca-Cola in postwar Germany, see Willett. For an analysis of popular culture in the Third Reich, see Eric Rentschler, *The Ministry of Illusion: Nazi Cinema and Its Afterlife* (Cambridge: Harvard UP, 1996); and Lutz Koepnick, "Unsettling America," *Modernism/Modernity* 2.3 (1995): 1–22. For a discussion of jazz between repression and co-optation in the regime, see Michael H. Kater, *Different Drummers: Jazz in the Culture of Nazi Germany* (New York: Oxford UP, 1992); and Bernd Polster, "*Swing Heil*": *Jazz im Nationalsozialismus* (Berlin: Transit, 1984).

48. Trommler 2:339.

that adolescent Germans came to idolize Elvis Presley, James Dean, and Marlon Brando. The wholehearted embrace of this popular culture has to be seen as part of a generational opposition against the problematic past of their fathers and mothers. To be sure, not all of the culture enlisted in the service of reforming the German soul can be called popular culture. Writers such as Ernest Hemingway, Ambrose Bierce, J. D. Salinger, Jack London, John Steinbeck, and Thornton Wilder were widely read or performed on the German stage. But their inspiration was largely taken up by members of the Gruppe 47, a group of authors a decade or more older than the generation under discussion here. Writers like Siegfried Lenz or Heinrich Böll were interested in creating a German version of the American short story, while Max Frisch sought to adapt Wilder's dramatic techniques for his own playwrighting. For those born during the war or later it was primarily American popular culture that mattered—or a popularized version of high culture, as, for instance, in the film adaptations of Hemingway's stories or in appreciation of Edward Hopper as elective affinity to Pop art. As Trommler underscores, this generation's approach to American popular culture showed an "almost existential identification" that clearly distinguished it from earlier periods in German history.[49]

Thus, while certain continuities between the 1920s and the late 1940s and 1950s exist, the latter period presents the problem of Americanization with added complexities. What is new here is that an entire generation—roughly those born after 1938—was brought up with American popular culture from its members' earliest childhood on. This generation is characterized by particularly complex and contradictory attitudes toward the culture and politics of the United States—complexities that only became apparent when this generation came of age in the late 1960s. Since the Americans liberated Germany from fascism—something the Germans had failed to do themselves—the Germans had internalized the American model to the point of siding with them against themselves. Thomas Elsaesser has compared this state of mind to what psychologists call the Stockholm Syndrome, in which "hostages become grateful to their captors for not exercising their power over life and death . . . [I]magine watching a Hollywood film, dubbed into German, where the audience saw John Wayne speaking impeccable stage-German fighting fiendish Germans speaking German with foreign accents. Who, in the audience, would not rather be American?"[50]

After 1968 the student protest movement inaugurated in Germany a tense debate about issues of German identity, its past, capitalism, and the relation of art to politics. In this debate it became apparent that America had mapped itself in complex ways over specifically German problems. The

---

49. Ibid. 2:341.

50. Thomas Elsaesser, "Germany's Imaginary America: Wim Wenders and Peter Handke," in *European Cinema Conference Papers,* ed. Susan Hayward (Birmingham: Aston UP, 1984) 32.

voices in this debate displayed a paradoxical attitude toward American politics and the country's popular culture: on the one hand, an attraction toward a culture that had been decisive in furnishing and shaping childhood images, tastes, and desires and, on the other hand, a rejection of American politics and the colonizing effect of its mass culture. Wenders, for instance, has explained how rock music offered him an alternative to all the *Kultur* forced on him in his youth. Because for him traditional German culture was stigmatized by fascism, rock 'n' roll expressed his generation's opposition to the past. Not only for Wenders but for many of his generation, popular culture corresponded to psychic needs at a time of cultural pessimism and historical skepticism. The writer Jörg Fauser laments that German culture had little to offer but good intentions:

> When I started to write, German literature wanted to be still more reasonable than it had already been. It set out to improve the world. At that time there wasn't a single interesting German language writer. They all were incredibly optimistic, obnoxiously well-intended, and extraordinarily caring about their profession. They and their productions had nothing to do with how I lived (and I certainly wasn't the only one). Our life style [*Lebensgefühl*] was determined by America even though we had never been there and had no intentions of going there.[51]

Fauser's targets are the members of the Gruppe 47, including Heinrich Böll, Siegfried Lenz, and Günter Grass, whose relentless probing into the German past may have made them models of moral integrity but whose works came up second to those American products that celebrated hedonism, consumerism, and the joy of life.[52] While the older generation was attracted to Hemingway's tales of war, fear, loneliness, and alienation as experiences that resounded with their own attempts to understand the incomprehensible, the younger writers and filmmakers made it clear that they could not get satisfaction from the efforts of the Gruppe 47 "to produce literature like others produce Volkswagens."[53]

Clearly, one has to distinguish the generation of artists under discussion here, all born between 1938 and 1946 (with the exception of Monika Treut, who was born in 1954)—Wim Wenders, Rainer Werner Fassbinder, Peter Handke, Wolf Wondratschek, Werner Herzog, Herbert Achternbusch, Wolf-

---

51. Jörg Fauser, *Blues für Blondinen: Essays zur populären Kultur,* ed. Carl Weissner (Frankfurt: Rogner and Bernhard bei Zweitausendeins, 1990) 43. This essay dates from 1979.

52. More than a decade earlier, in 1966, Peter Handke had attacked the members of the Gruppe 47 by saying that these writers had forgotten "that literature was made through language, not through the things which were described with language" (*Ich bin ein Bewohner des Elfenbeinturms* [Frankfurt am Main: Suhrkamp, 1972] 29). While Handke's call for more formal self-reflexivity has little to do with Fauser's call for being more contemporary, both challenged what they perceived to be the group's monopoly on literature.

53. Wondratschek, *Menschen, Orte, Fäuste* 278.

gang Bauer, Elfriede Jelinek, Rolf Dieter Brinkmann, Hans Christoph Buch, Marianne Rosenbaum, Botho Strauß, Jörg Fauser, Werner Schroeter—from writers like Martin Walser, Günter Kunert, Wolfgang Koeppen, Max Frisch, Uwe Johnson, and filmmakers like Alexander Kluge, Edgar Reitz, and Hans Jürgen Syberberg, whose works also deal extensively with the presence of American culture and politics but who were already adolescents when American troops first appeared in Germany.

The experience that brought into focus this generational gap was the Vietnam War. It was then that the American model of freedom and democracy that had thoroughly shaped the 1950s and mid-1960s came under scrutiny. As had always been the case in the long history of German-American relations, it was a military issue that caused the pendulum between pro- and anti-American sentiments in Germany to swing; more recently, it was the deployment of cruise missiles in the 1980s, the so-called *Nachrüstungsbeschluß,* and the Gulf War that divided German intellectuals. The Vietnam War caused the strongest swing of the pendulum, and it showed that the watershed between pro- and anti-American sentiments had less to do with politics—most authors discussed here would situate themselves on the Left in a very general sense—than with age.

Yaak Karsunke (born 1934) recapitulates in his autobiographic poem "Kilroy was here" (1967) his generation's childhood memories of the American occupation at a moment when the positive associations with things American take a dramatic turn, as the U.S. wages war in Vietnam:

Kilroy was here

> when I was 11
> "Kilroy is here"
> was written on the broken walls
> on collapsed pillars
> on tables in bars, on toilets
> the amis wrote it everywhere
>
> when I was 11
> my sisters wore red skirts
> my mother herself had
> taken off the white circle
> with the four times broken
> cross & burnt it
> now kilroy was here
>
> when I was 11
> the war was over & "Hitler kaput"
> like the houses the windows the jews

& germany (what was that?)
instead kilroy had come
taught us basketball
& chewing gum & cocacola

when I was 11
Kilroy taught me words like fairness
& democracy
slogans like never again war
he showed me jitterbug
& even Shakespeare sonnets
with a brooklyn accent

when I was 11
these were three golden words
"Kilroy is here"
almost as beautiful as the three
of the french revolution
about which he was talking
liberty & equality & fraternity

when I was 11
my parents
had raised me the wrong way
Kilroy was patient
to explain to me the human rights
& the uno charta
to re-educate me

when I was 11
Kilroy was the best
friend I had
his house was always open for me
in the basement
I listened to jazz & Stravinsky

:much of this was left behind
—years later—
when Kilroy boarded his plane
loaded it up with napalm & disappeared
now you can read on the pagodas
& on the smoking black remnants of villages
"Kilroy is here"

—we
are through with one another[54]

54. Kilroy war hier

als ich 11 war stand
"Kilroy ist hier"
auf den geborstenen mauern
auf gestürzten säulen
auf kneipentischen in klos
die amis schrieben
es überall hin

als ich 11 war trugen
meine schwestern rote röcke
den weißen kreis mit dem vierfach
gebrochenen kreuz
hatte meine mutter selber
abgetrennt & verbrannt
jetzt war Kilroy hier

als ich 11 war war
der krieg aus & "Hitler kaputt"
wie die häuser die fenster die juden
und deutschland (was war das?)
dafür war kilroy gekommen
brachte uns basketball bei
& kaugummi & cocacola

als ich 11 war lehrte
mich Kilroy worte wie fairneß
& demokratie
parolen wie nie wieder krieg
brachte mir jitterbug bei
& selbst an den Skakespeare-Sonnetten
noch den brooklyn-akzent

als ich 11 war waren
das drei goldene worte
"Kilroy is here"
fast so schön wie die drei
der french revolution
von der er erzählte
freiheit & gleichheit & brüderlichkeit

als ich 11 war hatten
meine eltern
/ mich falsch erzogen
Kilroy gab sich die mühe
erklärte mir die menschenrechte
& uno-charta
erzog mich um

The poem paints an impressive portrait of the immediate postwar situation in Germany as experienced by an eleven-year-old: a country and people in shambles, eager to forget and put behind twelve years of fascism and to accept wholeheartedly the culture of the liberator. Especially the children and teenagers are susceptible to the materialistic wealth, the new culture of jazz, jitterbug, and rock 'n' roll, and to the teachings of democracy and human rights that come with it. No longer a bomb shelter, the basement is now a place to enjoy this new material and intellectual freedom and a genuine friendship is struck up—until, two decades later, the same soldiers that brought chewing gum and Coca-Cola invade Vietnam. The separation of this friendship is the consequence of a serious disenchantment as philo-Americanism turns into anti-Americanism. As Michael Rutschky writes:

The Americans introduced humanity, civilization, and democracy. With many people of my generation I shared the conviction that these imports were clearly superior to the domestic products. But this conviction was precisely what determined the passionate protest against the war in Vietnam: only a people that had experienced the Americans as generous liberators, and that had learned to love them could have been so shocked by the way the great, free United States of North America could torture a small Asian people in such a cruel fashion. It must have been the disappointed love affair, together with the new, blinding images of misery, which led to an outbreak of anti-Americanism that could find no limit to unmasking that the "free and great America" was actually a phantasm— and thus everything else it ever taught us about humanity, civilization, and democracy.[55]

---

als ich 11 war
war Kilroy der beste
freund den ich hatte
sein haus stand mir offen
in seinem keller
hörte ich jazz & Strawinsky
& keine sirenen

:viel von dem blieb zurück
—jahre später—
als Kilroy sein flugzeg bestieg
es mit napalm belud & verschwand
jetzt steht auf pagoden
& den rauchschwarzen resten von dörfern
"Kilroy is here"

—wir
sind geschiedene leute
      (Yaak Karsunke, *Kilroy und andere* [Berlin: Wagenbach, 1967] 65f.)

55. *Erfahrunghunger* 192f.

Karsunke's and Rutschky's disenchantment with America is reiterated in a series of works published in the late 1960s and early 1970s about the U.S. involvement in Vietnam, ranging from Erich Fried's *und Vietnam und* (1966) and Peter Weiss' *Viet Nam Diskurs* (1968) through Reinhard Lettau's *Täglicher Faschismus: Amerikanische Evidenz aus 6 Monaten* (1971). What is most revealing about these texts is the way in which Americanization is linked to an assessment of the German's own past: American imperialism in Vietnam is seen as parallel to German fascism. In an open letter resigning from a scholarship at Wesleyan University in 1968, Hans Magnus Enzensberger compared the American situation of the 1960s to that of Nazi Germany and found mind-boggling parallels in the way in which both governments employed racial discrimination and persecution, support of counterrevolutionary wars, and alarming increases in the armament budget.[56] This harsh indictment is indicative of at least two things: first, the sudden swing of the pendulum from pro-American to anti-American sentiment showed that the positive perception of the United States was conditioned, once again, more on German postwar necessity than on a realistic assessment of America's political interests; and, second, that the specter of fascism and the concomitant need to be antifascist is far from over. What is really at stake in the debate about Vietnam is not so much the politics of the United States but a self-definition of German intellectuals in regard to issues of national identity, capitalism, and pacifism—a question, as I show in the epilogue, that has posed itself with renewed urgency after German unification.

The experience of the Vietnam War also led to a critical reevaluation of America's politics during the immediate postwar years, and to a rewriting of the myth of the "Zero Hour" from a post-1968 perspective. With hindsight it became clear that the historic chance for a new beginning, for a "start from scratch" with a "clean slate," had been squandered; perhaps it had never really existed in the first place. The questioning of the past by the student protests revealed that the United States had been far less altruistic in its mission in Germany than they had suggested. It became obvious now that the Americans had been less propelled by humanitarian or democratic goals than by political, ideological, and economic ones. De-nazification, for instance, had soon been less important than industrialization in order to strengthen West Germany as a bulwark against the East. Two examples may illustrate the retrospective critique of America that resulted from this crude awaken-

---

56. Cf. Hans M. Enzensberger, "On Leaving America," *New York Review of Books,* 29 February 1968, 31–32. For a critical discussion of Enzensberger's letter, see Karla Lydia Schultz, "'Think: You Could Become an American': Three Contemporary Poets Respond to America," *Yearbook of German-American Studies* 23 (1988): 153–63; for a self-critique of Enzensberger, see also Karla Lydia Schultz, "A Conversation with Hans Magnus Enzensberger," *Northwest Review* 21.1 (1983): 145–46. For a discussion of "American Fascism," see also the conversation between Enzensberger and Herbert Marcuse, "USA: Organisationsfrage und revolutionäres Subjekt," *Kursbuch* 22 (1971): 45–60.

ing. In his film *Stunde Null* (1976) Edgar Reitz depicts the transitional period at the end of the war in a small German village near Leipzig when the Americans withdraw to let the Soviet Army take over. While for the majority of the population the arrival of the Russians brings fear of rape and plunder, the young protagonist experiences the Americans as the greater of the two evils: his grand expectations of the Americans are deeply disappointed when they take away his girl and his gun. This critical sentiment is amplified considerably in Reitz's television series *Heimat* (1984). In the episode "The American" we see Paul, who had emigrated to the United States in the 1920s, visiting his hometown in the Hunsrück after the war. Now a rich American who speaks his native German only with a thick accent and who jingles his coins in the belief that money can buy anything, Paul presents a stark contrast to the rural life he left behind, a *Weggeher* (someone who went away) who does not fit in anymore. America has also corrupted him emotionally; "a cold land," as his mother calls it, has made him a cold man. For Reitz America is a country that has taken away the Germans' national identity.

Even more disconcerting, perhaps, than these stereotypes of an Americanized German bereft of his identity is the fact that, in the inner logic of a film about German history from the 1920s to the 1980s, the United States, and not National Socialism, assumes the role of the scapegoat. For Reitz "the real terror" is American television—after all, *Heimat* was Reitz's effort to reclaim a history "taken away" by the American TV series *Holocaust*—and "the deepest loss"[57] one can suffer is the loss of one's language experienced by Paul. For Reitz the *Weggeher* is part of a *Wegwerfgesellschaft* (a consumer society producing garbage), the most extreme example of which is Auschwitz: human beings become refuse. According to this reasoning, the Holocaust is but an epiphenomenon of this greater story of loss, and the Jews, who are linked to the *Wegwerfgesellschaft* both by the fact that many of them live in the United States and by the archaic symbol of the Wandering Jew, are seen as the force that led to their own destruction.

For Hans Jürgen Syberberg, too, Hollywood and the American culture industry are just as much to blame for the demise of German art after the war as the legacy of Nazism. Indeed, at the root of what Syberberg perceives as the ongoing crisis of national and cultural identity lies Americanization. In his monumental film *Hitler, ein Film aus Deutschland* (*Our Hitler* [1977]) and his essayistic work we witness how, in sweeping generalizations, Americanism and Jewish intellectualism are blamed for the denigration and the abysmal state of contemporary arts and letters.

---

57. Edgar Reitz, *Liebe zum Kino: Utopien und Gedanken zum Autorenfilm, 1962–1983* (Cologne: Verlag Köln, 1985) 142. For a detailed analysis of Reitz's anti-Americanism, see Eric L. Santner, *Stranded Objects: Mourning, Memory, and Film in Postwar Germany* (Ithaca and London: Cornell UP, 1990) 57–102. The following remarks retrace Santner's analysis, based in part on his own interview with Reitz (cf. *Stranded Objects* 80f.).

During the late 1960s and 1970s this critique of the United States as cryptofascist was something one could find not only in Germany but all over the globe, including in the United States. Articulated from within West Germany, however, this critique became entangled in the specific problem of postwar Germany's efforts to come to term with the past. The comparison between U.S. atrocities in Vietnam and Germany's organization of the Holocaust established a parallel that served to alleviate some of the burden of guilt Germans felt weighing on their shoulders. If the Americans showed similar capabilities for murder as the Germans had four decades earlier, then the Holocaust could not be as uniquely German as had been claimed. Enzensberger's statement that "fascism is not horrible because the Germans practiced it, but because it is possible anywhere" served to blur the line between Nazism of the 1930s and everyday fascism. Similarly, Max Horkheimer's famous statement that those who speak about fascism may not be silent about capitalism, written in American exile, became for the 1968ers a legitimation to conflate the two terms. It is important to note that this critique is yet again a generational critique and therefore only rarely found among the intellectuals I discuss here: by indicting American fascism, Germans of the immediate postwar generation (ranging from those who were born in 1929, like Enzensberger and Walser, to Karsunke, who was born in 1934) were able to demonstrate an antifascism that they would have liked to demonstrate under Hitler, had they only been old enough. They were thus able to show their conformist parents what *they* should have done—thus pointing the accusing finger once again in their direction.[58]

If Syberberg blames the United States as the corruptor of young Germans by saying that "the chocolate of enlightenment out of the hand of the victor smudges the brain of the defeated,"[59] for the generation under discussion here, accepting Hershey Bars or chewing gum from American GIs never caused a problem. Marianne Rosenbaum calls it "Peppermint Peace." Clearly, the time span that separates the two generations—as with Karsunke and Wenders the difference can be sometimes merely a decade—marks a generational difference. In most of the works discussed in this study one will not find the anti-American sentiment of Enzensberger, Karsunke, Lettau, Reitz, and Syberberg, nor do we find the alleged parallels between German Nazism and U.S. fascism. Instead, the younger generation's critique of America takes on a very succinct form that relies less on judgment from above or outside but

58. An important exception is Uwe Johnson (1935–84), who, in his four-volume novel *Jahrestage* (1970ff.), gives a very differentiated account of the United States from 1967 to 1968. Johnson explicitly accuses Enzensberger of arrogance and elitism for his public resignation from the fellowship at Wesleyan University as well as Enzensberger's naive support of the Cuban revolution.

59. Hans Jürgen Syberberg, "Wie man neuen Haß züchtet: Eine Stellungnahme von Hans Jürgen Syberberg zu den Angriffen in dieser Zeitung," *Frankfurter Allgemeine Zeitung,* September 6, 1990, 36.

employs American genres, styles, and topics to address issues of Americanization *at home*. Fassbinder's *American Soldier* (1970), for instance, portrays the return of a Vietnam veteran to Munich, but virtually no reference is made to his experience in the war. Likewise, Handke' novel *Short Letter, Long Farewell,* an autobiographical account of a trip across the United States, makes no mention of Vietnam. Instead, both narratives focus on how America as imaginary construct can take on political proportions. It is the America in the mind that matters, not the America in the news. As Handke explained: "The words Hitler, Auschwitz, Lübke, Berlin, Johnson, Napalm bombs are too loaded with meaning, too political for me as if to make any innocent [*unbefangen*] use of them for the writing of literature. When I read these words in a literary text, no matter in which context, they remain ineffective . . . and they prevent me from thinking or associating."[60]

As I argue in this study, the generational experience determines the way in which these authors address the United States and its popular culture in order to make sense of their own identities. German artists born during the war or immediately thereafter find themselves in the paradoxical situation in which their critique of American culture is often articulated in the idiom of that culture; it therefore also entails a critical assessment of their *own* upbringing, childhood memories, and thus their selves. Their works therefore render the presence of American culture a complex and problematic phenomenon, dramatically oscillating between a profound philo- and anti-American stance, sometimes in one and the same work. While Wenders, for instance, in a famous statement considered rock music a "life-saver,"[61] it has also been cited, in an equally famous line by one of the characters in *Kings of the Road* (1976), as a form of "colonization of the subconscious." In contrast to the colonialism of previous centuries, the American takeover of postwar German culture was much more voluntarily accepted, and any critique of this "colonization" is therefore often accompanied by elements of self-hatred and guilt. This particular form of colonization would make a statement like Karsunke's "We are through with one another," impossible for the postwar generation because they perceive of the United States not as a friend, as Karsunke writes in his autobiographic poem, but as a father. Having lost their German fathers in the war—either literally or figuratively, since they lost their integrity and credibility by fighting in Hitler's army—America provided ersatz fathers: for Wenders and Handke these father figures included John Ford, Sam Fuller, and Nicholas Ray; Fassbinder turned to Douglas Sirk (significantly, he never referred to Detlef Sierk!); Rolf Dieter Brinkmann praised William Burroughs and Andy Warhol. Others, like Herzog, called themselves fatherless and constructed the myth of starting out of a vacuum—

60. Handke, *Ich bin ein Bewohner des Elfenbeinturms* 25.
61. Dawson, *Wim Wenders* 11.

to be sure with considerable help from their grandfathers, including an Americanized F. W. Murnau.

No matter how appropriate the term *colonization* here really is, in the eyes of the colonized it established an oedipal relationship that clearly determined their artistic agenda: while you can divorce a friend, you can only rid yourself from the father by killing him. The oedipal construction also gave their relationship with America a definite gender aspect—which explains why among a plethora of male writers and filmmakers concerned with America and Americanization there are very few women who take up this subject. The ones who do have a significantly different story to tell. While Jelinek demonstrates that it is particularly women who are susceptible to and exploited by American movies and television, Marianne Rosenbaum in her film *Peppermint Peace* (1982) and Monika Treut in her films *Virgin Machine* (1988), *My Father Is Coming* (1991), and *Female Misbehavior* (1992) celebrate the liberating aspects of popular culture. For Rosenbaum the American liberation of Germany is also an erotic liberation in which a young Peter Fonda replaces morbid fascist bureaucrats and Catholic authorities, while American pornography provides Treut's protagonists with an escape from German patriarchy.

The Children of John Ford and Theodor W. Adorno

> Once upon a time there were the mass media, and they were wicked, of course, and there was a guilty party. Then there were the virtuous voices that accused the criminals. And Art (ah, what luck!) offered alternatives, for those who were not prisoners of the mass media. Well, it's all over. We have to start again from the beginning, asking one another what's going on.
>
> —*Umberto Eco*

The fairy tale that Umberto Eco tells us is a modern one. In Germany it begins in the 1920s, when the emerging mass media became a serious challenge to the arts, theater, and literature, and to the notion of *Kultur* in general—a challenge that has been considerably amplified ever since the end of World War II. As always in a fairy tale, the bad guys were the others. For German intellectuals from Oswald Spengler to Edgar Reitz they were the Americans: from its very beginning the threat of mass media has been virtually synonymous with Americanization. This threat forged alliances between people who could not be further apart in their view of cultural politics. Adorno and Goebbels converged in their utter distaste for American jazz.

Adorno, of course, is also *the* main proponent of the redemptive power of art Eco alludes to (and it goes without saying that, regarding *which* art possesses redemptive qualities, Goebbels and Adorno quickly part company). Adorno is the theorist of the great divide par excellence. His influential study of the culture industry in *The Dialectics of Enlightenment,* cowritten with Max Horkheimer and shaped by their exile experience in the United States, provides much of the vocabulary that ever since its (belated) German publication, in 1969, has determined the arguments about American mass media.[62] Instrumental to the student protest movement through his notion of *Ideologiekritik,* Adorno is both catalyst and antagonist for the authors under discussion here—someone who taught them to be critical only to become, implicitly or explicitly, the target of their own critique. If Jean-Luc Godard once called his generation the childen of Marx and Coca-Cola, the artists under discussion here could perhaps best be described as the children of John Ford and Theodor W. Adorno. (To be sure, only Wenders, Handke and Achternbusch have written about their fascination with Ford, while Brinkmann, Treut, Jelinek, and Fassbinder would have probably objected to Ford's portrayal of macho stars and the exclusion of women as narrative agents in many of his films; yet all these German and Austrian artists, whether critical or affirmative, share a strong interest in the period of Hollywood filmmaking of which Ford is a key proponent.)

Adorno was among the first to realize that the study of modernism has to entail the study of mass culture. For him modernism was a reaction to the commodification of culture advanced by the culture industry. Adorno always insisted on the separation of art and reality. Art for him was the negation of the negativity of reality—a negation through which the work of art preserved its autonomy and claim to truth. According to Adorno, the culture industry is a form of mass deceit that threatens this autonomy by forging a "false reconciliation" between art and reality. He understood this industry to be a centrally controlled force that produces standardized and homogenizing cultural commodities, that negates individuality and style, and that turns its receivers into a mass of duped consumers. Even when they recognize the manipulations of the system, its pervasiveness makes them obey nevertheless: "The triumph of advertising in the culture industry is that consumers feel compelled to buy and use its products even though they see through them."[63] The culture industry thus has the sole purpose of social control.

In the discussions surrounding the social configuration of mass media in contemporary culture Adorno's description of the culture industry has been criticized for its essentialism, reductionism, ethnocentrism, and elitism. Douglas Kellner, for instance, has argued that it is Adorno's theory that homogenizes and pacifies the culture industry, which in reality is more diversified and complex than the theory that describes it.[64] Jim Collins polemicizes that Adorno's centralistic vision of master-minded cultural productions resembles the 1920s surveillance models of Fritz Lang's *Dr. Mabuse,*

---

62. *The Dialectics of Enlightenment* was first published in Amsterdam and reprinted with changes in 1947 by Querido before being republished in Germany in 1969.

63. Theodor W. Adorno and Max Horkheimer, *The Dialectics of Enlightenment,* trans. John Cumming (London: Allen Lane, 1973) 167.

64. Douglas Kellner, "Critical Theory and the Culture Industries: A Reassessment," *Telos* 62 (1984–85): 196–206.

the Gambler and *Metropolis* but has little explanatory value for describing cultural production and consumption in contemporary societies.[65] To do justice to Adorno, it must be added that in some of his later writings—often neglected by his critics—he somewhat revised his monolithic account of the culture industry. These revisions to a certain extent acknowledge that the power of the culture industry is not as encompassing as previously believed. In the posthumously published essay "The Schema of Mass Culture," which was originally meant to be part of *The Dialectics of Enlightenment,* Adorno writes: "Since as subjects human beings themselves still represent the ultimate limit of reification, mass culture must try and take hold of them again and again: the bad infinity involved in this hopeless effort is the only trace of hope that this repetition might be in vain, that human beings cannot be totally controlled."[66] And in "Transparencies on Film," inspired by the emergence of young German filmmakers in the mid-1960s, especially the work of Alexander Kluge, Adorno concedes that in the cinema there *does* remain a gap between the intentions of the culture industry and their actual effects on the viewers. "The ideology provided by the industry, its officially intended models, may by no means automatically correspond to those that affect the spectators."[67]

Despite the serious problems with Adorno's description of the culture industry, his critique of mass culture is important for the purpose of this study for several reasons. Adorno's writing on the culture industry show that popular culture has to be considered in relation to questions of power and cultural imperialism and that therefore the notion of postmodernism cannot be one of mere style, as has so often been asserted (especially in Germany). Popular culture is political, even if more than in the one sense that Adorno thought, namely as repressive. In that respect any discussion of the role of mass media in contemporary society has (still) much to learn from Adorno. Furthermore, the literary and cinematic texts here considered revolve around a concern that was central to Adorno: the clashing of high and low. Although they seldom make reference to Adorno's work, they should be seen as critical responses to Adorno's view of the culture industry, a criticism amplified by the fact that its authors were politicized at a time when the Frankfurt School exerted its strongest sway among West German intellectuals. Only if this powerful influence of the Frankfurt School on the critical discourse of the 1960s and 1970s is kept in mind will certain seemingly apolitical texts—as, for instance, Handke's—reveal their polemic dimension.

Taking issue with Adorno's vision of modernism and his insistence on the great divide, the individual chapters in this study demonstrate how tradi-

---

65. Jim Collins, *Uncommon Cultures: Popular Culture and Post-Modernism* (New York and London: Routledge, 1989) 10.

66. Theodor W. Adorno, *The Culture Industry: Selected Essays on Mass Culture,* ed. J. M. Bernstein (London: Routledge, 1991) 80.

67. *Culture Industry* 156. Cf. also Miriam Hansen, "Introduction to Adorno, 'Transparencies on Film' (1966)," *New German Critique* 24–25 (1981–82): 186–98.

tional notions of culture have been challenged through the influx of American mass media and popular culture. What unites these artists is their validation of popular culture as a political force for attacking the canon of high art and bourgeois morals. But popular culture is not only the object of their discourse; it is also its mode of enunciation. To varying degrees and for different purposes the films, novels, plays, and poems under discussion here poach freely from the culture industry: images, styles, genres, are used as ways of addressing audiences reared on American popular culture and for establishing patterns of identification; sometimes ideologically suspect texts are subverted from within (as, e.g., in Wenders's transformation of the western); at other times the subversive elements of the American underground (pornography, camp, the writings of William Burroughs) are presented to challenge traditional German *Kultur;* impurity, playfulness, subversion, ambiguity, and irony dominate.

My own readings of these texts' dialogic relationship with American popular culture argue that they implicitly, if not explicitly, challenge Adorno's notion of the culture industry in four ways. First, while Adorno's claim that mass culture is the product of an industry that needs to be seen in connection to questions of capitalism and cultural imperialism is certainly valid, this should not preclude the fact that popular culture is not only about materialism but also always about meanings, pleasures, and identities. Therefore, Adorno's equation of functional artifacts and textual artifacts overlooks fundamental differences between the production and circulation of commodities and sign systems.[68] These meanings, pleasures, and identities are only realized or established in the act of reception. While Adorno argued that the reception of mass culture has a stupefying and homogenizing effect on its audience (except for his later modification concerning the cinema, quoted earlier), the texts examined in this study show that the reception of popular culture can be selective, discriminating, and creative. The main criteria determining their appropriation is their relevance.

Second, the reception of texts of popular culture is not exclusively passive; the texts considered in this study all demonstrate an active involvement with popular culture. Even if one agrees with Adorno that the culture industry articulates social contradictions in order to homogenize them, one still has to consider "this process of articulation . . . the field of contest and struggle,"[69] rather than mere subjugation.

Third, the products of the culture industry are far from homogeneous. While they cannot be radical or overtly subversive because they cannot describe an experience that is totally different from that of their viewers or

---

68. This point is made by Bernard Gedron, "Theodor Adorno Meets the Cadillacs," in *Studies in Entertainment: Critical Approaches to Mass Culture,* ed. Tania Modleski (Bloomington and Indianapolis: Indiana UP, 1986) 18–36.

69. Huyssen, *After the Great Divide* 22.

readers, they can still be progressive. This progressive potential relies very much on the way the viewers experience pleasure of recognition anchored in the text. In that respect popular culture can be political. For example, when rock 'n' roll first emerged in the 1950s, it was part of a generational, cultural, and class struggle and became instrument of opposition and liberation. This is certainly how it was read by most of the German authors discussed here. But even after its "commercialization" and "co-optation" by the culture industry, in the 1970s, it still retains that meaning for today's adolescents. It is not the mode of production but the creativity of consumption that is the determining factor.

Fourth, there are serious problems with Adorno's notion of intentionality. Just because audiences do not participate in the production of texts does not mean they do not participate in the production of meaning. As John Fiske has shown, people make their own meaning within, and against, what the culture industry provides.[70] While Adorno believed that "mass culture is a system of signs that signals itself,"[71] it is far more productive to study the proliferation and dissemination of meaning of the sign once it has been appropriated by the consumers. Consider the contemporary example of rioting young German skinheads and neo-Nazis donning hats and baseball caps with the insignia X. Their harassing of foreigners and minorities is the exact opposite of Malcolm X's political struggle against racism, since one of the targets of their hatred is the very group Malcolm X represented. Yet, nevertheless, they can identify with the position of being an asocial, disempowered minority, which the symbol X was first meant to represent. Malcolm X's original intentions have been drastically altered and even perverted, but it is also clear that certain affinities between the intended meaning of the sign and the interpretation of the recipient have to exist for this appropriation to take place. This process becomes more complicated as the sign undergoes further mediations: we may suspect that the skinheads got their idea of wearing X hats not from Malcolm X's writings but from Spike Lee's film *Malcolm X,* just as the very availability of the hats is part of the commercial promotion of the film. This mediation and medialization thus further problematizes the notion of intentionality: perhaps Malcolm X would have never agreed to have a commercial, mainstream film made about him or have his insignia become a consumer commodity. While the sign cannot mean just anything to anybody, it becomes clear from this example that intentions are multiple, and their modes of appropriation cannot be contained—a process that has been called a semiological guerilla warfare.[72]

As Eco concludes his fairy tale, the story of the great divide "is all over." And, indeed, Adorno's monolithic account of the culture industry is hardly

70. Cf. John Fiske, *Understanding Popular Culture* (Boston: Unwin Hyman, 1989).
71. Adorno, *Culture Industry* 71.
72. Eco, *Travels in Hyperreality* 135–44.

capable of describing our present condition, which is characterized by late-capitalist modes of production, decentered forms of reception, and eclectic borrowings from older styles. But, as Eco also points out, if we want to find out about our present situation, it is not enough to claim mere posteriority; we have to start again from the beginning. In other words, if we are to talk about postmodernism, we have to theorize the meaning of the prefix. Let me conclude, therefore, with a word on terminology and methodology.

As I employ the term here, *postmodernism* is understood as a development in literature and film that takes seriously the validation of popular culture as a challenge to the canon of high art, a development that can also be seen in architecture (in which the term was first applied), music, theater, performance, and dance. Beyond blurring the lines between mass culture and high art, it also questions the lines between past and present, between the canonized and the marginal, and between the simulated and the real. In the context of the late 1960s in West Germany this attack on binarisms implies furthermore a questioning of the divisions between the public and the private, the personal and the political, politics and art, and life and art. In that respect postmodernism has important (though often unacknowledged) roots in the avant-garde movements of the 1920s. As Andreas Huyssen has shown, the relationship between high modernism and mass culture has to be understood as a dialectical one, with the postmodern condition being marked by an increasing blurring of the boundaries. It can be seen as a radicalization and popularization of tendencies already at work in modernism. Postmodernism, however, takes complete leave of the modernist premise of art's apolitical autonomy. Whether this strategy implies an opening up to facile commercialization and co-optation or whether it presents a challenge to the totalizing forces of an increasingly uniform mass culture has been a central concern in the debates of the 1980s. As I argue in this study, the taking leave of the claim to autonomy of art does not necessarily lead to abandoning any claim to criticality or negativity. Even if, as Fredric Jameson claims, postmodern texts lose a critical distance, they do not forfeit the notion of critique per se, but they do force us to think of it differently. The postmodern tendency for appropriation, reappropriation, and revision also indicates that the tension between high and low still exists and that postmodernism's potential strength in fact relies on it. Only the boundaries have become more permeable and suspect, and the struggle over meaning has become more visible.

The discussion of postmodernism in German and Austrian literature and film presents further complications. They stem in part from the fact that, just like the popular culture under discussion here, the term *postmodernism* itself is an import from America. For both Wim Wenders and Jean Baudrillard, America embodies the postmodern condition par excellence, an anticipation of what is to happen in Europe and elsewhere as well. One of the first to apply the term was Leslie Fiedler, who used it to describe a literature that would close "the gap between elite and mass culture"[73] by learning from genres such as the western, science fiction, and pornography. As the ensuing debate in Germany about Fiedler's essay demonstrates, the understanding of postmodernism in Germany reverberates with questions of Americanization; many of the arguments then first brought forth still determine today's discussion of the term. While critics in the United States have emphasized that postmodernism is not merely a stylistic development but has to be linked to questions of late capitalism and to politics and culture at large, Germans have mostly limited the term to the field of aesthetics. For them its trademarks are fun, *Nivellierung* (leveling down), irreverence, or an apocalyptic relativism of anything goes. Jürgen Habermas's programmatic essay "Modernity—An Incomplete Project" depicts the postmodern condition as a neoconservative threat to an Enlightenment tradition of reason and universal morality. Not only the critics but also the writers themselves have been apprehensive of the label. Heiner Müller, whose *Hamletmachine* constitutes for many the postmodern play par excellence, has disqualified the term by saying, "I cannot keep politics out of the question of postmodernism"[74]—but why should he? It is obvious that this relegation of postmodernism to the realm of the aesthetic is unsatisfactory.[75]

If, despite the terminological problems and inconsistencies, and despite the threat of imposing a foreign theory (yet another unwitting Americanization), I insist on using the term for the writers under discussion here, it is for the following reasons. As Richard McCormick has demonstrated, applying the notion of postmodernism to the study of German literature and film serves a double purpose: first, it situates a particular German political, social, and artistic configuration in a larger international context—a context in which, for example, the student protest movement is seen as part of an encompassing challenge to modernism. Second, it shows what German works have to contribute to a debate that has largely focused on French and American works, despite its recourse to German thinkers including Nietzsche, Freud, Benjamin, and Heidegger.[76] Such a contribution may sharpen

---

73. Leslie Fiedler, "Cross the Border—Close the Gap," *Collected Essays*, 2 vols. (New York: Stein, 1971) 2:468.

74. Heiner Müller, "Reflections on Post-Modernism," trans. Jack Zipes with Betty Nance Weber, *New German Critique* 16 (1979): 56. Elsewhere, in a more playful manner, he has reiterated this refusal to take the postmodern seriously: "The only Postmodernist I know of was August Stramm, a modernist who worked in a post office" (Heiner Müller, "I Am Neither a Hope—nor a Dope—Dealer," *Hamletmachine and Other Texts for the Stage*, ed. and trans. Carl Weber [New York: PAJ, 1984] 137).

75. Cf., for example, Peter Handke's recent statement: " Yes, we are indeed in a situation that offers plenty of opportunities. We can start anew—not postmodern, but in the sense of a new modernism. We have the chance to be universal, without ideologies" ("Gelassen wär ich gern," *Der Spiegel* 49 [1994]: 170–76; here 170).

76. Richard W. McCormick, *Politics of the Self: Feminism and the Postmodern in West German Literature and Film* (Princeton: Princeton UP, 1991).

our sense about what exactly the postmodern is; it especially may clarify some of the severe discrepancies between the understanding of postmodernism in Germany and the United States.[77]

My field of inquiry is the confrontation and appropriation of American popular culture by German filmmakers, novelists, playwrights, and poets in a historically defined period, and my methodology attempts to account for this interdisciplinary, if not eclectic, approach. Since I cross boundaries, and since I put emphasis on reception and transformation rather than on the autonomous aesthetic product, my approach emphasizes the dynamic and fluid relationship between literary and social life; it focuses on the circulation and adaptation of representations; and it attempts to integrate literary and film studies in cultural studies.

With these introductory remarks about the complex and contradictory historical, intellectual, and political impact of American popular culture for German intellectuals in mind, we are now in a better position to understand the significance of Edward Hopper's "Nighthawks" for the argument of this study. Hopper's painting clearly foregrounds the framing alluded to in the title of this study—obviously, the four characters are framed by the huge window of the diner, reinforced by the neon lights, which highlight their status of being presented to the viewer: a veritable fishbowl effect. The characters in "Nighthawks" are trapped: all escape routes are eliminated; doors and other viable exits are simply nonexistent. The frame imposed on them sets them up. To be sure, the German artists attracted to the painting felt that they, too, had been set up—namely, by an American culture and society that had colonized, as Wenders said, their subconscious. But framing the vision also means bringing something into focus and into perspective—both to adjust the lens in order to see better and to relate this image to the larger picture. Clearly, as popular culture helped these artists challenge traditional European notions of cultural production and reception, it served this focusing function too. As is perhaps typical for the quasicolonial predicament of the postwar German intellectuals, popular culture is therefore both catalyst and antagonist; the target of their critique and its very motor. But there is yet another, perhaps meta-, level on which "Nighthawks" can be read, for it is also a painting about the circulation of images. As an image about the artificial, theatrical nature of images, it reminded its German observers of their imaginary relation to the United States, a country to which they entertain a decidedly observing and voyeuristic position—which should remind us that when they talk about nighthawks, they really talk about themselves.

---

77. A detailed analysis of this issue is found in Hoesterey, *Verschlungene Schriftzeichen* 130–63.

Between Avant-Garde and
Popular Culture

CHAPTER 2

From Andy Warhol to
Rolf Dieter Brinkmann

I like ordinary things because they don't mean anything—and that's their depth.

—*Rolf Dieter Brinkmann*

Surface is an illusion, but so is depth.

—*David Hockney*

In an essay on the American poet Frank O'Hara, Rolf Dieter Brinkmann states: "We live in the surface of things, we make up this surface, there is nothing on the other side—the back is empty. Therefore, we finally have to accept this surface; the iconography of the everyday [*das Bildhafte täglichen Lebens*] has to be taken seriously."[1] Inspired by O'Hara's poetry and that of other contemporary American writers, Brinkmann proclaims an aesthetics of the surface that validates the beauty and significance of the everyday. Central to this aesthetics is the attempt to fuse the visual and the verbal. Incorporating elements from film, photography, porn magazines, comics, and the fine arts, Brinkmann's own work presents a vigorous attempt to validate popular culture as a challenge to the canon of high art. His poetry, fiction, essays, and diaries entertain obvious parallels to the work of American Pop artists, especially the paintings and films of Andy Warhol, who also strove to represent objects immediately recognizable by, and appealing to, large audiences. Beyond the similarities concerning the objects of their artistic representation, Warhol and Brinkmann both questioned the very relation between art and society by challenging what they perceived as the elitism and esotericism of high modernism. It is in this context of redefining the function of art and its modes of production, distribution, and reception that the political implications of the aesthetics of the surface emerge.

---

1. "Die Lyrik Frank O'Haras," *Der Film in Worten: Prosa, Erzählungen, Essays, Hörspiele, Fotos, Collagen 1965–1974* (Reinbek: Rowohlt, 1982) 207–22; here 215.

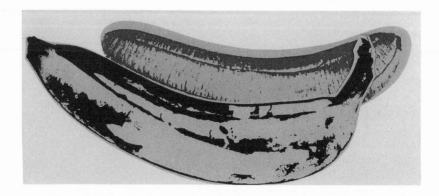

"One moment it is a banana / One moment it is not."—Rolf Dieter Brinkmann, "Andy Harlot Andy"

Andy Warhol, *Banana* (1966). Copyright © 1998 Andy Warhol Foundation for the Visual Arts / ARS, New York.

Taking issue with recent discussions about postmodernism and the notion of surface, this chapter contrasts Brinkmann's poetic and essayistic work with Andy Warhol's notion of Pop in order to fathom the radical aspect of their respective aesthetics. This comparison implies an understanding of the political and cultural context of post-1968 West Germany into which Brinkmann transferred Warhol (and the misreadings it produced) as well as a look at the historical avant-garde, which Brinkmann intended to redefine for his own purposes. A reading of selected texts by Brinkmann reveals the contribution his work has to make in the context of the present debate about postmodernism.

Learning from Andy Warhol

In his influential study on the cultural logic of postmodernism Fredric Jameson identifies the fascination with the surface as one of the main constituents of contemporary postmodernism: "The emergence of a new kind of flatness or depthlessness, a new kind of superficiality in the most literal sense [is] perhaps the supreme formal feature of [postmodernism]."[2] Comparing Vincent van Gogh's painting "A Pair of Boots" with Warhol's "Diamond Dust

---

2. Fredric Jameson, *Postmodernism, or The Cultural Logic of Late Capitalism* (Durham: Duke UP, 1991) 9. Cf. also Todd Gitlin, "Postmodernism Defined, at Last!" *Utne Reader* (July–August 1989): 52–61; and Ihab Hassan, "Toward a Concept of Postmodernism," *The Postmodern Turn: Essays in Postmodern Theory and Culture* (Columbus: Ohio State UP, 1987) 84–96. Both Gitlin and Hassan emphasize the notion of surface as constitutive for postmodernism.

Shoes," Jameson argues that Warhol's replacement of depth through surface endows the image with a "glacéd X-ray elegance [which] mortifies the reified eye of the viewer."[3] Warhol's conflation of inside and outside is indicative of the disappearance of other oppositions that are at the core of modernism, including the dialectics of essence and appearance; the Freudian model of latent and manifest, or of repression; the existential model of authenticity and inauthenticity (alienation and disalienation); and the great semiotic opposition between signifier and signified.[4] The disappearance of these oppositions has radically changed our understanding of the relation of art to politics. Culture can no longer claim an autonomous or semiautonomous sphere in the practical world and has thus lost the utopian character Herbert Marcuse once ascribed it. Thus, the question arises whether art still retains a "critical distance" from what it represents or whether is has expanded into, or been co-opted by—according to how one wishes to evaluate this development—the social realm.

Warhol's paintings are quite explicit about the connection between art and consumer culture and turn around the commodification of objects and subjects alike—from the Coke bottles and Campbell soup cans to the Marilyns and Elvises. One of the most famous pronouncements of *The Philosophy of Andy Warhol,* after all, is that "business art is the step that comes after art."[5] Calling his studio "The Factory," Warhol tried to imitate the mass production of industrial manufacturing and throughout his prolific career took pride in his work ethic. As Christin J. Mamiya writes, there can be no doubt that "Pop art not only depicted and reflected [consumer culture] but also appropriated the mechanisms and strategies of corporate society, ensuing the effective marketing of this movement and its absorption into the matrix of consumer institutions."[6] The question of to what degree Warhol's work retains a "critical distance" is therefore a difficult one. While from a modernist standpoint one may argue that Warhol's work and much that goes under the label of postmodern art abandons critical negativity because it delights in the excesses and contradictions of late capitalism, from a postmodernist standpoint one could praise its anti-elitist attitude that foregrounds inclusion rather than exclusion while highlighting the fetishization of consumer culture. I would argue that the continuing attraction of Warhol's paintings and his films (which are neglected by Jameson) consists precisely in the playful exploitation of their own ambiguities, thereby denying the viewer or spectator the security of a fixed position. This ambiguity, I would further argue, is the effect of Warhol's fascination with the surface, a

---

3. Jameson 9.

4. Ibid. 12.

5. Andy Warhol, *The Philosophy of Andy Warhol: From A to B and Back Again* (San Diego: Harcourt, 1977) 92.

6. Christin J. Mamiya, *Pop Art and Consumer Culture: American Super Market* (Austin: U of Texas P, 1992) 1.

fascination that is at the core of his paintings and films, his lifestyle, and his self-fashioned "philosophy." As Stephen Koch puts it: "Famous for being famous, [Warhol] is pure image."[7]

Warhol's best-known paintings show film stars or soup cans as they appear on the screen or advertising billboards; that is, the "original" (if one may call it that at all) is already two-dimensional, from which Warhol's silkscreens seem to subtract a further dimension. Films like *Sleep, Eat,* or *Haircut* depict precisely what their titles promise—"protagonists" that sleep, eat or get a haircut. If one looks, furthermore, at the many interviews and autobiographical statements reflecting Warhol's lifestyle and forms of self-promotion, it becomes clear that his fascination with the surface takes on fetishistic proportions. As he said in an interview: "I don't read much about myself, anyway, I just look at the pictures in the articles, it doesn't matter what they say about me; I just read the textures of the words. I see everything that way, the surface of things, a kind of mental Braille, I just pass my hand over the surface of things."[8] And he goes on: "When I read magazines I just look at the pictures and the words, I don't usually read it. There's no meaning to the words, I just feel the shapes with my eye and if you look at something long enough, I've discovered the meaning goes away."[9] And, finally: "If you want to know about Andy Warhol, just look at the surface: of my paintings and films and me, and there I am. There's nothing behind it."[10] In their provocative superficiality these statements are not without logic. The denial of depth is first of all a polemic against the elitism and esotericism of abstract expressionism and against the legacy of modernism in general. But it is also a personal defense mechanism: "I'd prefer to remain a mystery," says Warhol, using the surface as camouflage, with the paradoxical effect that this mystery further arouses the curiosity of the beholder, whose unfulfilled desire it will be to distinguish the real from the fake. (It should be added that throughout his career the pale master has cleverly used his shyness and passivity as a tool to exert power over his entourage and workers.) Most important for our purposes, the cult of the surface propagates an aesthetics of absolute legibility, instant disclosure of "meaning," naïveté, immediacy of the unobstructed view, and total presence.

Clearly, then, Warhol made use of the notion of surface both as aesthetic credo *and* as provocative and polemical tool for establishing his own artistic identity (even if it was an identity that insisted on having no identity). It was precisely this combination of the aesthetic and the political that made him

---

7. Stephen Koch, *Stargazer: The Life, World and Films of Andy Warhol* (New York: Marion Boyars, 1991) 24.

8. Gretchen Berg, "Nothing to Lose: An Interview with Andy Warhol," in *Andy Warhol: Film Factory,* ed. Michael O'Pray (London: BFI, 1989) 54–61; here 54.

9. Ibid. 61.

10. Ibid. 56.

attractive for Brinkmann. Since Pop art led to radical changes not only about what we consider to be art but also about how we think about art's role in society and the institutionalization of art, the notion of surface became instrumental for the radical changes Brinkmann projected in the modes of production, distribution, and reception of art and its function in the social realm. As he made clear in his programmatic essay "Der Film in Worten" ("The Film in Words"), Brinkmann understood his fascination with the sensuality of the surface and the suggestive power of images as directly opposite the emphasis on rationality and reason dominant among the German Left: "For a long time European intellectuals have proudly claimed the monopoly on enlightened consciousness; but this consciousness has no value in itself—it has to extend itself through images, it has to become a surface. The example of sexuality shows the small effects of Western rational thought: advertising has made more of an impact . . . a long flow of images which have put their own momentum before the product which they advertise."[11] Those, like Martin Walser, who felt attacked by Brinkmann were quick to condemn this kind of irrationalism as fostering "the latest form of fascism,"[12] and Yaak Karsunke called him a "front yard dwarf [*Vorgartenzwerg*] of the U.S. Pop scene."[13] To be sure, Brinkmann's plea to leave behind the "usual accumulation of words"[14] in favor of a growing flow of images and to take as his role model contemporary American poets and artists provided a calculated provocation in 1969, when the student movement and its indictment of U.S. politics in Vietnam were at a high point. But, beyond the intent to provoke, Brinkmann's aesthetics were part of a much larger challenge to the modernist conception of art that endowed art with a certain autonomy and thus separated it from the concerns of everyday life. (As I will show in chapter 3, Elfriede Jelinek also began her literary career by combining Pop art and the strategies of literary avant-garde, but her work engages the reader in rather different ways than that of Brinkmann.)

This autonomy was supposed to prevent art from turning into a commodity or into something useful to the aims of society, but it also isolated and removed art from society. While some of his contemporaries thought that the solution should be to abolish literature altogether, Brinkmann thought to revitalize literature by closing the gap between high culture and mass culture and by creating works that would be available to, and understood, enjoyed, and further circulated by, large portions of the general public. "I imagine a city with poetry readings, billboards with poems, poems being handed out at the bus stop in the morning . . . I imagine a city where poets teach students

---

11. "Der Film in Worten," *Der Film in Worten* 223–48; here 225.
12. Martin Walser, "Über die Neueste Stimmung im Westen," *Kursbuch* 20 (1970): 19–41; here 36.
13. Yaak Karsunke, *Frankfurter Rundschau,* 27 June 1970, vi.
14. "Der Film in Worten" 223.

how to write poetry, I imagine a city with rock 'n' roll concerts in relaxed places, warm, casual summer evenings when the faces are relaxed."[15] In his own writings he strove to abandon exclusivity by appropriating materials and styles from many different cultures, subcultures, media, and literary and non-literary genres. Their subject matter dealt with the everyday and with objects of immediate recognition (like Warhol's canvases), described in a style that allowed the reader instant understanding. As Brinkmann wrote in the pre-amble to *Westwärts 1 & 2,* it was his intention "to make poems simple, like songs, or like opening a door."[16] His overall goal was not to change the genre of poetry but, rather, its function. Understanding poetry no longer as a criti-cal reflection of existing social realities but as an active participation in the everyday and endowing poetry with the task and the ability to transcend con-ventional patterns of perception and experience, Brinkmann conceives of the writing of poetry as a political act. While Walter Benjamin thought that the aestheticization of the everyday was fascism, Andy Warhol thought that it was just fun. Clearly, Rolf Dieter Brinkmann learned more from the latter than the former.

After the Historical Avant-Garde

In order to assess how radical the implications of Brinkmann's work really are, two important historical qualifications have to be made. The first per-tains to the reception of American culture in Germany in the late 1960s. As I have argued, Warhol's work as painter and filmmaker, and his role as single-handed inventor of Pop, both as art and as lifestyle, made him attractive for Brinkmann's search for revitalizing German cultural life—especially Warhol's wholesale rejection of art history, his interest in the everyday, film, mass media, and consumer culture. But, of course, Brinkmann's fascination with Pop was by no means unique among German youths. In the mid-1960s a wave of enthusiasm for British and American rock music, poster art, the flower child cult, and the drug scene swept the Federal Republic in which *Pop* became the synonym for a counterculture that rebelled against the constrict-ing norms of society. As Andreas Huyssen has shown, much of the belief in the radical and subversive force of Pop has proven to be rather naive.[17] The democratization of art that many German Leftists saw promised by Warhol, Lichtenstein, and others never materialized, as Pop art was easily assimilated

15. "Ein unkontrolliertes Nachwort zu meinen Gedichten," in *Literaturmagazin 5: Das Vergehen von Hören und Sehen. Aspekte der Kulturvernichtung,* ed. Hermann Peter Piwitt and Peter Rühmkorf (Reinbek: Rowohlt, 1976) 228–48; here 240.

16. "Vorbemerkung," *Westwärts 1 & 2* (Reinbek: Rowohlt, 1975) 5–7; here 7.

17. Andreas Huyssen, "The Cultural Politics of Pop," *After the Great Divide: Modernism, Mass Culture, Postmodernism* (Bloomington: Indiana UP, 1987) 141–59; here 141. See also Jür-gen Wissmann, "Pop Art oder die Realität als Kunstwerk," in *Die nicht mehr schönen Künste: Grenzphänomene des Ästhetischen,* ed. Hans Robert Jauß (Munich: Fink, 1968) 507–30.

by consumer culture.[18] Brinkmann shared, at least to a certain degree, this utopian belief in Pop art and its subsequent disappointment. After 1971 Brinkmann became disenchanted with American popular culture and especially with the German reception of the underground literature for which his work as editor and translator had been so instrumental: "I was pretty depressed and shocked and I was filled with disgust when I saw how the—admittedly somewhat euphoric—anthology *Acid* was absorbed by the mainstream!"[19] As he writes in *Rom, Blicke*, by 1972 America had become the evil empire: "This exhaustion and sucking up of the Western world through Americanism, through the onslaught of the foreign (*Überfremdung*), through trance";[20] and in *Erkundungen für die Präzisierung des "Gefühls" für einen Aufstand: Reise Zeit Magazin (Tagebuch)* he calls the United States a "decrepit country of smiling faces."[21] But, while his own writings of that period—most of them published posthumously—are more critical about the capitalist and imperialist implications of American popular culture, and while a stay in Austin, Texas, in 1974 forced him to square his imaginary America with the lived experience abroad (reflected in the poetry volumes *Westwärts 1 & 2* and *Eiswasser an der Guadelupe Str.*), Brinkmann never abandoned his project of surface art with its fusion of the visual and the verbal as a means of recording the complexities of the everyday. The depth of Brinkmann's surface art clearly transcends that of American Pop art or at least of its reception in West Germany.

This leads me to the second historical qualification concerning the contemporaneity of Brinkmann. Brinkmann's vision about radical changes in the relation between art and society, about the infusion of high art with popular culture, and the validation of the everyday is not without important precursors in the first two decades of this century. A short historical digression is in order here to map Brinkmann's relation to the historical avant-garde; only then will the label *postmodern* as a description for both his style and his cultural politics—or, rather, his politics of style—acquire any meaning.

---

18. For a particular indicative indictment of Pop, see Jost Hermand, "Pop oder die These vom Ende der Kunst," *Die deutsche Literatur der Gegenwart: Aspekte und Tendenzen,* ed. Manfred Durzak (Stuttgart: Reclam, 1971) 285–99; *Pop International: Eine kritische Analyse* (Frankfurt am Main: Athenäum, 1971); and Paul Konrad Kurz, "Beat-Pop-Underground," *Über moderne Literatur: Standorte und Deutungen,* 3 vols. (Frankfurt am Main: Knecht, 1971) 3:233–79.

19. *Rom, Blicke* (Reinbek: Rowohlt, 1979) 93. Brinkmann's disenchantment with American Pop is already prefigured in Warhol's artistic decline in the 1970s. This decline has been read by Klaus Theweleit as a political sellout in the Nixon years, also noticeable in Elvis Presley. (See the second volume of Theweleit's, *Buch der Könige: Recording Angels' Mysteries* [Frankfurt am Main: Stroemfeld / Roter Stern, 1994]). Stephen Koch, still Warhol's most perceptive critic as far as the films are concerned, explains Warhol's "degradation" with the increasing artistic control of Paul Morrissey and Warhol's retreat from the Factory after he was shot, and almost killed, by Valerie Solanas in June 1968.

20. *Rom, Blicke* 164.

21. *Erkundungen für die Präzisierung des "Gefühls" für einen Aufstand: Reise Zeit Magazin (Tagebuch)* (Reinbek: Rowohlt, 1987) 365.

As Peter Bürger has shown in *Theory of the Avant-Garde,* the avant-garde movements of first two decades of this century such as dadaism and surrealism took issue with the notion of autonomous art, which they perceived to be without any social or political consequences. The radical remedy they suggested was to turn art into something practical while at the same time aestheticizing the social and political realm, thus closing the gap between art and life. As these movements realized, it is not the content of a work of art but the way it is situated within institutions that determines its reception, and they therefore strove to change the ways in which art was produced, distributed, and received. As Bürger argues, this attack on the institution of art has failed—which leads him to speak of the *historical* avant-garde—as these institutions continue to exist to this day without having undergone significant changes; the avant-garde's only lasting achievement is a heightened sense of awareness of the function of art in bourgeois society. Contemporary movements and artists who take up ideas and strategies of the historical avant-garde are thus doomed to repeat its mistakes and to fail:

> An art no longer distinct from the praxis of life but wholly absorbed in it will lose the capacity to criticize it, along with its distance. During the time of the historical avant-garde movements, the attempt to do away with the distance between art and life still had the pathos of historical progressiveness on its side. But in the meantime, the culture industry has brought about the false elimination of the distance between art and life, and this allows one to recognize the contradictoriness of the avant-gardiste undertaking.[22]

The notion of "critical distance," alluded to earlier in connection with Jameson's discussion of the postmodern, appears here again as Bürger insists that, without this distance, art will be co-opted by commercialism. While the historical avant-garde considered the overcoming of the gap between art and life a form of progress, the ultimate failure of these movements teaches us that this strategy is not to be emulated. Following Adorno's *Ästhetische Theorie* (which he criticizes elsewhere for its lack of historical understanding), Bürger thus reiterates the great divide between progressive art and the culture industry. In regard to the work of Andy Warhol, which he labels "neo-avant-garde," he writes: "The painting of 100 Campbell soup cans contains resistance to the commodity society only for the person who wants to see it there."[23]

22. Peter Bürger, *Theory of the Avant-Garde,* trans. Michael Shaw (Minneapolis: U of Minnesota P, 1989) 50. Published in German as *Theorie der Avantgarde* (Frankfurt am Main: Suhrkamp, 1974).

23. Ibid. 61. This argument is developed in more detail in Russell A. Berman, "Konsumgesellschaft: Das Erbe der Avantgarde und die falsche Aufhebung der ästhetischen Autonomie," trans. Birgit Diefenbach, in *Postmoderne: Alltag, Allegorie und Avantgarde,* ed. Christa Bürger and Peter Bürger (Frankfurt am Main: Suhrkamp, 1987) 56–71.

A similar critique is also found in the work of Hans M. Enzensberger. Anticipating Bürger's argument about the aporias of the avant-garde by more than a decade, Enzensberger expressed as early as 1962, "Any avant-garde today is repetition, conceit, or self-conceit."[24] Like Bürger, Enzensberger believed that the historical avant-garde had not made good on its promise "to shake off political and aesthetic ties, to overturn traditional forms of domination, to set repressed forces free."[25] Those who today still lay claim to being "ahead" of the others are either the creators of the consciousness industry (Enzensberger's term for the culture industry)[26] or those who take pride in belonging to a cultural elite that only speaks to the initiated. Enzensberger's own way out of the aporia of the avant-garde later in the decade was a call to abolish literature altogether.[27]

While I would agree with Bürger and Enzensberger that the avant-garde's reliance on novelty and shock poses an inherent dead-end because these strategies quickly exhaust themselves, and while I would also agree that much of the radical impetus of the historical avant-garde has been swallowed, digested, and thus leveled by the big stomach of cultural institutions (both public and private), I would insist that the avant-garde's most important achievement—namely, recognizing the necessity for bridging the gap between high art and popular culture by questioning the autonomy of art—continues to be of utmost importance. This line of questioning was also what led Brinkmann to take issue with Hans M. Enzensberger's critique of the avant-garde. While Brinkmann shared Enzensberger's indictment of the elitism of experimental and hermetic poetry as an avant-garde gone stale, he heavily criticized the fact that Enzensberger had lumped Jack Kerouac into the same category. According to Brinkmann, Enzensberger's critique remains caught in a Eurocentric school of thought that prematurely applies historical-aesthetic categories, because its emphasis on intellect blinds it to the sensual

---

24. Hans Magnus Enzensberger, "Die Aporien der Avantgarde," in *Einzelheiten II: Poesie und Politik* (Frankfurt am Main: Suhrkamp, 1984) 50–80; here 79.

25. Ibid. 67.

26. A similar critique of contemporary movements labeled "avant-garde" is found in Hans Platschek. He writes: "By constantly cashing in on the value of its novelty, the avant-garde has succumbed to the laws of the art market. Without market, it wouldn't even be an avant-garde in the first place" ("Schüsse in Hornberg oder Der Streit um die Avantgarde," in *Stichworte zur "Geistigen Situation der Zeit."* vol. 2: *Politik und Kultur,* ed. Jürgen Habermas [Frankfurt am Main: Suhrkamp, 1979] 615–35; here 630).

27. In his famous article " Gemeinplätze, die Neueste Literatur betreffend" Enzensberger extended his critique to contemporary attempts to politicize literature: "All efforts, so far, to break out of the ghetto of cultural life by force and to 'reach the masses,' say, through agitprop songs or street theater, have failed. As far as literature is concerned, they have been irrelevant; politically, they have made no impact whatsoever" (*Kursbuch* 15 [1968]: 187–97; here 192). If Enzensberger understood this call for political action as the latest reincarnation of the historical avant-garde, it was obviously a misreading: dadaism and surrealism had not claimed an art that was politically or socially relevant; instead, they wanted to change the very function of art in order to integrate art and life better.

quality of Kerouac's and other Beat writers' works. And, while Brinkmann agrees that certain elements of the historical avant-garde have been taken up by American writers, he feels that Enzensberger (and others) fail to see "that European literary movements like Surrealism, Expressionism, Dada . . . have been transformed and adjusted to the new material."[28] This particular new American movement in literature and the arts presented a vitality that Brinkmann meant to transfer to Germany to provide his own society with much needed inspiration, an alternative to Enzenberger's swan song on literature: "The 'death' of literature can only happen in literature—if writing ceases to conform to this definition (*indem Geschriebenes sich nicht mehr dem zuordnet*). Therefore: let's stop talking about 'literature' . . . literature, literature, as if it still mattered."[29]

The Depth of the Surface

The question to be asked, then, is: to what degree do Brinkmann's own appropriations of the new American sensibility present an "adjustment" of the material that he admired in the work of American writers and artists? Or to return to the focus of my argument: to what degree does his adaptation and transformation of Warhol's surface art transcend both the pop fad of the late 1960s and the aporias of the historical avant-garde and contribute to what certain critics have called—for better or worse—an "un-co-opted post-modernism"[30] or "a postmodernism of resistance"[31] that preserves a certain utopianism while moving beyond the binary oppositions typical of modernism and much of the avant-garde?[32]

Let us consider the following poem taken from *Godzilla* (1968), a book of poetry printed entirely on posters of magazine advertisements showing women in their swimsuits.

28. "Der Film in Worten" 231.

29. Ibid. 236f.

30. E. Ann Kaplan, intro., *Postmodernism and Its Discontents: Theories, Practices,* ed. E. Ann Kaplan (London and New York: Verso, 1988) 1–9; here 3ff.

31. Hal Foster, "Postmodernism: A Preface," in *The Anti-Aesthetic: Essays on Postmodern Culture,* ed. Hal Foster (Port Townsend, WA: Bay Press, 1983) ix–xvi; here xii.

32. While there are now a number of interesting studies on Brinkmann, few situate his work in the larger debate about postmodernism. Notable exceptions are Sibylle Späth, *"Rettungsversuche aus dem Todesterritorium": Zur Aktualität der Lyrik Rolf Dieter Brinkmanns* (Frankfurt am Main: Peter Lang, 1986); and Thomas Gross, *Alltagserkundungen: Empirisches Schreiben in der Ästhetik und in den Materialbänden Rolf Dieter Brinkmanns* (Stuttgart: Metzler, 1993). In Rolf Renner's account of postmodern German literature, Brinkmann assumes primarily the role of someone who, through his reception of American literature and editorial work, paved the way for others. See Rolf Günter Renner, *Die postmoderne Konstellation: Theorie, Text und Kunst im Ausgang der Moderne* (Freiburg: Rombach, 1988) 144–51.

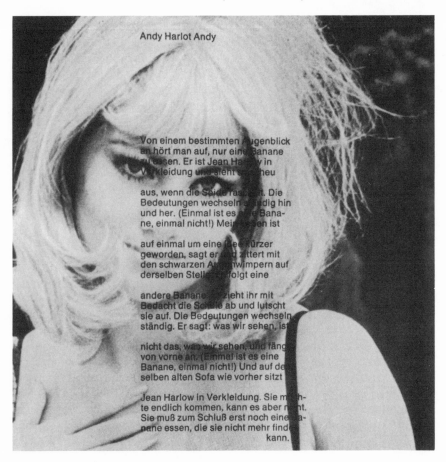

Andy Harlot Andy

Von einem bestimmten Augenblick
an hört man auf, nur eine Banane
zu essen. Er ist Jean Harlow in
Verkleidung und sieht so scheu

aus, wenn die Seide raschelt. Die
Bedeutungen wechseln ständig hin
und her. (Einmal ist es eine Banane, einmal nicht!) Mein Leben ist

auf einmal um eine Idee kürzer
geworden, sagt er und zittert mit
den schwarzen Augenwimpern auf
derselben Stelle. Folgt eine

andere Banane zieht ihr mit
Bedacht die Schale ab und lutscht
sie auf. Die Bedeutungen wechseln
ständig. Er sagt: was wir sehen, ist

nicht das, was wir sehen, und fängt
von vorne an. (Einmal ist es eine
Banane, einmal nicht!) Und auf dem-
selben alten Sofa wie vorher sitzt

Jean Harlow in Verkleidung. Sie möchte endlich kommen, kann es aber nicht.
Sie muß zum Schluß erst noch eine Banane essen, die sie nicht mehr finden
kann.

"We should no longer think (and live) in words but in images."—Rolf Dieter Brinkmann, from the preface to his volume of poems *Godzilla* (Rowohlt, 1968)

"Andy Harlot Andy," from *Godzilla.*

Andy Harlot Andy

From a certain moment
on you stop eating a mere
banana. He is Jean Harlow in
drag and he looks so shy

when the silk rustles. The meaning
constantly changes back and

forth. (One moment it is a banana, one moment it is not!) My life

is suddenly one idea shorter,
he says, and he bats his
black eyelids in the
same place. It follows an-

other banana. Carefully, he
takes off its peal and sucks
it up. The meanings constantly
change. He says: what we see is

not what we see and begins
from anew. (One moment it is a
banana, one moment it is not.) And
on the same old sofa as earlier sits

Jean Harlow in drag. She finally wants to come, but she can't.
She must first eat a bana-
na which she can't find anymore.[33]

The title of the poem refers to Andy Warhol's first sound film, *Harlot* (1964),
featuring the transvestite Mario Montez dressed up as the sex symbol Jean

---

33. Andy Harlot Andy

   Von einem bestimmten Augenblick
   an hört man auf, nur eine Banane
   zu sehen. Er ist Jean Harlow in
   Verkleidung und sieht so scheu

   aus, wenn die Seide raschelt. Die
   Bedeutungen wechseln ständig hin
   und her. (Einmal ist es eine Banane, einmal nicht!) Mein Leben ist

   auf einmal um eine Idee kürzer
   geworden, sagt er und zittert mit
   den schwarzen Augenwimpern auf
   derselben Stelle. Es folgt eine

   andere Banane. Er zieht ihr mit
   Bedacht die Schale ab und lutscht
   sie auf. Die Bedeutungen wechseln
   ständig. Er sagt: was wir sehen, ist

Harlow, who, in the course of the seventy minutes of the film, devours one banana after the other. The "plot" of the film revolves around the repetitive exploitation of ambiguity: Is it a banana or a phallus? Is it a woman or a man? Is *Harlow* a stand-in for *Warhol?* "The meaning constantly changes . . . what we see is not what we see." Obviously, Brinkmann is fascinated with Warhol's anarchic imagination—his destruction of traditional sexual behavior, and his playful subversion of the dominant modes of cinematic representation.[34] Warhol's homemade Factory superstar Mario Montez acts out his (her!) sexual fantasies in front of the running camera, unrehearsed and unedited. This pretense to realism—everything is equally worth recording and storing, and anybody can be a star—is essential to Warhol's art. Equally essential is the amateurism of its execution (e.g., shaky camera movement, out-of-focus shots, actors looking directly into the camera, and at times inaudible sound). As Warhol comments: "The Pop idea, after all, was that anybody could do anything."[35]

Imitating the serial quality of *Harlot* (one banana is eaten after another), Brinkmann's poem simply recounts in chronological order the scenes and lines of the film and refrains from interpreting it. The film invites, or even demands, a reception in which the viewer enjoys the sensuality of the viewed without intellectual reflection. Interpretation is a no-no because it destroys,

---

nicht das, was wir sehen und fängt
von vorne an. (Einmal ist es eine
Banane, einmal nicht!) Und auf dem
selben alten Sofa wie vorher sitzt

Jean Harlow in Verkleidung. Sie möchte endlich kommen, kann es aber nicht.
Sie muß zum Schluß erst noch eine Banane essen, die sie nicht mehr finden kann.

(Rolf Dieter Brinkmann, *Godzilla* [1968]; rptd. in
Standphotos: Gedichte, 1962–1970 [Reinbek: Rowohlt, 1980] 165)

The original edition of *Godzilla* consisted of two hundred copies; the reprinted version is only in black-and-white.

34. Dieter Wellershof recalls Brinkmann's own experiments with filmmaking: "The films, which he shot with his Super-8 amateur camera and which he showed to a small circle of friends, were mostly imitations of the fixed camera of Andy Warhol. For example, he mounted the camera on a tripod and asked several people, one after the other, to sit motionless and without music in front of the running camera. It was a silent interrogation, and the result was not uninteresting. It was an imitation of American underground movies" (*Too Much: Das lange Leben des Rolf Dieter Brinkmann*, ed. Gunter Geduldig and Marco Sagurna [Aachen: Alano, 1994] 85). What is missing in Brinkmann's poetic adaptation of Warhol's film (and what by all accounts seems to be missing from Brinkmann's own films as well) is the deconstruction of rigid opposition of gender, which is central to Warhol's notion of camp and his use of the drag queen. Biographical information about Brinkmann reveals his ridiculing and often contemptuous behavior toward gays—for example, his friend and coeditor, Ralf Rainer Rygulla.

35. Andy Warhol and Pat Hackett, *POPism: The Warhol '60s* (San Diego: Harcourt, 1990) 134.

but it is also futile because it can never contain the unlimited dissemination of meaning. As Ronald Tavel, the "writer" of *Harlot,* commented: "A hundred meanings depart in every direction from out of its meaninglessness."[36] In the early poem "Zwischen den Zeilen" (Between the Lines) Brinkmann also refutes this hermeneutic digging for meaning:

> Between the lines
> there is nothing
> written.
>
> Each word
> can be checked
> in black
> and white.[37]

Significantly, the poem does so in form of a verdict, while most of his later texts, much like Warhol's *Harlot,* celebrate the absence of meaning in a more playful manner.

By mounting his poem on an advertisement poster, Brinkmann further enhances the visual element already present in his purely descriptive text. This translation of images into prose as well as the infusion of texts with images is at the core of Brinkmann's surface art. Warhol's serial paintings of coke bottles, soup cans, and Mona Lisas introduced the element of reading, and thus temporality, while his paintings of newspapers transformed the printed word into an object to be looked at. In Brinkmann this fusion of image and text is achieved through a highly descriptive prose interspersed with movie stills, photographs (often taken by the author himself) and cut-outs from magazines. According to Brinkmann, poetry is the most suited form "to capture, in a concrete snapshot, spontaneously recognized events and movements, and a sensibility which reveals itself only momentarily."[38] Accordingly, it is to imitate "*Zooms . . . over-exposure, double-exposure . . .* unpredictable *turns* (thought turns) *cuts:* an image track."[39] Brinkmann's poems are therefore often very short and attempt to catch a random observation like a camera would.

But what are the implications of Warhol's and Brinkmann's respective

---

36. Ronald Tavel, "The Banana Diary: The Story of Andy Warhol's *Harlot,"* in O'Pray, *Andy Warhol: Film Factory* 66–93; here 68. The quotation marks framing *writer* are based on the fact that Warhol did not want Tavel to produce an actual script for the actors; the soundtrack written by Tavel and spoken by him and two other men off-camera is largely inaudible and used merely as counterpoint to the images.

37. *Standphotos* 60.

38. Ibid. 185.

39. "Notizen 1969 zu amerikanischen Gedichten und zu der Anthologie *Silverscreen,"* Der *Film in Worten* 248–69; here 267.

claims to realism: What do their works do to the objects they represent? And what bearing do these representations have for the social function of their art? To address these questions means to map Brinkmann's departure from Warhol. The minimalism of Warhol's films and paintings (with their emphasis on duration, repetition, and random elements) and of Brinkmann's poetry (consider the many poems simply titled "Gedicht" [poem] or "Photographie" [photograph] that consist of little more than a sentence describing a single image) suggests that anything is worthy of attention and can enter a work of art. Warhol's factory superstars can be seen as the becoming-flesh of the objets trouvés and the ready-mades of Marcel Duchamp that Brinkmann time and again alludes to in the poem "Vanille" (Vanilla) and elsewhere. With approval Brinkmann quotes the last line of Warhol's novel *a*—"From the garbage into the book!"—as a strategy for incorporating found materials into one's own work.[40] But this superficiality is deceiving. Both Warhol's and Brinkmann's surface art transforms those elements of the everyday it selects. In Warhol's silkscreen of stars, and even in his paintings of soup cans or two dollar bills, there is a materialistic envy of the unattainable, further enhanced through the voyeuristic detachment of its objects. Marilyn and Liz are frozen in their "image *as stars:* no more soul, nothing but a strictly imaginary status, since the star's being is the icon."[41] While his paintings pretend to be totally legible, Warhol himself is mute; while they emphasize immediacy, he withdraws. Having abandoned the third dimension, he is no longer the artist behind his work but the artist beside it. According to Warhol, the paintings mean what they are; there's no hidden intention, no signified. "I don't know where the artificial stops and the real begins," he says,[42] conflating not only art and reality but also art and artifice. But Warhol's unintentionality is precisely that, an intention. The aestheticization and fetishization of meaninglessness, executed in bold colors on huge canvases magnifying the everyday— and thus changing our perception—is what makes Pop into art. As Roland Barthes observes, "Pop is an art because, just when it seems to renounce all meaning, consenting only to reproduce things in their platitude, it stages, according to certain methods proper to it and forming a style, an object which is neither the thing nor its meaning, but which is: its signifier, or rather: the Signifier."[43]

Rolf Dieter Brinkmann's portrayal of stars shows that his intention of changing our perception is headed in a different direction. While poems like "Eine übergroße Photographie von Liz Taylor" (A Larger-than-Life Photograph of Liz Taylor), "Der nackte Fuß von Ava Gardner" (The Naked Foot

---

40. "Anmerkungen zu meinem Gedicht 'Vanille'" 144.
41. Roland Barthes, "That Old Thing, Art . . . ," in *Post-Pop Art,* ed. Paul Taylor (Cambridge: MIT UP, 1989) 21–31; here 24.
42. Andy Warhol, quoted in Jonas Mekas, "Notes after Reseeing the Movies of Andy Warhol," in O'Pray, *Andy Warhol: Film Factory* 28–41; here 37.
43. Barthes 28f.

of Ava Gardner), and "Brief an Humphrey Bogart, schon weit entfernt" (Letter to Humphrey Bogart, Now Far Away) make good on Leslie Fiedler's call that the "new anti-Gods and anti-heroes" of postmodern literature should come "out of the world of Jazz and Rock, of newspaper headlines and political cartoons, of old movies immortalized on T.V,"[44] these poems are never content with just reproducing the glamorous image of the stars. They insist that the significance of their presence depends on being experienced by a subject. And they relate that presence to the world of the experiencing "I":

> Better
> with no money in Tobruk
> with Rock Hudson on
> the screen than with no
> money lost in
> the trolley
> to Müngersdorf
> where nothing's happening
> anyway.[45]

A note in *Die Piloten* dedicates the volume to all those "who time and again like to sink into the cheap seats in front of the screen. They are the pilots to which the title refers."[46] As the metaphor of the pilot indicates, in the cinema one can "take off" into the realm of fantasy, but the spectators determine the course themselves by combining their imagination with the one presented on the screen.

In contrast to the glamorization of the star, the poem "Graham Bonney oder das komplizierte Gefühl" (Graham Bonney or the Complicated Feeling) explores what happens when we are suddenly face to face with a star. The lyrical I and a friend suddenly run into the pop singer as they walk down a street, but, surprised by the unexpected encounter, they let the situation pass. As the verses "we both / didn't know what to do / for Graham Bonney was so close to us"[47] indicate, it is *because* of the proximity of the star that they do not know what to do. Contrasting the myth of the star with the banality of the encounter—which, as the "Nachtrag zu dem Gedicht über Graham Bonney etc." (Postface to the Poem about Graham Bonney) explains, is based on a real experience—it becomes clear that, outside of a certain setting such as a rock concert, the star is just "ein Mensch wie du und ich" (a human being like you and I).[48] Harald Hartung has correctly pointed to the formal parallel

44. Leslie Fiedler, "Cross the Border—Close the Gap," *Collected Essays,* 2 vols. (New York: Stein, 1971) 2:461–85; here 481f.
45. *Standphotos* 240.
46. Ibid. 187.
47. Ibid. 233.
48. Ibid. 234.

between Brinkmann's poem and Warhol's prints, arguing that the metric and typographic arrangement of the poem deliberately imitates techniques of Pop art:

> The separation of the verses, which follows neither rhythm nor syntax, emphasizes the mechanical aspect of reproduction. In contrast to Celan, the cutting up of words does not emphasize meaning or sound but rather it marks the edges that are produced when a verbal perception is cut to fit to the mold "poetry" (lines, stanza). Just as Warhol used the silk screen technique to transpose an authentic model, for example a photo, the form of the poem can do the same.[49]

While I agree with Hartung that Brinkmann's narrative poem strives to be as easily understood as Warhol's prints of stars and consumer icons are recognized, it needs to be emphasized that there remains an important difference regarding the material they use and its arrangement. For, whereas Warhol reiterates the iconographic aspect of the star photo or billboard reproduction—which can hardly be called authentic, as Hartung suggests, for Warhol is precisely interested in their inauthenticity—Brinkmann is demonstrating that stars can be banal. Warhol, on the one hand, is especially interested in the very packaging of images of commodities, and his own work can be seen as "re-packaging packaging as a commodity itself";[50] Brinkmann, on the other hand, tells us in his poem about Graham Bonney what happens when the commodity appears without package or the package is unwrapped: nothing.

A further example that may demonstrate what distinguishes Warhol from Brinkmann is the way in which they adapted the avant-garde's emphasis on democratizing art by showing their audience how to become artists themselves. Warhol's definition of Pop as the idea "that anybody could do anything" suggests this very notion of democracy. As noted earlier, almost all of his films foreground their dilettantism and amateurism, and many of them can be given the credit "directed by Andy Warhol" only in a very remote sense, as he neither directed the actors nor operated the camera. Nor was there any editing, for that matter; sometimes Warhol was not even around for the shooting. While this may be seen as a critique of the Romantic notion of creative genius, the execution of this critique still relied on Warhol's genius for organization and promotion. As Stephen Koch and others have argued, it was precisely because of his conspicuous absence that Warhol exerted both artistic and political control—not to mention the economic control, since it was always Warhol who footed the bill. Similarly, while his homemade super-

49. Harald Hartung, "Lyrik der 'Postmoderne': Vier Beispiele zu einer Ästhetik der Oberfläche," in *Abhandlungen aus der Pädagogischen Hochschule Berlin,* ed. Walter Heistermann (Berlin: Colloquium Verlag, 1974) 303–28; here 313.
50. Peter Wollen, "Raiding the Icebox," in O'Pray, *Andy Warhol: Film Factory* 14–27; here 19f.

stars such as Mario Montez, Ingrid Superstar, International Velvet, Candy Darling, and others may be considered parodies of Hollywood's star system, the parody cannot escape the need to imitate its target of ridicule. This proximity includes processes of medialization and imaging that can hardly be called democratic (even if subverted through a camp sensibility) and fame's toll on the personal lives of many members of the Warhol entourage. Warhol's do-it-yourself paintings further demonstrate the limits of parody. Depicting a half-finished paint-by-numbers sailboat or violin, these works suggest that anyone can produce a masterpiece. While this could be seen as an assault on high art, Warhol's parody in fact elevates its object onto the level of high art. Taking its inspiration from the immediacy of the everyday, the do-it-yourself paintings in fact reinstall an aesthetic distance: no one, after all, would dare to go to the museum and complete Warhol's work. As this new, and much more profound, aesthetic distance shows, Warhol may have crossed the border into the popular, but he has not closed the gap. These paintings do not represent the end of art and its disappearance into the everyday—merely the end of art as we knew it.

In this respect Brinkmann's call to reduce the distance between author and recipient of a literary work seems truer to the spirit of the historical avant-garde. While Brinkmann, like Warhol, criticized the Romantic notion of a creativity and inspiration anchored in a prophetic or visionary author, he followed the Dadaists' and Surrealists' lead to activate the response of the recipient, something Warhol's do-it-yourself paintings can only *imitate*. Both Tristan Tzara's *Pour faire un poème dadaïste* and André Breton's *Manifeste du surréalisme* tell their readers how they themselves can produce texts, as does Brinkmann in his literary journal *Der Gummibaum;* significantly, all three texts do so in the form of a recipe: "Why not write a tasty recipe for cookies. That's a nice poem. Add 10 grams of pot, and the cookies will be even better, and the poem 'Cookies' too."[51] As Brinkmann explained elsewhere: "A subjectivity which leaves behind literary conventions . . . has the liberty to include a recipe into a poem; it thus makes the poem more relevant because it can be shared better."[52] Postmodern literature is thus a literature that "no longer understands itself in competition with the 'great' literary products"—a competition that is still implied in Warhol's notion of parody—and that can focus on the everyday without fear of being criticized for its banality.

---

51. "Ein paar Hinweise," *Der Gummibaum: Hauszeitschrift für neue Dichtung* 1 (1969), quoted in Sibylle Späth, "Die Entmythologisierung des Alltags: Zu Rolf Dieter Brinkmanns lyrischer Konzeption einer befreiten Wahrnehmung," *Text + Kritik* 7 (1981): 37–49; here 39. As Späth points out, this article mentions no author but most likely was written by Brinkmann, who was the main editor of the journal. Contributors to the short-lived journal (only three issues were circulated in the form of pamphlets) included Nicolas Born, Peter Handke, Ernst Jandl, and Dieter Wellershof.

52. "Notizen" 251.

A crucial distinction, then, between Brinkmann's and Warhol's aesthetics—and a much-debated question in the discussion about postmodernism in general—is the role of subjectivity. If the gap between authors and readers is (to be) closed, if the traditional concept of what constitutes a work of art is (to be) abandoned because everything is considered material and potentially a work of art, what, then, is the position of the creative subject? What respective strategies do Brinkmann and Warhol adopt to work toward their own disappearance? It is here that the notion of a postmodernism of resistance takes on its distinctive features.

Toward a New Realism

Like Warhol's paintings, Brinkmann's poems acknowledge that visual media such as film, photography, and television have radically changed our modes of perceiving and understanding the world. These changes clearly transcend the realm of these media and have to have an impact on the way we write or paint or live. Warhol's and Brinkmann's respective attempts to come to terms with the significance of images acknowledge that this is not just a question of style but of staging subjectivity itself. Warhol's answer to the proliferation of images has been to become one—an attempt to interface with the surface of his art. What his silkscreen portraits and films like *Empire,* an eight-hour shot of the Empire State Building taken from a static camera, attest to is the process of extreme dehumanization that the society of the spectacle has brought about. "*Empire* is a massive, absurd act of attention, attention that nobody could possibly want to give or sit through. Indeed, nothing could possibly tolerate it—and here's the point—but a machine, something that sees but cannot possibly care."[53] Perhaps Warhol's insight into the totality and ubiquity of the surface contains something of the "winner loses" logic that Jameson describes (in a different context): the more powerful Warhol is in describing an increasingly closed and terrifying environment, the more his work loses any critical capacity, any impulses of negation and revolt.[54] In the end Warhol reinvents the autonomy of art that seemed to have been overcome: "I think we're a vacuum here at the Factory. It's great."[55]

In line with his negation of subjectivity, Warhol stated that everybody should become a machine, a statement frequently and approvingly quoted by Brinkmann. And yet Brinkmann's understanding of the notion of surface differs significantly from Warhol's disembodied images. Although Brinkmann refrains from interpreting the implications of Warhol's art[56] and reads

---

53. Koch 61.
54. Jameson 5.
55. Quoted in Koch 3.
56. Cf. the following passage: "Today, the sensibility which is expressed—both 'positively' and 'negatively'—in the empty, metal-like landscapes of Roy Liechtenstein, and in the images of Andy Warhol . . . can no longer be grasped with yesterday's interpretations" ("Der Film in Worten" 226).

Empire in terms of a modernist self-reflexivity ("Warhol's film *Empire* is a meditation on film and filmic time"),[57] his appropriation of Warhol's notion of surface indicates that he is interested in going beyond the dissolution of subjectivity by searching for the ways in which even in an image-dominated and constituted reality the subject *can* interface with other surfaces and texts. As he writes in "Notes Written in 1969 on American Poems and on the Anthology *Silverscreen*": "Life is *a complex network of images [ein komplexer Bildzusammenhang]*. What matters is *in* which images we live and *with which images we combine our own images.*"[58] This emphasis on *our own* images indicates that Brinkmann is not willing to relinquish subjectivity as completely as Warhol, because he realizes that the total abstraction from the self is as fictitious as the belief in the self-contained, rational subject position against which they both polemicize.

In *After the Great Divide* Andreas Huyssen has argued that this reintroduction of subjectivity is one of the decisive elements that distinguishes the postmodernism of the 1970s from that of the 1960s. For Huyssen the American Pop, rock, and sex movements of the 1960s had exhausted themselves by the end of the decade. The postmodernism of the 1970s, by contrast, loosened its ties—acknowledged or unacknowledged—to the historical avant-garde, thus avoiding the Scylla of repeating its aporias and the Charybdis of being co-opted by the culture industry. "What was new in the 1970s was, on the one hand, the emergence of a culture of eclecticism, a largely affirmative postmodernism which had abandoned any claim to critique, transgression, or negation; and, on the other hand, an alternative postmodernism in which resistance, critique, and negation of the status quo were redefined in non-modernist and non-avant-gardist terms."[59] While I would argue that Pop art, especially Warhol's work, is more than just the "endgame of the historical avant-garde"[60] that Huyssen sees in it because it already prefigures ways out of the avant-garde's aporias, Huyssen's distinction is useful for describing Brinkmann's appropriation of Pop. Extending Huyssen's work to recent developments in West Germany, Richard McCormick has shown that writers and filmmakers including Peter Handke, Botho Strauß, Karin Struck, Wim Wenders, and Helke Sanders stage a return to subjectivity as a response to the predicament of modernism. McCormick calls their various strategies to redefine inwardness, to overcome the excesses of rationalistic modernism, and to merge personal memory and historical discourse "postmodern responses."[61] While Brinkmann differs from these authors and from what has

---

57. Ibid. 236.
58. "Notizen" 249.
59. Huyssen, "Mapping the Postmodern," *After the Great Divide* 178–221; here 188.
60. Cf. Huyssen, "The Search for Tradition: Avantgarde and Postmodernism in the 1970s," *After the Great Divide* 160–77.
61. Richard McCormick, *Politics of the Self: Feminism and the Postmodern in West German Literature and Film* (Princeton: Princeton UP, 1991).

been called the "New Subjectivity," his insistence on subjective agency, however fractured or fragmented, shows rather similar strategies about how to fuse the personal and the political. Immediacy in his poems always means being immediate to an experiencing subject. When Brinkmann favors the replacing of sense with sensuality, he is attempting to still "the hunger for experience"[62] and not to ridicule experience altogether. The poet at the heart of his poetry is still a person, not, as in Warhol's art, a persona.

Similarly, while Brinkmann shares the anti-intellectualism and anti-rationalism of Pop art and the celebration of the seductive power of images because they challenge the confinements of discourse, he insists that a literature that opens itself to the everyday and the banal still has to reflect its means of incorporation; what is called for is "a sensibility . . . that knows how to react to contemporary impulses [*Reizmuster*] without feeling guilty, and yet without losing itself in these impulses so that it would produce a mere doubling."[63] As a writer interested in images, the threat of duplication is, of course, always diminished by the fact that images have to be translated—and thus interpreted—into words, but even the photo collage "Wie ich lebe und warum" (How I Live and Why), which apart from the title contains no words, highlights the I/eye behind the camera. The photos are often out of focus or taken at odd angles as if taken rather hastily; they show the banality of Brinkmann's apartment, individual rooms such as bath or study, its drab Cologne surroundings, and in one memorable instance the feet of the photographer. Rather than duplicating the reality in front of the lens, these photos emphasize the mode of experience of the photographer—hence Brinkmann can claim that they not only demonstrate how he lives but why.

While this insistence on subjectivity distinguishes Brinkmann from Warhol, it is important to note that the experiencing I/eye of Brinkmann's work is no longer the alienated subject of modernism, as a brief comparison of Brinkmann's strategy to fuse the visual and the verbal with modernist precursors shows.[64] When writers like James Joyce, John Dos Passos, or Wolfgang Koeppen imitated the use of film montage, they assembled the individual elements in such a manner that a certain narrative continuity still remained intact. In Brinkmann's notion of montage—most radically demonstrated in the posthumously published volumes *Rom, Blicke, Erkundungen für die Präzisierung des "Gefühls" für einen Aufstand: Reise Zeit Magazin (Tagebuch)*, and *Schnitte*—the sudden zooms, reversing of angles, close-ups,

---

62. This is the title of Michael Rutschky's perceptive study of the 1970s, *Erfahrungshunger: Ein Essay über die siebziger Jahre* (Cologne: Kiepenheuer and Witsch, 1980).

63. "Die Lyrik Frank O'Haras" 213.

64. For an introductory discussion of the influence of film on modern literature and art, see Arnold Hauser's chapter on "The Film Age," in *The Social History of Art,* 4 vols., trans. Stanley Godman (New York: Vintage, 1958) 4:226–59; for a discussion of the relation of film to Expressionist poetry (much appreciated by Brinkmann), see Anton Kaes, "Literary Intellectuals and the Cinema," *New German Critique* 40 (1987): 7–34.

Cartoon from Rolf Dieter Brinkmann, *Die Piloten* (Rowohlt, 1968)

"'I don't understand! I hit the animal right between the eyes, and yet I didn't kill it!

"'Did all the running around in the outer world make me impotent?'

"Meanwhile, in Kitschland: 'What the cop doesn't know is that we (the products of American bourgeois culture) refuse to admit the reality of death . . . and thus we're immune to it!'

"'Like god and art and silly goose.'"

and cuts leave the reader disenfranchised. In these later texts Brinkmann's surface is no longer the polished, aestheticized and removed surface of Warhol but, instead, a mimicry of the brutal, aggressive, and overbearing image-word combinations found in newspapers, comics, and advertising. Nothing is integrated and brought into coherence; everything is simply added on and piled up. Florian Vaßen has pointed out that the montage of *Rom, Blicke* (which incorporates letters, postcards, photos, newspaper clips, train tickets, and other found objects) denies the reader a position within Brinkmann's text, thus producing an uncanny exposure. "By dissecting reality into single, isolated details, and by reducing it to mere facts, the relating of experience becomes impossible—in the end, experience is being destroyed."[65] Yet, as Brinkmann insists in the same text, he understands (his) writing as vehement opposition to a rapid "loss of experience" ("Erfahrungsverlust und Erlebnisverlust").[66] To accept the iconographic quality of everyday life— "das Bildhafte täglichen Lebens"—thus always means both a fragmentation of the subject *and* a mapping of its terrain, a description of the explosion of the self *and* a collecting of the pieces. His descriptions of Rome as garbage heap of Western civilization interspersed with his minute drawings of the terrain covered in his daily walks and travels entail both the long list of postmodern "no-longer-possibles" as well as first steps toward an "aesthetic of cognitive mapping," which is Jameson's answer to the transformations of space, time, and cultural politics in the postmodern era: "a yet unimaginable new mode of representing . . . in which we may again begin to grasp our positioning as individual and collective subjects."[67]

There is no doubt for Brinkmann that this "new realism," as Jameson somewhat confusingly calls it, is one that has to come to terms with the surface and the superficiality of our image-dominated everyday culture. As Brinkmann's works never tire of demonstrating, the persuasive power of images will not go away, even if couched in so many words. What matters, today perhaps more than ever, is "*in* which images we live and *with which images we combine our own images.*"

---

65. Florian Vaßen, "Die zerfallende Stadt—Der "zerfällende" Blick: Zu Rolf Dieter Brinkmanns Großstadtprosa *Rom, Blicke," Juni: Magazin für Kultur und Politik* 5 (1991): 189–97; here 195.

66. *Rom, Blicke* 417.

67. Jameson 54.

CHAPTER 3

Watching Television with
Elfriede Jelinek

Media determine our situation which (in spite of that or because of that)
deserves an analysis.

—*Friedrich Kittler*

Life follows the lead of television, and television is an imitation of life.

—*Elfriede Jelinek*

In Don DeLillo's novel *White Noise* Murray Jay Siskind, a visiting lecturer in
the Department of Popular Culture at the College on the Hill, shares with his
colleague Jack Gladney his bewilderment about the research interests of his
fellow scholars: "I understand the music, I understand the movies, I even see
how comic books can tell us something. But there are full professors in this
place who read nothing but cereal boxes." To which Gladney replies: "It's the
only avant-garde we've got."[1] DeLillo here offers an ironic comment on the
aporias of the contemporary avant-garde, which in order to remain "ahead"
have to reinvent its relation to consumer culture in ever more "radical" ways
until the two have in fact become indistinguishable from each other.

According to Peter Bürger's *Theory of the Avant-Garde,* which provides
one of the most sustained though not uncontested accounts of the avant-
gardes of the beginning of this century, it is the postwar culture industry (in
Adorno's sense of the term) that has produced today's homogeneity between
culture and commerce described by DeLillo. The culture industry has thus
perverted the goals of the historical avant-garde, which, by attacking the
institutionalization of art, intended to close the gap between art and life. For,
as Bürger argues, the most important insight of the historical avant-garde
was to understand how the production and reception of art was (and continues to be) shaped by institutions. What mattered most, therefore, was attacking the ways in which these institutions determined and in fact limited the
function and reception of art—an experiment that, according to Bürger, ultimately failed because the avant-garde's reliance on shock and its complicity

---

1. Don DeLillo, *White Noise* (New York: Penguin, 1986) 10.

in the logic of creating the New turned out to be artistic aporias. In the end the institutions of art proved to be stronger than expected and did not crumble. All that the historical avant-garde really achieved, Bürger concludes, was to heighten our awareness for the power of these institutions.

The subject of Bürger's book are such movements as Dada, French surrealism, and Cubism, but the context of his work is the emergence of Pop art and its reception in Germany during the 1960s. As I discussed in the previous chapter, the problematic tension between art and life again became important when Pop challenged traditional notions of what we consider art and of art's role in society. For Rolf Dieter Brinkmann and many other German and Austrian writers and artists of the late 1960s and early 1970s, Pop held the promise of a democratization of art. Bürger, however, did not share this optimism. For him Pop was but a ahistorical and apolitical copy of the movements of the first two decades of the century: "The neo-avant-garde institutionalizes the *avant-garde as art* and thus negates genuinely avant-gardiste intentions."[2] Yet, as I have argued with regard to Rolf Dieter Brinkmann and as I want to reiterate in this chapter with regard to a very different writer, the insistence of the historical avant-garde to close the gap between high and low by rejecting the elitism of modernism and its hostility to mass culture has survived the demise of the avant-garde. It can be seen as the most important feature for defining today's postmodernist art. Andreas Huyssen, for instance, agrees with Bürger's assessment of the failure of the *historical* avant-garde but insists that the increasing blurring between high art and mass culture that we presently witness in a variety of cultural manifestations cannot be seen exclusively in terms of the commodification and reification of art, as Bürger claims; instead, it has to be seen as an opportunity rather than a loss of quality.[3] It is in this triangle of mass culture, the historical avant-garde, and postmodernist literature that the early works of Elfriede Jelinek need to be situated.

Like the literary works of Brinkmann, Peter Handke, Wolf Wondratschek, Wolfgang Bauer, Peter Chotjewitz, Ror Wolf, F. C. Delius, Urs Widmer, Gerhard Roth, and many others who first emerged in the late 1960s and early 1970s, Jelinek's novel *Michael: Ein Jugendbuch für die Infantilgesellschaft* (*Michael: A Youth Book for the Infantile Society* [1972]) as well as her first published novel *wir sind lockvögel baby!* (*we are decoys, baby!* [1970]) try to revive a European avant-garde tradition by infusing it with contemporary American Pop art and popular culture. Jelinek's works show a fascination with American films, comics, cartoons, and the "cut-up and fold-in" technique of the underground literature of William Burroughs, which she combines with the radical poetic experiments of the Wiener Gruppe (the

2. Peter Bürger, *Theory of the Avant-Garde,* trans. Michael Shaw (Minneapolis: U of Minnesota P, 1984) 58.

3. Andreas Huyssen, *After the Great Divide: Modernism, Mass Culture, Postmodernism* (Bloomington: Indiana UP, 1986) ix.

Viennese Group consisting of avant-garde writers working together from 1952 to 1964 and which experimented with new forms of literary representations) and the Grazer Gruppe (the Graz Group, a more contemporary group of experimental writers with which Jelinek and also Handke were associated).[4] *Michael,* a very poignant example of this trend, portrays the devastating influence of television programs on two teenage women. Jelinek calls her text a novel but in fact suspends any traditional notions of unity of plot or character (let alone character development) and, instead, stages a cacophony of discourses drawn from TV series, advertising, pop psychology, and the confused consciousness of her struggling protagonists. Her satire displays an intimate knowledge of the programs made for the first Austrian and German television generation as well as their potential for violence and exploitation. Jelinek's work can therefore be read as an example of an avant-garde literature searching to incorporate critically elements from consumer society and popular culture. The question to be addressed is the one outlined earlier: Can Jelinek's tendency for appropriation, reappropriation, and revision of various discourses of popular culture—often considered a trademark of postmodernism—negotiate a path between, on the one hand, the aporias of the historical avant-garde, which instead of bridging the gap between art and the everyday (*Lebenswelt*) ultimately had nothing to offer but innovations of form, and, on the other hand, the complete dissolving of the differences between art and commerce of DeLillo's cereal box-reading scholars who confirm the old saying that "die wahre Kunst" (true art) has become "die Ware Kunst" (art as commodity).

Addressing these question means addressing the function of literature in the age of mass media. Here Jelinek's experimental prose provides a fascinating case study of the possibilities and limitations of the literary avant-garde vis-à-vis the most encompassing contemporary mass medium: television. Since a changed relation between art and popular culture has been identified as one of the main characteristics of postmodernism, an analysis of Jelinek's appropriation and critique of television will shed some light on the question of whether she really should be considered a postmodern writer, as so many critics have suggested,[5] or whether she remains imbedded in a modernist tradition that insists on the great divide between high and

---

4. Jelinek also translated Thomas Pynchon's novel *Gravity's Rainbow,* which is often considered a prime example of American postmodern literature.

5. Cf. Allyson Fiddler, "There Goes That Word Again, or Elfriede Jelinek and Postmodernism," in *Elfriede Jelinek: Framed by Language,* ed. Jorum B. Johns and Katherine Arens (Riverside, CA: Ariadne P, 1995) 129–49; John Pizer, "Modern vs. Postmodern Satires: Karl Kraus and Elfriede Jelinek," *Monatshefte* 86.4 (1994): 500–513; and Ingeborg Hoesterey's two articles, "Postmoderner Blick auf österreichische Literatur: Bernhard, Glaser, Handke, Jelinek, Roth," *Modern Austrian Literature* 23.3–4 (1990): 65–76; and "A Feminist 'Theater of Cruelty': Surrealist and Mannerist Strategies in *Krankheit oder Moderne Frauen* and *Lust,*" in Johns and Arens, *Elfriede Jelinek* 151–65.

low. Before turning to an analysis of Jelinek's novel *Michael: Ein Jugend-buch für die Infantilgesellschaft*—a satire on the effects of television *and* a comment on the relationship between literature and television—I want to map key arguments about the relation between literature and television prominent in Germany during the early 1970s. I will conclude with some remarks about questions of cultural imperialism as the hidden referent of Jelinek's critique of television.

German Intellectuals and Television

In the essay "Welt ohne Fernsehen" (World without Television [1979]) the critic Jörg Drews claimed that television has no social or artistic value and called for its abolishment: "Television must disappear, there are no grounds for its existence, it is an evil, a dead-end. Except for the fact that it does exist, there is no serious argument that could be made in its favor, and everybody knows that."[6] Drew's polemic assessment summarizes *in nuce* a long tradition of German thought regarding the threats of mass culture and mass media. As outlined in chapter 1, this tradition can be traced back to the first emergence of cinema as mass medium during the Weimar years. In postwar Germany the discussion of the relationship between mass culture and high culture was shaped in decisive ways by Adorno and Horkheimer's study of the culture industry. Theirs was an ideological analysis that aimed at understanding culture as a form of social expression. According to this approach, specific cultural texts are analyzed in order to comprehend how these texts embody and enact values, beliefs, and ideas. Adorno and Horkheimer defined ideology as false consciousness: the ruling class attempts to promulgate its own values as universal ones, thereby leading others to adopt their values as their own and thus participating in their own exploitation and oppression. The more successful the ruling class is in describing its own beliefs as "natural" beliefs, the more successful it will be in perpetuating the status quo and continuing the class system of oppression. According to the Frankfurt School, the task of the intellectual becomes teaching the oppressed about their state of oppression. In one of his few comments on television, when discussing who should decide about the programming on television, Adorno stresses the importance of the intellectual. The question raised in the title of his speech, "Kann das Publikum wollen?" ("Can the Audience Have a Will?") is answered in the negative: since the web of manipulation is so tightly woven that it produces in the audience a false consciousness, television viewers, had they a choice in programming, would pick only those programs already forced on them. Adorno therefore concludes: "Not the plebiscitary majority should decide over cultural affairs geared towards the masses . . . but instead only people

---

6. Jörg Drews, "Welt ohne Fernsehen," *Merkur* 33.6 (1979): 593–97; here 593.

who are competent, and who know as much about art as about the social implications of mass media."[7]

Following Adorno and Horkheimer's account of the culture industry as forging a false reconciliation between art and reality by producing standardized and homogenizing cultural commodities, two strategies of the critique of mass media emerged in the 1970s. On the one hand are those who insist on the great divide between mass culture and high culture; in the spirit of Adorno's modernism they feel that literature, music, and the arts have to be protected from an encroaching commercialization and reification. So as not to facilitate a false reconciliation between art and commerce, serious art, Adorno believes, is meant to negate the negativity of reality. This approach underlies the work of Botho Strauß, whose novels frequently turn to a discussion of television. Strauß's intellectual protagonists usually despise what is shown on television and define their own tastes and identities in opposition to it. In *Die Widmung (Devotion* [1989]) the narrator laments: "I have seen too much disappear into the TV for my heart still to cling to images;"[8] and in *Paare, Passanten (Couples, Passerby* [1984]) we read: "No one has been more deprived of their powers of deception, not by the church, not by war, than we who have been made dull through irradiation [*wir matt Bestrahlten*], we who still want to think and want to see can only do it in flash-fade, lonesome voyeurs whose world vision is ruled by the jump cut, the way a slotted aperture makes a one-dollar peep show flicker."[9] Like Adorno and Horkheimer, Strauß sees television as a medium that has exploited any relation between reality and representation, and it has conditioned our ways of seeing and perceiving the world. Like the invention of radio and cinema, television has dramatically altered the social and aesthetic function of literature. "Whoever is writing these days may try to artificially shut himself off, and make things different, but these remain the true conditions under which he will write."[10] Whether we like it or not, television determines the conditions of writing— how one writes, for whom, and for what reasons, as well as its modes of distribution and reception. Strauß's own "answer" has been to produce a literature that radically focuses on the construction of subjectivities, developing a verbal economy with which visual media such as film and television cannot rival. (Significantly, none of his works has been made into a film yet.)

---

7. Theodor W. Adorno, "Kann das Publikum wollen?" in *Vierzehn Mutmaßungen über das Fernsehen: Beiträge zu einem aktuellen Thema,* ed. Anne Rose Katz (Munich: Deutscher Taschenbuch Verlag, 1963) 55–60; here 57. Cf. also Theodor W. Adorno, "Television and the Patterns of Mass Culture," in *Television: The Critical View,* ed. Horace Newcomb (New York: Oxford UP, 1976) 239–59; "How to Look at Televison," in Theodor W. Adorno, *The Culture Industry: Selected Essays on Mass Culture,* ed. J. M. Bernstein (London: Routledge, 1991) 126–53; and "Prolog zum Fernsehen" and "Fernsehen als Ideologie," in Theodor W. Adorno, *Eingriffe* (Frankfurt am Main: Suhrkamp, 1963) 69–80, 81–98.

8. Botho Strauß, *Die Widmung* (Munich: Deutscher Taschenbuch Verlag, 1980) 31f.

9. Botho Strauß, *Paare, Passanten* (Munich: Deutscher Taschenbuch Verlag, 1984) 178.

10. Ibid. 178.

To be sure, a critique of television such as Strauß's is not really addressed to television viewers but, rather, seeks approval from the readers of his books. Those who make it through Strauß's dense prose in all likelihood will applaud him for the insight and acumen of descriptive detail, but they are rarely the ones that Strauß describes as television addicts. If one really wants to address the evils of mass media, one has to do so by using a mass medium. This, I would argue, is the strategy behind Strauß's essay "Anschwellender Bocksgesang" ("Increasing Tragedy" [1993]), published in *Der Spiegel,* and the reasons for the tremendous response to Strauß's essay have much less to do with its content—much of what Strauß here writes about the reversal of politically Right or Left positions, about questions of national identity, or about television he had already said years before—than with the fact that a recluse for once stepped out of hiding and gave a rare "public" performance (a fact, of course, that *Der Spiegel* did not fail to mention). I will return to the political implications of this essay in the epilogue; here I want to focus only on its critique of mass media. One can read "Anschwellender Bocksgesang" as the reaction of the solitary, romantic believer in the power of the word against the magic of the new media: with self-hatred Strauß here acknowledges that he only gets his message across if he uses the very media he despises. This message, again, is that contemporary media society has made it impossible to experience reality without mediation and thus to have any real understanding of it. As Strauß reiterates with unprecedented furor:

> These commentators, debaters, and info-tainers endlessly belabor thoughts which we only mentioned in passing; they fill up their time slots with questions which they would never even ask themselves. They even incorporate enigmas and hieroglyphs into their shallow, see-through language—these mediators and world-moderat-makers. The disgrace of the modern world is not that it is full of tragedies—in this it hardly differs from other eras—but the incredible process of moderating, the inhuman down-scaling through mediation . . . The regime of the telecratic public sphere is the least bloodiest reign of terror and at the same time the most encompassing totalitarianism in history.[11]

The only remedy for Strauß is to turn one's back on mainstream media society, to find "the magic places of separation" (*die magischen Orte der Absonderung*),[12] to educate oneself through reading. In the end Strauß redraws the line between the masses and the intellectual, between mass culture and *Kultur:* "If we only stopped talking about culture [*Kultur*] and instead would distinguish categorically between what keeps the masses content from what belongs to the stragglers [*den Versprengten*] (who do not even form a com-

---

11. Botho Strauß, "Anschwellender Bocksgesang," *Der Spiegel* 6 (1993): 202–7; here 206–7.
12. Ibid. 206.

munity any more)—and that both are separated forever by the notion of the sewer, the channel of television."[13]

Although Strauß stresses his isolated position in his attacks on television, he is representative of a large number of German intellectuals from both sides of the political spectrum. Lutz Hachmeister has argued that much of the hostility of intellectuals toward television can be explained through the fact that television tends to draw attention away from the print-dominated culture of writers and academics.[14] Indeed, this kind of resentment seems to underlie a series of critiques of television by American writers, including Jerry Mander's *Four Arguments for the Elimination of Television* (1978), Marie Winn's *The Plug-in-Drug: Television, Children, and the Family* (1977), and Neil Postman's *Amusing Ourselves to Death: Public Discourse in the Age of Show Business* (1985), many of which are widely read in Germany and Austria.

A different critique of mass media is represented by Hans Magnus Enzensberger. In the wake of the failed student protest movement Enzensberger scolded intellectuals for their disinterest in and rejection of television, radio, and the press. The widespread media hostility among intellectuals only proved to Enzensberger that they felt the threat of losing their privileged position as spokesperson for others. Following a different leftist tradition, namely the work of Walter Benjamin and Bertolt Brecht from the 1920s, Enzensberger argued in his "Baukasten zu einer Theorie der Medien" ("Constituents of a Theory of the Media"[(1970]) that the media can serve an emancipatory cause if they can be made to act as agents of communication and not only distribution. Against fellow leftists who perceived mass media as a mere tool for manipulation, Enzensberger wrote that there was no "pure," or uncontaminated, writing, filming, or broadcasting to be had. What mattered, instead, was to participate in, rather than refrain from, the mass media: "A revolutionary plan should not require the manipulators to disappear; on the contrary, it must make everyone a manipulator."[15] Enzensberger thus implicitly rejects Adorno's notion of false consciousness, which would presuppose the possibility of a true consciousness; for Enzensberger there is no "outside" of ideology.

Despite their ideological differences regarding the mass media, Strauß and Enzensberger coincide in the evaluation of the power of the media to shape the public sphere in historically unprecedented ways. For both, however, their insights prove to be without benefit. The irony of Strauß's foray into the world of journalism is that his *Spiegel* essay, at least for now, has thoroughly eclipsed his novelistic and dramatic oeuvre. His intention was to

---

13. Ibid. 207.

14. Cf. Lutz Hachmeister, "Der Gesamtschuldner: Das Fernsehen als Antipode intellektueller Orthodoxie," *Merkur* 534–35 (1993): 841–53.

15. Hans Magnus Enzensberger, "Constituents of a Theory of the Media," *New Left Review* 64 (1970): 13–36; here 20.

save literature from the fangs of the mass media, yet the result has been the opposite. Reading Strauß today, we always and foremost read the author of "Anschwellender Bocksgesang" and its media hype. As Benjamin Henrichs comments, "those who enter the media will die in the media."[16] In a similar vein Enzenberger's proposal about the progressive potential of the media remained just that, a proposal, as his lead was not taken up by others. The proliferation of the media in Germany in the 1980s, especially the introduction of cable TV and the increased number of weekly magazines, have further marginalized intellectual thought and decreased the potential for democratic exchange, at least in the way Enzensberger had envisioned it. In his 1988 essay "Das Nullmedium oder Warum alle Klagen gegen das Fernsehen gegenstandslos sind" ("The Zero Medium, or Why All Complaints against Television Are Futile") he mocked with self-irony the 1970s optimism of his "old constituents theory"[17] and radically reversed his view of television. Enzensberger now describes television as a technological version of a psychotherapy for the masses, a truly buddhistic machine that allows its viewers to enter meditation precisely because it is devoid of content and meaning.[18] If in "Constituents Theory" he attacked Marshall McLuhan for his lack of analytical tools for understanding social relations (a common Marxist critique at the time), he now seems to adhere to McLuhan's slogan that the medium is the message and that television as a zero medium therefore broadcasts nothing but zero messages. Reverting back to the insistence on the great divide of his teacher Adorno, Enzensberger, in a logical short-circuit, considers those programs inappropriate for television that still do contain a residue of meaning: religious services, operas, chamber concerts, and feature films.

While McLuhan makes a surprising return in Enzensberger's description of television of the late 1980s, his influence also informs the media theories of Jean Baudrillard[19] and, closer to home, Friedrich Kittler. Following McLuhan, Kittler claims that it is impossible to understand the content of the media, because all understanding is determined by technology, of which human subjects are but an effect. "Humans exist only to the degree that they can be stored and transmitted by the media. Thus, what matters are not the content or the message with which broadcast technology outfits so-called

---

16. Benjamin Henrichs, *Die Zeit,* March 12, 1995, 17.

17. Hans Magnus Enzensberger, "Das Nullmedium oder Warum alle Klagen über das Fernsehen gegenstandslos sind," *Der Spiegel* 20 (1988); reprinted in Hans M. Enzensberger, *Mittelmaß und Wahn: Gesammelte Zerstreuungen* (Frankfurt: Suhrkamp, 1991) 89–103; here 98.

18. It should be added that, in true Enzensbergerian fashion, he recently again changed his mind about television. In light of the news coverage of civil wars and brutal carnage all over the globe, Enzensberger called television "the most corrupt of all media"—a claim that only makes sense if one attributes meaning to its representations ("Ausblick auf den Bürgerkrieg," *Der Spiegel* 25 [1993]: 170–75; here 174).

19. Cf. Andreas Huyssen, "In the Shadow of McLuhan: Baudrillard's Theory of Simulation," *Twilight Memories: Marking Time in a Culture of Amnesia* (New York: Routledge, 1995) 175–90.

souls for the duration of a technological era but (adhering strictly to McLuhan) only their switches (*Schaltungen*), this schematism of perception per se."[20] The popularity of McLuhan's message with these intellectuals and its astonishing perseverance into the 1990s (at least in Germany but, if the popularity of Baudrillard in this country is any indication, also in the United States) can perhaps be explained through one simple observation: if the medium is indeed the message, then there is no need to bother with that message itself. Instead of asking what television teaches or tells its audiences, or what meanings they derive or poach from it, one can simply focus on the media-determined possibility conditions of meaning (Kittler), refortify the last bastions of high art (Strauß), or enjoy the buddhistic bliss of the medium as message and massage (Enzensberger).

Since Jelinek describes herself as a Marxist (she belonged to Austrian Communist Party [ÖKP] until 1991) we should not be surprised to see significant parallels between descriptions of the relation of art, mass media, and society in her writings and those of the Frankfurt School. In her novel *Michael* we witness two naive, working-class women falling victim to illusions about love and life created by television. According both to Jelinek and to Adorno and Horkheimer, the culture industry serves as palliative by suggesting that there exist no real differences of class or gender. Both *The Dialectics of Enlightenment* and *Michael* portray mass culture as a homogeneous, centrally controlled and organized system intended to keep its consumers immature and uninformed; its promises create druglike dependencies that make its helpless consumers come back for more. Gerda and her friend Ingrid are indeed just like the *Ladenmädchen,* or shop girls, of Siegfried Kracauer's famous essay of 1920s who gullibly buy into the fantasies enacted in the moving images in front of them.[21]

Jelinek's method in the novel, as in almost all her writings, is to make visible how certain patterns of oppression are masked by the ideology of capitalism and bourgeois society. While this society wants to portray certain aspects of life as unchangeable, Jelinek points to the ways in which they are constructed, thus allowing us to ask who constructs them and for what reasons. Drawing on Roland Barthes's work on mythology,[22] Jelinek calls her strategy an "Entmythologisierungsvorgang" (process of demythologization).[23] If myth, according to Barthes, is a form of language that makes things seem natural, given, eternal, and immutable, demythol-

---

20. Kittler, *Grammophon, Film, Typewriter* (Berlin: Brinkmann and Bose, 1986) 5.

21. Siegfried Kracauer, *Das Ornament der Masse: Essays,* ed. Karsten Witte (Frankfurt: Suhrkamp, 1977) 279–94. Incidentally, the volume is dedicated to Theodor W. Adorno.

22. Cf. Roland Barthes, *Mythologies,* trans. Annette Lavers (New York: Farrar, 1972).

23. "Warum ist das Schminken für Sie wichtig, Frau Jelinek? Ein Interview von Agnes Hüfner," *Frankfurter Allgemeine Zeitung,* 31 October 1986, 94–95; here 94.

ogization is the attempt to expose the "natürlichkeitsschleim der alles überzieht und überklebt" (the slime of naturalness that covers and clogs up everything), as she writes in her programmatic essay "die endlose unschuldigkeit" (the eternal innocence [1970]).[24] Both in the essay and in the novel Jelinek's key device is montage. Throughout the essay Jelinek juxtaposes theoretical remarks or quotes about the mechanisms of television and mass media with excerpts from TV series such as "The Flintstones," "Der Kommissar," "Flipper," "Lassie," and "Daktari." Read side by side with psychoanalytic or Marxist observations, the TV clips suddenly appear in a strange new light. Through exaggeration and the sudden insertion of violent or sexually explicit material into the clips, a distantiation is achieved that reveals the hypocrisy of seemingly harmless programs: "oh simon, you're bleeding! don't mention it. but I must find a second exit before it's too late. quickly! come! but before we get out let's fuck again, then everything will go easier!"[25] The same montage principle informs *Michael,* in which scenes from familiar television shows are suddenly made strange when the child-loving Uncle Bill of "Family Affair" unexpectedly sexually molests his niece; when Porter Ricks from "Flipper" sadistically tortures animals; or when Inge Meise, a parody of Inge Meysel, the German TV mother par excellence, surprises her guests by exclaiming, "I'm so horny." These scenes from television are imbedded in a narrative that revolves around the two shop girls, Gerda and Ingrid, and that constantly juxtaposes the fiction of the TV programs with the lives of Jelinek's fictional characters. Yet the division implied by intertitles such as "reality" and "story" or "retelling" quickly collapses as Ingrid and Gerda interact with the TV characters. It remains undecidable—and it ultimately matters very little—if they step into a fantasy world or if the TV characters enter theirs. What does matter is that reality quickly punishes those who hold television to its promises, because they dare to venture beyond the positions of class and gender ascribed by society. While the media seduces them to want "more," reality does not allow it. Like Adorno and Horkheimer, television is for Jelinek a mass medium that ultimately only serves as a "kontrollinstanz"[26] and a "massenkommunikatorische[s] über ich"[27] that perpetuates patriarchal society.

Since its belated publication in West Germany, in 1969, Adorno and Horkheimer's account of the culture industry has undergone profound criticism by contemporary film and television scholars who have challenged its monolithic account of a systematically organized, all-encompassing

---

24. Elfriede Jelinek, "die endlose unschuldigkeit," in *Trivialmythen,* ed. Renate Matthei (Frankfurt am Main: März, 1970) 40–66; here 45.
25. Ibid. 50.
26. Ibid. 43.
27. Ibid. 42.

machinery of mind control.[28] Indeed, if Jelinek's early novel *Michael* were nothing but a rehearsing of Adorno's critique of ideology, it would be hardly worth considering today. But Jelinek's text is first and foremost a *literary* text and therefore addresses the question of the function of literature in the age of television. Besides Jelinek's crude basis-superstructure model, and in clear contradiction of it, there is a fascination with mass media that points toward a collapsing of Adorno's binary thinking. This is the point I want to turn to now.

Literature in the Media Society

Elfriede Jelinek's discussion of television in *Michael* contains elements of both Strauß's modernist critique of television as well as Enzensberger's belief of his 1970 essay that the Left can no longer ignore the mass media—a paradoxical concoction that brings Jelinek closer to the postmodern sensibility that recognizes the aporias of modernism without really being able to go "beyond" them, since the notion of a beyond relies on an understanding of progress with which postmodernism disagrees. Instead, *Michael* can be read as an attempt to come to terms with television from within. In order to engage with Jelinek's contradictory and ambiguous appropriation of television, let me quote a longer scene from the novel:

> stop! isn't that the young mr. boss? gerda secretly calls him michael when she talks about him with mommy. sometimes she imagines that she can call him that in front of everybody.

---

28. Scholars such as Stuart Hall and John Fiske in England; Jim Collins, Mimi White, and Douglas Kellner in the United States; and Knut Hickethier and Lutz Hachmeister in Germany have shown how Adorno's theory of mass media needs to be revised in two important ways: more emphasis needs to put on the reception because audiences are extremely heterogeneous and therefore produce, or "poach," a variety of equally valid meanings from one and the same program. Furthermore, and beyond the act of reception, these programs themselves have to be seen as reflecting a struggle of *competing* ideologies and therefore contain breakages and ruptures. Both of these important points are not considered by Jelinek; according to her portrayal of television, *all* programs contain the same repressive message, and *all* working-class women derive the same meaning from them.

The Austrian-German family game show "Wünsch Dir was," which Jelinek mentions frequently in her novel, would have provided a good example to explore the breakages in the game show genre. Hosts Dietmar Schönherr and Vivi Bach pushed the envelope of this genre by repeatedly including games or gestures previously not seen on TV. In contradiction to federal policy that TV may not be used to advance a certain political party, Schönherr wore a red carnation, a symbol of the Austrian Socialists, on the eve of the election. Jelink herself mentions the famous incident when in a fashion show game the daughter of one family wore a transparent blouse. Rather than understanding this as an attack on the puritanical codes of society *through* television, and therefore crediting television with a modest degree of rebellion, Jelinek assumes that television viewers felt embarrassed, rather than challenged, provoked, or amused, by the incident (cf. Elfriede Jelinek, *Michael: Ein Jugendbuch für die Infantilgesellschaft* [Reinbek: Rowohlt, 1972] 137).

yes right. it is michael. the young mr. boss has a problem. he is desperately trying to maneuver his new jaguar into a garage door which belongs to a villa with the same name. it doesn't work. michael i help you. gerda rushes towards him the mother follows a bit slower. after all the young folks want to be alone. mother eyes are watching. gerda stretches and signals with her hands and shows him the way in and twists almost unnaturally and shows and yells and makes faces and almost tears herself up. more to the right! (michael) she adds softly inaudibly. michael reverses and tries for the tenth time. gerda indicates with her fingers the millimeters michael has to go further to the right. there! krrracks. a scream from several voices. the left front light is broken. gerda turns as white as snow. her mommy hits gerda's face with her fist. you mean woman, go and apologize to your mr. boss. gerda sobs. in these few seconds her entire life passes by. in front of her inner eye. everything she's ever seen on tv. for instance the scene where gerda bends over so that one can see her long tanned legs and where she gets a bag from the back seat of the low sports car.
the beautiful new car. the super sports car has a dent. mother has turned white as snow. if she has to pay for this! but gerda knows right away what must & will happen. after all why else does she watch the entire tv program until late at night? this is what will happen next: she lies down in front of the driveway like a board in her new winter coat. in a moment michael will rush to her and ask: girl are you hurt? then he will pick her up. something like understanding will flash across his face. then he will hold her tight and never let her go again. she will wait for the divorce from patrizia in a country house in the mountains. she will be well taken care of there. she will be all alone there and yet not alone after all because she's got MICHAEL.[29]

This scene exploits the incongruity between the dull reality of the young protagonist and an imaginary dreamworld that could relieve her from the monotony of the everyday—a dreamworld that, like the good-looking, prosperous, dynamic junior executive Michael, is derived from television shows. This is a world in which class conflicts, psychological, social, and economic problems are easily resolved and dramatic conflicts are followed by the inevitable happy end. As the continuation of the scene shows, however, those who confuse facts with fiction will be punished. Gerda's eagerness to act out "everything she's ever seen on tv" leads to tragedy. Instead of seducing Michael by showing him "her long tanned legs," Michael himself reverts to the kind of violence typical of a television character: "mr. michael the junior boss steps on the gas. puts it in reverse. the car jumps backwards across gerda. as if she were nothing. she is nothing. gerda looks like a rolled and tied-

---

29. Ibid. 62f.

up piece of ham. only mountain and valley. some caterpillars look this disgusting too."[30] The episode concludes with Gerda's realization that she will have to wear her old coat to the office tomorrow, as her new one is now ruined.

The scene presents an ambiguous notion about what the function of literature would be in regard to television. On the one hand, and following Adorno, the intention of Jelinek's satire is apparently to show how seemingly innocuous television programs can control and manipulate their consumers with sometimes devastating effects. Time and again, Gerda and Ingrid, the two "protagonists" of a narrative without progression, experience aggression and brutality when their TV-induced fantasies collide with a harsh reality. Television is therefore but a tool in the systematic coercion of its easily duped consumers; entertainment becomes synonymous with keeping the viewers complacent, docile, and easily exploited. Since Jelinek's novel empowers its readers to see through their modes of manipulation and infantilization, it has been read as an example of "a literature that enlightens by new means."[31] According to this view, the novel's imitation of the language of television creates an awareness for the latent violence of seemingly harmless children programs like "Flipper," "Daktari," and "Family Affair," family shows like "Ida Rogalski," and game shows like "Wünsch Dir Was." Yet there are also problems with considering *Michael* a piece of literature that enlightens its readers. As in the case of Strauß, one would have to ask whether those who watch TV will actually be the ones to read Jelinek's novel; does her message, in fact, reach those whom she addresses?

But there is a more important question to be asked: even if we would accept that Jelinek's message about the manipulative forces of television gets across, one would have to wonder if anything can be done about this manipulation. As the episode here shows, television erases in Gerda the ability to distinguish fictional characters or events from real life. The fact that the only consequence to come of the accident is that Gerda will have to wear her old coat to work tomorrow renders the violence done to her a kind of cartoon violence—a graphic and exaggerated violence with only momentary effects and which seems to imply that Gerda is not only a consumer of television but also that she herself has become a TV character. It is not only that the characters can no longer decide if they are confusing fact and fiction; we as readers can no longer be sure if Gerda and Ingrid are the creation of Jelinek's literary discourse or of the discourse of television. In this respect, then, the line between the real and the hyperreal has disappeared and with it any possibility of ideology critique that could reveal the manipulative power of the media. We have entered Baudrillard's simulacrum, in which any distinction

---

30. Ibid. 64.

31. Sibylle Späth, "Im Anfang war das Medium . . . : Medien- und Spachkritik in Jelineks frühen Prosatexten," in *Elfriede Jelinek,* ed. Kurt Bartsch and Günter Höfler (Graz: Droschl, 1991) 95–120; here 113.

between the real and the simulated, essence and appearance, truth and lie, has become impossible. Television has drained the real out of its commodities and characters, and images now only refer to other images.

The predicament described in Baudrillard's media theory has been equated with the postmodern condition in general. In a similar vein certain stylistic and formal aspects of Jelinek's prose (and of her plays) have been identified as distinctively postmodern. Her radical intertextuality, which combines often unacknowledged quotes and materials from a wide variety of artistic and nonartistic sources, has been read as a strategy for questioning modernist conceptions of the purity of language and for refusing to elevate art into a realm separated from the world. As one critic observed about *Michael:* "She really knows how to imitate the optimistic, friendly, public and yet so marvelously private tone of the mass-medialized shows for children, quiz shows, and family shows. Those who would not have believed that this short, sweet, self-assured and untruthful way of speaking can be reproduced in print have been proven wrong."[32] Making ample use of reproduction and imitation, her collages reassemble disparate elements in striking fashion, thereby asking readers to question previous assumptions about their meanings while simultaneously effacing the role of the author as creator and organizer.

It is not only the subject matter—in the case of *Michael* the portrayal of a televised hyperreality—that seems constructed but also the subjectivities of the two main characters, Ingrid and Gerda. Unlike the heroes or heroines of a realist narrative, these are protagonists without *Innenleben,* without independent agency, without a voice of their own. If the postmodern condition is indeed characterized by the death of the subject, as so many commentators have claimed, then the two women are prime examples of that condition. Only rarely do we glimpse a potential escape route out of the hyperreality of television, as, for instance, when Gerda believes that she is in the wrong movie.[33] As the mere projection screen of an endless flow of images, the two women remain two-dimensional; their words are prompted by the programs they watch. A similar flatness characterizes Jelinek's style, which is devoid of symbolism and allegory and instead highlights surface or depthlessness: "I have a tendency to make things flat [*flächig*],"[34] Jelinek said in an interview, and a programmatic essay about her theater plays is entitled "Ich möchte seicht sein" (I Want to Be Shallow).[35]

Jelinek's willingness to take seriously the iconography of contemporary

---

32. Joachim Kaiser, "Meine lieben jungen Freunde," *Süddeutsche Zeitung,* November 16, 1972.

33. Jelinek, *Michael* 31.

34. "Warum ist das Schminken für Sie wichtig, Frau Jelinek?" 45.

35. Elfriede Jelinek, "Ich möchte seicht sein," *Theater Heute* (Jahrbuch 1983) 102; reprinted in a longer version in: Christa Gürtler, ed., *Gegen den schönen Schein: Texte zu Elfriede Jelinek* (Frankfurt am Main: Verlag Neue Kritik, 1990) 157–61.

popular and consumer culture has been read as further indication of her post-modern sensibility.[36] Especially *lockvögel,* a novel populated with characters from comics, film, advertising, television, show business, and Austrian folk tradition (including Batman and Robin, who here appear as a gay couple; White Giant; Mickey Mouse; Ringo Starr; the Easter Bunny; and Kasperl), has been interpreted as a literary text that challenges traditional hierarchies of high and low, attempts to integrate art into the everyday, and therefore seems to follow Leslie Fiedler's call to "cross the border and close the gap" as the prerequisite for a postmodern literature.[37] Even more than *Michael, lockvögel* shocks the reader by revealing the underlying brutality and sexual aggression of seemingly innocuous teenage culture. The voice of a narrator who guides the reader through *Michael* is absent in this earlier novel, leaving us alone amid a stream of increasingly incoherent ministories. As if surfing across TV channels, we follow a never-ending series of events involving innumerable characters that ultimately lead nowhere; conventional notions of time, place, or plot have ceased to exist in this media universe, and all that remains is an endless flow of images. Striking juxtapositions recall the jump-cut technique from film or the sequence of drawings in cartoons, while Jelinek's endless mininarratives seem to imitate Andy Warhol's fascination with serialist art. As in Warhol's paintings, *lockvögel* constantly contrasts high art or serious literature with advertising, thereby challenging the function and autonomy of both discourses.

Yet, despite these obvious allegiances with postmodernism in regard to questions of style and form, and despite her apparent congruity with Baudrillard's nihilistic view of television, there are elements in Jelinek's work that seem to situate her more in the tradition of critical modernism. These include her notion of satire; the strategies according to which she positions the reader; and her focus on texts as representations rather than on textuality itself. All these elements inform Jelinek's notion of "referentiality," a key term for her work. Understood as a practice of literary representation that emulates verisimilitude, referentiality seems to be the prime target of Jelinek's literary montages. With its ability for presenting things through seemingly unedited images, often "live," television is a medium particularly prone to obfuscate its modes of representation and thus come across as "the real thing." As indicated earlier, the critique of television articulated in *Michael* insists that this mass medium erases in its consumers the ability to understand the representations shown on television as fictional or constructed, and tele-

---

36. Cf. Barbara Alms, "Triviale Muster—'hohe' Literatur: Elfriede Jelineks frühe Schriften," *Umbruch* 1 (1987): 31–35; and Sigrid Schmidt-Borenschlager, "Gewalt zeugt Gewalt zeugt Literatur . . . *wir sind lockvögel baby!* und andere frühe Prosa," *Gegen den schönen Schein* 30–43; cf. also the articles by Späth and Hoesterey cited earlier.

37. Leslie Fiedler, "Cross the Border—Close the Gap," *Collected Essays,* 2 vols. (New York: Stein, 1971) 2:461–85.

vision therefore makes it difficult to relate them in a meaningful way to consumers' private lives.

In her own novels and plays Jelinek, in contrast, highlights the text as artifact and metafictional, and in interviews she has explained how she uses makeup and fashion in order to foreground modes of constructing her own gender identity.[38] If the mass media attempt to create verisimilitude by narrativizing events, and thus suggesting closure and wholeness, Jelinek, on the other hand, is at pains to emphasize fragmentation and dislocation. Realism, for her, is a concept never to be used without quotation marks. And yet referentiality enters through the back door. The function of the narrator in *Michael* is a clear indication that, while the protagonists are trapped in the world of representation and simulacra, there is indeed a position outside to be had, even if we should be careful not to confuse the authorial voice with the author herself. But even in the more radical *lockvögel,* in which no such authorial voice appears, there is a bond established between reader and writer by virtue of the selection of *what* is chosen as the subject of satire—namely, the latent violence of popular culture characters that reflects the repressive mechanism of capitalist society. As Dagmar Lorenz has shown: "Jelinek's texts have an effect on the readers . . . because they are caught in a net of silently accepted premises and one-sided perspectives to which the texts offer no alternatives."[39] Without this unspoken agreement about a certain reality, the satire would not work. And Konstanze Fliedl has added, "without a solid notion of reference we would not be able to speak of a satire in the first place."[40] Thus, a significant contradiction in Jelinek's oeuvre becomes apparent: while texts such as *Michael* and *lockvögel* foreground their own constructedness out of a multiplicity of discourses, thereby pointing to the encompassing power of representation(s) in shaping our world, Jelinek's notion of satire presupposes the very unified worldview that her texts question. It seems that Jelinek wants to have a referent and eat it too.[41]

The importance of a certain notion of referentiality or realism for Jelinek, which her radical intertextuality only seemingly questions, indicates

---

38. "Ich will mich durch Bekleidung und Kosmetik nicht eigentlich schön-machen. Ich möchte eine ironische Distanz zu mir gewinnen" ("Warum ist das Schminken für Sie wichtig, Frau Jelinek?" 94).

39. Dagmar C. G. Lorenz, "Humor bei zeitgenössischen Autorinnen," *Germanic Review* 62.1 (1987): 28–36; here 30.

40. Konstanze Fliedl, "'Echt sind nur wir!' Realismus und Satire bei Elfriede Jelinek," *Elfriede Jelinek* 57–77; here 57.

41. As noted earlier, Jelinek's understanding of the text as the manifestation of an underlying system, as evidenced in *Michael,* is rooted in Barthes's work on myth. It should be added here that Barthes's turn to poststructuralism in *S/Z* can be read as a self-critique of his earlier work, in which the focus now shifts away from questions of representation and toward the production of meaning. Barthes now becomes interested in how texts outplay the codes on which they seem to rely. Significantly, Jelinek never quotes from Barthes's later work.

her indebtedness to a modernist notion of being and appearance. Indeed, a long list of other binarisms, all subordinated to the master narrative of ideology critique, now become visible: a clear separation of what is morally right or wrong; of elite and masses; of victim and victimizer. While the working-class protagonists are trapped, the intellectual author-narrator clearly is not, at least not to the degree that she couldn't see through the mechanism of deception. But it remains questionable whether this message of *Michael* will reach the little shop girls. This novel and, even more so, *lockvögel* are highly abstract texts whose complicated wordplays and allusions to a wide variety of intertexts make them difficult to read for those who are not intimately familiar with *both* the icons of contemporary popular culture (which can be very short-lived) and the experimental techniques of the Viennese Group and the Graz Group.[42] Unlike Rolf Dieter Brinkmann, for whom learning from popular culture meant "making poems simple, like opening a window"[43] and who therefore echoes Leslie Fiedler's notion of postmodern literature, Jelinek's fusing of high and low does not really impinge on the function of literature but only on its form and in that respect remains closer to a modernist avant-garde (and its aporias) than to a postmodern literature that would indeed question the role of writing in the postmodern condition.

Jelinek's "gebrauchsanweisung" (user's manual), with which she prefaces *lockvögel,* may further illustrate this point. Here she asks the readers to substitute the name of the novel, inserted in a plastic pocket on the book's shiny black cover, with one of the other six title cards supplied on a perforated sheet of paper: "you are supposed to change this book immediately. you are supposed to change the subtitles." And she adds: "you are supposed to let yourself get carried away to make CHANGES outside legality," a call to combine politics and art. Paradoxically, while the author asks her readers to be disobedient, she herself takes on an authoritative voice. The real paradox of the "gebrauchsanweisung" is that it can only *play* at letting the reader participate in creating the novel (i.e., in choosing its title), thus rendering Jelinek's innovation a mere formal one. Not surprisingly, in the paperback edition of the novel the alternate titles are no longer perforated (one would have to take scissors now to cut them out), and there is no longer a plastic pocket on the cover in which to insert them. It is safe to assume that Jelinek's idea of engaging the readers in acts of "changes" simply required a too expensive layout.

The Discourse of Cultural Imperialism

If in *Michael* television is shown to have no referent, it does however have a clear sense of historical, political, and geographical origin. The majority of

---

42. Cf. Fiddler 136.
43. Rolf Dieter Brinkmann, *Westwärts 1 & 2* (Reinbek: Rowohlt, 1975) 7.

shows such as "Daktari," "Flipper," "Family Affair," "Lassie," "Bonanza," "Dynasty," and "Dallas" discussed in *Michael, lockvögel,* and numerous interviews come from the United States, while Austrian and German television shows, including "Ida Rogalski," "Salto Mortale," and "Der Kommissar," seem merely to emulate their American models. Given Jelinek's ideological indebtedness to Adorno's notion of the culture industry—which, after all, is shaped by his exile experience in the United States—it is not surprising that she perceives these TV programs to be part of an encompassing "media imperialism of the U.S.A,"[44] which also includes American film, rock music, advertising, and consumer culture.[45] Like Wim Wenders, who has claimed that Germans used Polaroids and chewing gum to cover up the hole left by twelve years of fascism, Jelinek explains the great effectiveness and popularity of American mass culture with the Austrians' eagerness to put behind their complicity with Nazism.

Like many of her generation, Jelinek considers the 1950s a period when the crucial chance to build an antifascist democratic society was squandered because the eagerness to start anew prevented a coming to terms with the past. Questions of guilt and responsibility were swept aside: "After 1945 History decided to begin all over again; innocence came up with the same decision."[46] In her novel *Die Ausgesperrten* (*The Outsiders* [1985]) she portrays the Vienna of the late 1950s as a time when this amnesia is being propelled by the *Wirtschaftswunder* ("a German expression, manifested in numerous movies with house bars and kidney-shaped coffee tables, as well as in numerous fat blond women whose great bosoms are held up by wiry contraptions").[47] As the novel makes clear, while the term *economic miracle* is German, the concept of a democratic consumer society in which everybody can enjoy wealth, health, and beauty is primarily a creation of the American media—an image, of course, that, like the television programs of *Michael,* "proves to be no more than consciously manipulated deception."[48]

If the 1950s can be seen as a period of strong American cultural imperialism following the withdrawal of U.S. troops—("Hobby is a rapidly accepted foreign word. The Americans [*Amis*] are gone, their language stays. Hurray")[49]—the late 1960s witness the coming of age of a generation that

44. Josef-Herrmann Sauter, "Interviews mit österreichischen Autoren," *Weimarer Beiträge* 27.6 (1981): 109–17; here 112.

45. Similarly, the ultimate referent of Baudrillard's theory of the media is the United States, as *America* and *Cool Memories* make very clear.

46. Elfriede Jelinek, *Die Ausgesperrten* (Reinbek: Rowohlt, 1985) 98.

47. Ibid. 28.

48. Ulrike Rainer, "The Grand Fraud 'Made in Austria': Economic Miracle, Existentialism, and Private Fascism in Elfriede Jelinek's *Die Ausgesperrten,"* in Johns and Arens, *Elfriede Jelinek* 176–93; here 179. As Rainer points out, the French existentialist philosophy of Sartre and Camus, which Jelinek's title parodies, is shown to be a mere fashion too, offering the same false model to be imitated as the mass media.

49. Jelinek, *Die Ausgesperrten* 109f.

questions both its parents' involvement with Nazism and the political dimension of America's seemingly harmless popular culture, which had played such an important role in their own upbringing. *Lockvögel* is a novel that not only reveals the underlying brutality and aggression of Pop icons such as Batman and Superman and reads them as reflecting a repressive patriarchal society; *lockvögel* also equates America's *cultural* imperialism with its *military* involvement in Vietnam: "the bat person cocks the weapon and silently glides behind the broad trunk of a gigantic tree. a smile flashes across his face when he sees the yellow-skinned subhuman [*untermensch*] who is squatting next to a hanging branch and watches him. he finishes him off quickly man-to-man and climbs over a wall of corpses torsos and limbs."[50] As the racist rhetoric of the *untermensch* indicates, the war in Vietnam reiterates the military aggression of Nazi Germany three decades earlier: in Jelinek's account of history Batman is the revival of the SS officer as cartoon character.

Beyond concealing the aggressive reality of contemporary society, television programs, according to Jelinek, also transport aggression to its viewers: "i claim that salto mortale [a TV show about a circus family] and similar products are fascistic without any disguise."[51] As I pointed out in chapter 1, it needs to be stressed that this ideological indictment of television and its country of origin, the United States, was a far-spread sentiment among German intellectuals in the wake of the Vietnam War. But still in 1989 Wenders claimed that "television is pure fascism" because it lacks both morality and aesthetics.[52] (As I discuss in chapter 7, Wenders's films are full of attacks on television, often connected with criticism of American cultural imperialism.) *Michael* is further linked to fascism by the intertextual reference to Josef Goebbels's novel *Michael: Ein deutsches Schicksal in Tagebüchern* (1934), which also revolves around the life of an adolescent protagonist. The point to be made here is not whether such accusations of fascism are accurate or not but, rather, what happens to discussions of Nazism and its victims if the notion of German and Austrian fascism becomes instrumentalized and dehistoricized in order to criticize contemporary media society or sexism.

The reductiveness of Jelinek's (and Wenders's) approach of equating the United States, television, and fascism and the blindspots of their critique become clearer if we consider the debates surrounding the 1979 screening of the American TV series *Holocaust* in Germany. While many critics, from both sides of the political spectrum, argued that the format of a TV melodrama could not do justice to the historical complexities in question, the tremendous impact of the show with German audiences made any

---

50. Jelinek, *lockvögel* 50.
51. Jelinek, "die endlose unschuldigkeit" 52.
52. Reinhold Rauh, *Wim Wenders und seine Filme* (Munich: Heyne, 1990) 240. His film, *Lisbon Story* (1995), opens with an obituary of German television printed in *Die Wochenpost,* suggesting that the reign of TV may be over.

simple discrediting impossible. If one accepts the emotional reception of the show in Germany as an indication that there is indeed a strong desire among Germans to engage with a difficult past, and if one considers that the show succeeded in confronting Germans with the Holocaust to a degree that no artistic production—let alone scholarly discourse—had previously achieved, claims such as Jelinek's that television is a mere tool for deception and in itself complicitous with fascism become highly dubious. As I argued in chapter 1, this displacement onto a foreign culture of the fascism one cannot face at home is a strategy intended to alleviate the burdens of history and is in fact much more common among the generation that preceded Jelinek and Wenders.

The lack of historical differentiation is an important blindspot in Jelinek, Wenders, and many other leftists of the 1968 generation and has to be understood as a powerful, but naive, desire to be antifascist. More important for my discussion here is a different point: the emotional impact of the TV series *Holocaust* was based on the fact that identification with the victims was possible, something Jelinek's novels are at pains to avoid. Indeed, the success of the TV melodrama questions much of the dominant aesthetic of postwar German theater and literature and its politics of identification. As Andreas Huyssen has argued, "the key problem with critical appraisals of *Holocaust* in Germany lies in their common assumption that a cognitive rational understanding of German anti-Semitism under National Socialism is *per se* incompatible with an emotional melodramatic representation of history as the story of a family."[53] As Huyssen goes on to show in an analysis of *Andorra* by Max Frisch, *The Deputy* by Rolf Hochhuth, and *The Investigation* by Peter Weiss, these plays succeed in analyzing the economic, social, psychological, and ideological continuities between the Third Reich and the Federal Republic and, in Frisch's example, also Switzerland (a claim that Jelinek extends to Austria), but they disallow an audience identification with the historic specificity of Jewish suffering under Nazism. Huyssen concludes by saying that the vehemence of Leftists attacks on *Holocaust* is indicative of a refusal to accept that a Brechtian aesthetic based on distanciation, rationality, and universality may have become obsolete. (This revision of Brechtian aesthetics is explored in detail in the following chapter, in which I discuss Rainer Werner Fassbinder's idiosyncratic re-fusing of Brecht for his own cinematic practice.)

Huyssen's critique of postwar plays by Weiss, Frisch, and Hochhuth in light of the tremendous impact of the TV series *Holocaust* poses the question of whether Jelinek's critique of television, which emphasizes constructedness and distanciation, does not also come up short in comparison to the powers of the new medium. Jelinek may have realized "that the printed word cannot

---

53. Huyssen, *After the Great Divide* 95.

keep up with the effectiveness of the electronic media,"[54] but her insistence on *Sprachkritik* (critique of language) as the most effective form of critique of the media offers very little to remedy the situation. In the end it seems that Jelinek's literary texts are less open to competing and divergent readings than some of the television programs that she satirizes.

---

54. Jelinek, "die endlose unschuldigkeit" 50.

Hollywood Made
in Bavaria

CHAPTER 4

The Gangster Film and Melodrama
of Rainer Werner Fassbinder

The best thing I can think of would be to create a union between something
as beautiful and powerful and wonderful as Hollywood films and a critique
of the status quo. That's my dream, to make such a German film—beautiful and extravagant and fantastic, and nevertheless go against the grain.
Besides, there are many Hollywood films which are not at all apologies for
the establishment, as is always superficially maintained.
                                                    —*Rainer Werner Fassbinder*

Only through plagiarism can we become authentic.
                                                    —*Pedro Almodóvar*

An important aspect of German and Austrian literature of the late 1960s and
1970s is the attempt to fuse the tradition of the European avant-garde of the
first two decades of this century with elements of contemporary American
popular culture and Pop art. As I have argued in previous chapters, I consider Rolf Dieter Brinkmann to be more successful in this endeavor than
Elfriede Jelinek because his works are able to negotiate a path that avoids
mere repetition of the American model as well as the trap of reiterating the
aporias of the historical avant-garde. While the critique of popular culture
may be articulated more radically in the works of Elfriede Jelinek, they do
not escape the contradictions that also mark the modernist critique of mass
culture of Adorno and Horkheimer. The works of the filmmaker and playwright Rainer Werner Fassbinder have to be situated within a similar context
of competing traditions; Fassbinder's gangster films and melodramas, but
also his plays, are indebted to the avant-garde theater of Bertolt Brecht and
his notion of "eingreifendes Denken"—a strategy of interventionism—as
well as the Hollywood cinema of the 1930s to 1950s. Like Brinkmann, Fassbinder is able to overcome the modernist binarism of "progressive high art"
and "regressive popular culture." As I will show, he does so by exploiting the
inherent subversiveness of Hollywood genres.

Ever since Fassbinder first articulated this desire to create a "German

89

Hollywood" by making films that would be commercially viable while at the same time not uncritical of the society that they reflect, critics have commented on the impact classical Hollywood cinema and narrative patterns of genres such as the thriller or the melodrama have had on his work. To most of them it has been of particular interest how Fassbinder has managed to combine or reconcile Hollywood's formulas of recognition and identification with distanciating techniques in order to preserve a space for social critique. Choosing between either a Brechtian or a Sirkian interpretation—in some cases even reading Douglas Sirk as a Brechtian director—many critics confine themselves to an antithetical setup, either hailing Fassbinder as a high art political director in a Brechtian tradition or labeling him a Hollywood entertainer with, at the most, a critical edge. Yet, while it is standard fare to see Fassbinder as somehow displaced between Sirk and Brecht, the question of *how* this transmission works must remain at issue.[1]

To answer this question it is not enough, as most critics have done, to limit oneself to a comparative analysis of the formal aspects of Fassbinder's films and their respective models. While such approaches may provide valuable insights into Fassbinder's artistic originality, they often fail to address the ideological aspects of his work and ultimately depoliticize it, because they exclude the larger historical issues of postwar and, more precisely, post-1968 cultural politics, which propelled these rewritings and which lends Fassbinder's turn to Hollywood its provocative and hence political status. The political dimension of Fassbinder's relationship to America only emerges if situated within the complex patterns of reception that inform the dialogue between American and West German art and culture from the late 1960s onward, particularly the revived interest in Hollywood cinema of the 1940s and 1950s. Out of this dialogue emerged a postmodern sensibility in German literature and film—belatedly, when compared to the United States—one example of which is Fassbinder's idiosyncratic displacement of American popular culture, and particularly the classical Hollywood idiom, onto his own work.

Re-fusing Brecht

There are good reasons why a discussion of Fassbinder's cultural politics should begin with Bertolt Brecht. Fassbinder's efforts to politicize popular culture are indebted to Brecht's pioneering work about art and politics during the Weimar period. As part of the left-wing Weimar avant-garde, Brecht was among the first to question the great divide between (bourgeois) art and

---

1. Cf. Brigitte Peucker, "High Passion and Low Art: Fassbinder's Narrative Strategies," in *Ambiguities in Literature and Film,* ed. Hans Braendlin (Tallahassee: Florida State UP, 1988) 65; Thomas Elsaesser, "Primary Identification and the Historical Subject: Fassbinder and Germany," in *Narrative, Apparatus, Ideology: A Film Theory Reader,* ed. Philip Rosen (New York: Columbia UP, 1986) 538.

politics and to set faith in the politically subversive power of the popular. These are, perhaps, the more postmodern aspects of a playwright who for many—including Fassbinder in his interviews—seems to be the incarnation of high modernism. Yet, while Brecht's belief in the master narrative, of "science" or "history," as well as his belief in a truth-guaranteeing position outside of language appear untenable from a postmodern point of view, his involvement of the spectator in the text, his open admission of his own position, his interruption—but not elimination—of dramatic illusion, and his rejection of purity and harmony in favor of the fragmentary, the episodic, and the open made him part of a Weimar avant-garde that anticipated much of what has now, for better or worse, been labeled postmodern.[2] It is precisely through a recovery of these elements in Brecht that Fassbinder is able to fuse strategies of the avant-garde with Hollywood cinema in order to install and subvert both kinds of discourses.

Like Fassbinder, who had already made two short films before he joined the Action Theater in 1969, Brecht's beginnings lie as much with film as with theater. In the first years of the 1920s Brecht was a prolific filmscript writer, and even after turning his full attention to the stage, after his success of *Trommeln in der Nacht,* he remained interested in film and radio as technologies that should support the politicization of art. Throughout his career Brecht continued to write scripts for the film, few of which, however, made it onto the screen. Although Brecht's theoretical writings on film are negligible compared to the ones on theater, they have made a considerable impact on the film theory of the late 1960s and 1970s (much of which was first associated with the British journal *Screen*), reviving interest in questions of representation and realism.[3]

The formation of the New German Cinema and the striving for an *Autorenkino,* in which filmmakers possess a maximum degree of artistic freedom while controlling the means of production and distribution, cannot be understood without Brecht's notion of "eingreifendes Denken"—a strategy of interventionism rehearsed on all levels of cultural production. It is perhaps best exemplified by Brecht's confrontation with G. W. Pabst about the adaptation of *Die Dreigroschenoper* and the ensuing lawsuit, the so-called

---

2. For a discussion of the postmodern aspects of Brecht, see Richard McCormick, *Politics of the Self: Feminism and the Postmodern in West German Literature and Film* (Princeton: Princeton UP, 1991); Linda Hutcheon, *A Poetics of Postmodernism: History, Theory, Fiction* (New York: Routledge, 1988); and Elizabeth Wright, *Postmodern Brecht: A Re-Presentation* (New York: Routledge, 1989). The relation of Weimar avant-garde to American postmodernism is explored in Andreas Huyssen, "The Search for Tradition: Avantgarde and Postmodernism in the 1970s," *The Great Divide: Modernism, Mass Culture, Postmodernism* (Bloomington: Indiana UP, 1986).

3. Brecht's relation to film is analyzed in great detail by Wolfgang Gersch, *Film bei Brecht: Bertolt Brechts praktische und theoretische Auseinandersetzung mit dem Film* (Berlin: Henschel, 1975); John Willett, *Brecht in Context* (New York: Methuen, 1983); and Roswitha Mueller, *Bertolt Brecht and the Theory of the Media* (Lincoln: U of Nebraska P, 1989).

Dreigroschenprozeß, in which Brecht tried to expose the mechanisms of cinema production. Anticipating that he would lose the lawsuit, Brecht staged the trial as a sociological experiment that meant to prove that the cinema's model of authorship was one of industrial production and not a bourgeois model of creative authorship.

Fassbinder himself, it should be noted, has always deflected the influence of Brecht not only on his work as a film director but also on his work with the theater. In an oft-quoted interview he dismissed Brecht as someone "who made the audience think. I make the audience feel *and* think."[4] This typecasting of Brecht as a dry and didactic rationalist (which is certainly unjust if one considers such emotional and complex characters as *Mother Courage* or *Shen Te*) was rather common in a post-1968 literary and film culture, when, after the failure of the student movement, political theater in the Brechtian tradition was on its way out. Equally important for Fassbinder's depreciation could be the fact that after his death, in 1956, Brecht had quickly become a modern classic and hence a target for any critique that aimed at knocking over the pedestal of high art and its institutions. Furthermore, since many playwrights of the 1960s and early 1970s and several directors of the New German Cinema, including such diverse figures as Alexander Kluge, Harun Farocki, Hans Jürgen Syberberg, Jean-Marie Straub and Danièlle Huillet, and Helma Sanders-Brahms had explicitly or implicitly situated themselves within a Brechtian heritage, the provocative force of Brecht's theater had entered the mainstream and the ubiquitous reference to his work had often led to a leveling of once radical positions.[5] Denouncing Brecht served the additional purpose of highlighting one's own originality and creativity. If one considers, finally, that Brecht detested the very kind of cinema Fassbinder admired most—Hollywood productions of the 1940s—it is surprising that their work should be discussed under the same heading at all.

And yet the affinities between Brecht and Fassbinder, especially those of Fassbinder's theater work[6] and early films, are too strong and too obvious to be brushed aside. The *action-theater,* which Fassbinder joined in 1967, and the *antitheater,* its 1968 successor founded by him and nine other original members, were conceived as underground theaters that revolted—as their

---

4. Norbert Sparrow, "An Interview with Rainer Werner Fassbinder," *Cineaste* 8.2 (1977) 20.

5. Cf. the following statement by Max Frisch: "Millions of people have seen the works of Brecht and will see them time and again, yet I doubt that only one of them has changed his political thinking or even considered it . . . We all know that Brecht is a genius, and he has the powerful ineffectiveness of a classic" ("Der Autor und das Theater," *Gesammelte Werke* 5.2 [1976]: 342).

6. Cf. Yaak Karsunke, "anti-theatergeschichte: Die Anfänge," in *Rainer Werner Fassbinder,* Peter Iden et al. (Munich: Hanser, 1974) 7–16; Peter Iden: "Der Eindruck-Macher: Rainer Werner Fassbinder und das Theater," *Rainer Werner Fassbinder,* 17–28; Denis Calandra, "The Antitheater of R. W. Fassbinder," *Plays,* ed. and trans. Denis Calandra (New York: PAJ Publications, 1992) 9–18.

telling names indicate—against state-subsidized stages and bourgeois notions of art. Like Brecht's early plays, Fassbinder's first own works for stage and screen display a fascination with demonic city jungles devouring their inhabitants, and in Volker Schlöndorff's TV adaptation of Brecht's play *Baal* (1969) Fassbinder fittingly played the title role. The *antitheater's* radical adaptations of plays by Sophocles, Büchner, or Goethe followed Brecht's practice of reading classics against the grain, as outlined in his poem "Fragen eines lesenden Arbeiters" ("Questions of a Reading Worker") and the novel fragment *Die Geschäfte des Herrn Julius Cäsar* (*The Business Affairs of Mr. Julius Cesar*) (which itself became the basis for a Brechtian film adaptation by Straub/Huillet). The *antitheater's* production of *Iphigenie auf Tauris,* for instance, was a montage of Goethe's text, pop songs, excerpts from comic strips, Mao, and the Living Theater, with Orestes and Pylades playing a gay couple while shouting lines from the courtroom scenes of two recently indicted left-wing radicals, Fritz Teufel and Rainer Langhans. As the program notes made clear, the *antitheater* understood itself as socialist theater that meant to provoke and disturb while at the same time informing and educating its audience—a Brechtian position that, during a period that demanded the death of literature, was considered by many leftists an anachronism.

These borrowings from Brecht's epic theater were fused with elements from Antonin Artaud's theater of cruelty, which Fassbinder first came to know by way of the Living Theatre, an American collective ensemble that had been exiled from its home and was touring through Europe. When the Living Theatre first presented Artaud's theory on stage it had an electrifying effect on a German theater scene, in which younger directors such as Claus Peymann, Peter Stein, and Zadek were taking over from the generation of Gründgens, Hilpert, and Kortner. What seemed to impress Fassbinder was also the group's practice to write, direct, perform, and live together and to turn the theater into an arena of shared experience and utopian vision. While the use of meditation, ritual, excessive violence, provocation, action, and shock by the Living Theater became the model and namesake for the Action Theater, the *antitheater* experimented to combine Brechtian episodic plots, didacticism, the refusal of psychological explanations, and a sober and distancing acting style with Artaudian violence, energy, and spontaneity. As Michael Töteberg writes, "Combining the impulse of enlightenment with experimental aesthetics, the *antitheater* has developed a new type of play which integrates the different efforts of Artaud and Brecht in a more convincing fashion than the plays of the Living Theater."[7]

7. Michael Töteberg, "Das Theater der Grausamkeit als Lehrstück: Zwischen Brecht und Artaud—Die experimentellen Theatertexte Fassbinders," in *Rainer Werner Fassbinder,* ed. Heinz Ludwig Arnold (Munich: Text + Kritik, 1989) 24.

Gangsters in Munich

While Fassbinder's indebtedness to Brechtian aesthetics is perhaps most obvious in his theater work, it also informs his entire cinematic oeuvre, using and abusing Brecht to varying degrees. These at times radical transformations of Brechtian aesthetics set Fassbinder's cinema off from that of more orthodox postwar Brechtian filmmakers such as Jean-Luc Godard, Alexander Kluge, or Jean-Marie Straub and Danièlle Huillet. Two films, *Der Americanische Soldat* (*The American Soldier*), a 1970 gangster film, and the 1974 melodrama *Angst essen Seele auf* (*Ali: Fear Eats the Soul*) are especially suited to demonstrate Fassbinder's different attempts to wed German political theater with Hollywood genres.

Together with the early features *Love Is Colder than Death* (1969) and *Gods of the Plague* (1970), *The American Soldier* forms a trilogy of gangster movies that demonstrate in exemplary fashion the multiple paradoxes of Fassbinder's enterprise—paradoxes that are neatly contained in the name Franz Walsch. Frequently used by Fassbinder as a pseudonym for editing his films, it is also the name of the only character to appear in all three gangster films (twice played by Fassbinder, once by Harry Baer), although the Franz Walsch character dies in *Gods of the Plague.* A composite of Hollywood director Raoul Walsh and Franz Biberkopf, protagonist of Alfred Döblin's novel *Berlin Alexanderplatz* (1929), the name epitomizes Fassbinder's efforts to position himself between Hollywood gangster milieu and Weimar *Proletariat,* between American popular culture and German literary tradition. In *The American Soldier* Franz Walsch is the boyhood friend of Ricky, the protagonist who spells the name as follows to an operator: "I want a Munich number. The person's name is Franz Walsch. Walsch. —W as in war, A as in Alamo, L as in Lenin, S as in science fiction, C as in crime, H as in hell."

All three films were produced by the *antitheater* as low-budget, low-key, black-and-white movies; all three are set in Munich and depict the life of outsiders on the fringes of the big city underworld: small-time pimps, professional killers, bar girls, porn dealers, and policemen who are almost indistinguishable from the gangsters they pursue. *The American Soldier* is a simple tale of a German-American Vietnam veteran, Ricky/Richard, who returns to his native Munich as a hired killer, carrying out his assignments with mechanical precision. He calls up his old friend, visits the scenes of his youth, and, in a pivotal scene, goes to see his mother and younger brother, before he is killed in a showdown with those who hired him and no longer need his services.

The fundamental incongruity of setting an American thriller in Munich is quickly established at the beginning of the film and then exploited throughout. The film opens with a scene of three shady characters—later revealed to belong to the police force—playing cards under the smoke-filled light of a single low-hanging lamp. These are familiar types: the full-bearded, muscular boss, understated, obviously in command and winning, the sweaty and over-weight underling who loses, and the subservient intellectual with glasses, referred to as "Doc." A blonde moll in the background rounds out the picture of this underworld quartet. The traces of heavy drinking are everywhere. The phone rings, and the music flares up: "He's here." Cut to Ricky, whom the rolling credits introduce as the protagonist. He is entering town in a big white American cruiser, drinking Whiskey from a bottle with a blonde next to him. Yet the film never delivers the drama that it promises, strangely subverting the traditions from which it so obviously borrows: unlike in film noir, the killer/protagonist reveals no moralist concerns underneath his macho shell, killing his victims at random and without remorse. The police are just as cor-rupt as he is. Moreover, the film contains virtually no suspense, not because it lacks action but because of its slow pace. While the first scene contains all the "makings" of a thriller, it doesn't come off the ground: the close-up of the phone is just a little too long, the phone rings just a little too loud. The hero enters triumphantly, but we are not shown his face, which remains in the dark while that of the woman next to him seems lit by an artificial light source from below. When he throws her out of the car, he shoots her—but the bul-lets are blanks, thus strangely undercutting his image of a professional killer.

The kind of displacement created here is quite different from Brecht's plays, in which the drama is set in historic times or distant places in order to provoke comments or establish parallels on contemporary society (a tech-nique that Fassbinder uses in *The Marriage of Maria Braun,* in which a set of portraits links Nazi Germany and the reconstruction period of the 1950s to the Federal Republic under Chancellor Helmut Schmidt). The Hollywood formula is invoked in a fashion that vacillates between nostalgia and par-ody—a homage to past times and the awareness of the pastness of those times that cannot be recuperated. One of the first things the American soldier says is: "In the beginning, there was Germany . . . Once upon a time, there was a little boy who flew over the Big Pond—Shit." It is as if the Vietnam War, invoked by the film's title but never developed as a theme, is the landmark where for German postwar intellectuals the United States lost its innocence. Significantly, Fassbinder abandoned the genre after this film.

Like the other two gangster films, to which it provides a loose sequel, *The American Soldier* is a bleak, drab, and dingy film, shot in long takes with smooth, long pans and creating the feeling of sadness, emptiness, and tremen-dous monotony. This sensation of flatness makes no pretense to realism, nor does the performance of the actors and actresses who recite their lines with-out identifying with their roles. The dead-pan diction and primitive epic form bear the mark of Brecht. Since these early films offset viewer identification, they have been read as examples of Brechtian strategies of *Verfremdung,* intending to maintain the viewers' awareness of watching a performed real-ity. The stylized acting and mannered dialogues of these films undercut emo-tional involvement with the characters. As Anna Kuhn comments, "Unable to respond emotionally to the characters on the screen, the viewer tends to analyze the situation and to call into question the society responsible for it."[8] Even Kaja Silverman's Lacanian reading of *Gods of the Plague* implies a recourse to Brechtian *Verfremdung* when she argues that Fassbinder refuses to naturalize the concept of identity by concealing its external scaffolding. By shifting the focus away from spectator-character relation, Silverman claims, the film draws attention to the role of reflection and identification in the construction of identity.[9] Yet the question arises whether the space created by offsetting viewer identification is at all available for productive criticism. In other words, do these films really provide the viewer with access to a viewpoint above or outside the performed reality?

It is therefore important to understand to what degree films such as *The American Soldier* share Brecht's notion of realism. We may recall that the Brechtian *Verfremdungseffekt* works to counter audience identification with the characters by foregrounding the artificiality of the performance in order to make the audience aware that it is watching "a play, a mode of communication, a message."[10] The connection between play and reality is however reestablished when the engaged audience is impelled to investigate the characters' behavior and pass a moral judgment relevant to a reality that can and should be changed. The didactic purpose of epic theater is to instigate intellectual reflection upon, and social intervention into, the existing conditions. This connection between reality and representation is undermined in Fassbinder's pessimistic and fatalistic gangster films, because they foreground how images and modes of representation *constitute* a certain reality rather than understanding representation as a mere reflection or disguise thereof. Thomas Elsaesser has shown how one aspect of Brecht's work, his notion of anti-illusionism, today seems particularly problematic, because it is based on an understanding of the real that our media culture has rendered obsolete. Television, film, and photography are media that no longer reflect or, as Brecht believed, distort truth but, rather, create events—not in the sense that everything we see on TV is pure invention. But for a political event to attain credibility it must be expressed through images and therefore must "pass through the process of sometimes intense specularity, with the paradoxical effect that, in order to become recognizable as political, events have to be staged as spectacle."[11] This development from anti-illusionism to hyperreal-

8. Anna K. Kuhn, "The Alienated Vision," in *New German Filmmakers*, ed. Klaus Phillips (New York: Ungar, 1984) 80.

9. Kaja Silverman, "Fassbinder and Lacan," *Camera Obscura* 19 (1989): 54–84.

10. Hans-Bernhard Moeller, "Brecht and 'Epic' Film Medium: The Cineast, Playwright, Film Theoretician and His Influence," *Wide Angle* 4.3 (1980): 5.

11. Thomas Elsaesser, "From Anti-illusionism to Hyper-realism: Bertolt Brecht and Contemporary Film," in *Re-interpreting Brecht: His Influence on Contemporary Drama and Film*, ed. Pia Kleber and Colin Visser (Cambridge: Cambridge UP, 1990) 179.

Liebe – kälter als der Tod
Ein Film von Rainer Werner Fassbinder

"I was not trying to imitate an American gangster film, but to make a film about people who have seen a lot of American gangster films." — Rainer Werner Fassbinder

Fassbinder as Franz in *Love is Colder than Death.* (Publicity still, Stiftung Deutsche Kinemathek Berlin.)

ism has significant repercussions for the Brechtian notion of critique. Since a position outside or above representation is no longer available, the mechanisms of identification that representation generates become highly ambiguous and paradoxical.

In an interview Fassbinder once explained, "I was not trying to imitate an American gangster film, but to make a film about people who have seen a lot of American gangster films."[12] This statement indicates that Fassbinder is more interested in mechanisms of identification and the construction of imaginary relationships than in undercutting viewer identification or the dismantling of the representation of false realities. It also stresses the historic dimen-

---

12. Quoted in John Hughes and Brooks Riley, "A New Realism," *Film Comment* 11.6 (1975): 14.

sion of Fassbinder's infatuation with Hollywood cinema—often overlooked in psychoanalytic analyses such as Silverman's—because it indicates how this cinema served, for him and his contemporaries, primarily as an imaginary, a medium for reflection and speculation, and crucial for establishing and maintaining an entire generation's sense of identity.

Excluding the real as ideological, Fassbinder's remedy is to portray the artificiality of the artificial. All three gangster films abound with Hollywood clichés and icons. *Love Is Colder than Death,* for instance, features Bruno's Ford Mustang and his stolen Caravelle and Cadillac; Bruno's hat à la Alain Delon, who in turn seems to emulate Humphrey Bogart's performance of Philip Marlowe; and Franz's desire to have exactly the kind of sunglasses worn by the policeman approaching Janet Leigh in *Psycho.* In one of the film's funniest scenes Bruno, Franz, and Joanna go to a department store to steal sunglasses as the essential trademark of the Hollywood gangster. Putting on these sunglasses and taking them off becomes a self-conscious and ritualistic act, repeated many times throughout the film. Yet the subjects that mold themselves after Humphrey Bogart and James Cagney are taciturn and shabby and show none of the heroic aura that surrounds Hollywood's lonely heroes. They speak a language that is not theirs, turning the classical idiom and affirmative Hollywood discourse into a noncommunication of platitudes. The few dialogues are punctuated by long silences, rendering any verbal exchange a monologue in which no one cares for a response.

The American Soldier is extremely self-conscious in its quotation of Hollywood gangster rituals and icons of popular culture. It is not only the abundance of quotes, allusions, and references that startle—ranging from characters named Frau Lang, Murnau (as a voice on the phone), Rosa von Praunheim, Magdalena Fuller, Ricky (Rick being the name of Humphrey Bogart in *Casablanca*) over icons like a Batman comic read by a woman and shown in extreme close-up, the poster of a rock band decorating the police headquarters, and a pinball machine in the bourgeois home of Ricky's mother—it is not this enumeration of quotes and objects, but their mode of employment, that matters here. While individual scenes like Ricky's shooting of the prostitute with blank bullets might be considered parodies, Fassbinder's patchwork makes, on the whole, no satiric comment on its original material; if there is laughter, it is not a laughing about the characters but with the characters about the incongruity of their situation and their inability to cope with it. Rather than calling the film a parody—a term that Fassbinder refused—it might better be understood in terms of what Fredric Jameson, in distinction to parody, has called pastiche: "Pastiche is, like parody, the imitation of a peculiar mask, speech in a dead language: but it is a neutral practice of such mimicry, without any of parody's ulterior motives, amputated of the satiric impulse, devoid of laughter and of any conviction that alongside the abnormal tongue you have momentarily borrowed, some healthy linguis-

Ulli Lommel, with Hanna Schygulla, imitating Alain Delon imitating Humphrey Bogart in *Love is Colder than Death.* (Publicity still, Stiftung Deutsche Kinemathek Berlin.)

tic normality still exists."[13] The underlying theoretical assumption is that parody, just as Brecht's notion of anti-illusionism, is still informed by some belief in a master narrative that would legitimize a privileged critical stance. In Fassbinder's cinematic reality this vantage point has vanished. The Brechtian search for truth and falsehood is acted out and confined to the level of the image. If politics have to be representable in order to be effective, then all that is left are politics of representation.

Melodrama and Gay Camp

In many ways *The American Soldier* was a calculated provocation, not only because of the conspicuous absence of any direct political comment about Vietnam in a film about a veteran of that war—all that Ricky has to say when asked, How was the war? is "loud"—but perhaps even more because of its aesthetics. Its stylized surface quality, its polish and deliberate flatness—

---

13. Fredric Jameson, *Postmodernism, or The Cultural Logic of Late Capitalism* (Durham: Duke UP, 1991) 17.

which it shares with the avant-garde beginnings of Wim Wenders—is intended to deflect interpretation by rendering things and characters self-evident.[14] In its aestheticism and minimalism the film comes close to the position taken by Susan Sontag in her famous essay "Against Interpretation," in which she challenged the view that interpretation is necessary in order to achieve a resolution between the meaning of the text and the demands on the reader. Refusing the controlling and confining implications of a hermeneutics of suspicion, Sontag favored an "erotics of art" that would "reveal the sensuous surface of art."[15] Written in 1964, Sontag's essay today reads like a program for post-1968 West German literary and cinematic production, when after the failed student protest movement writers and filmmakers abandoned the concept of literature as social critique and political investigation and of documentary literature. Instead of following H. M. Enzensberger's call for the "death of literature," they staged a powerful resurrection of texts that turned their attention inward, onto themselves, seeking emotional authenticity and sensual experience. Sontag had believed film to be the most suitable medium to create an art "whose surface is so unified and clean, whose momentum is so rapid, whose address is so direct that the work can be . . . just what it is."[16] The directors she singled out for their works' "liberating anti-symbolic quality"[17]—Walsh, Hawks, Cukor—were precisely those instrumental for Fassbinder's, and also Wim Wenders's, sensibility. The young Germans reconsideration of classical Hollywood cinema was led by their appreciation of its immediacy and transparency, together with what they saw as its rejection of interpretation and simple-minded social critique—in Michael Rutschky's phrase: a replacing of sense through sensuality.[18] Writing about the Westerns of Raoul Walsh, Wenders marveled at how these films "brought out . . . tenderness in a dreamily beautiful and quiet way. They respected themselves: their characters, their plots, their landscapes, their rules, their freedoms, their desires. In their images they spread out a surface that was nothing else but what you could see. 'I'm never going back to El Paso,' says Virginia Mayo in a film by Walsh, and that's all that is meant when she says that."[19]

The American Soldier is a film that reflects the Brechtianism of Godard and Straub but is also quite aware of the aporias of their position, as the vacillating between pastiche, nostalgia, and self-indulgence shows. It therefore already anticipates the coming change in Fassbinder's position vis-à-vis Hol-

14. This refusal to explain things can also be seen in Fassbinder's interviews of this period, in which he often assumed the pose of being "too lazy" to speak about the political implications of his films.

15. Susan Sontag, *Against Interpretation* (New York: Delta, 1961) 13.

16. Ibid. 11.

17. Ibid.

18. Michael Rutschky, *Erfahrungshunger: Ein Essay über die siebziger Jahre* (Cologne: Kiepenheuer and Witsch, 1980).

19. Wim Wenders, *Emotion Pictures: Reflections on the Cinema,* trans. Sean Whiteside and Michael Hoffmann (London: Faber and Faber, 1989) 24.

lywood cinema and prepares the turn toward more audience-oriented films. The implications of this turn are illustrated by the changes the story of Emmi and Ali underwent from episodic insert in *The American Soldier* to the plot of the 1974 melodrama *Ali: Fear Eats the Soul.* Here is the version the chambermaid (played by Margarethe von Trotta) tells to Ricky, whom she has been trying to seduce, shortly before she commits suicide because her lover left her:

Happiness is not always fun. In Hamburg there lived a cleaning woman by the name of Emmi and she was 60 or 65; and one day when she was walking home from work it started to rain cats and dogs, and she went into a bar, one of those bars for the foreign workers, and she sat down and drank a Coke. And suddenly a guy asked her to dance, a really big fellow with incredible broad shoulders. And she thinks he is handsome and so she dances with him. And he sits down with her and they talk. He says that he has no apartment and so Emmi asks him along. Well, at home he slept with her and a few days later he said they should get married. And so they did. And suddenly Emmi became really young, from behind she looked like thirty or so, and for half a year they lived it up and were incredibly happy. They had lots of parties and so forth. And one day Emmi was murdered. And on her neck there were these marks from a signet ring. The police arrested her husband. His name was Ali, and there was an "A" on his ring. But he said that he had many friends whose names were Ali and who had a signet ring. And so they questioned all the turks in Hamburg by the name of Ali. But many of them had already gone back to Turkey, and the others didn't understand.[20]

In contrast to the gangster movie, the melodrama of the film Fassbinder made later is no longer a love story turned violent for reasons that remain unexplained but, instead, focuses on the pursuing of an improbable love affair and particularly on how the people surrounding the couple (family, neighbors, fellow workers) exert power and social pressure. Abandoning the latent misogyny of film noir and the thriller, in which women are the victims of male violence, Ali no longer kills Emmi. Instead, the couple's love affair becomes the target of society's rage and envy, ultimately taking its toll in an increasingly conflict-ridden relationship when Ali and Emmi begin to interiorize the hostility that surrounds them. Yet, unlike the guest worker in the chambermaid's tale, and unlike Herr R. of an earlier film, Ali does not run amok but represses the sufferings inflicted by a racist society to the point of collapsing from a stomach ulcer, ending the film with the question about the couple's future unanswered.

Fassbinder's shifting position toward American cinema, reflected in the thematic differences and continuities between *The American Soldier* and *Ali:*

---

20. "Der amerikanische Soldat," in *Fassbinders Filme 2,* ed. Michael Töteberg (Frankfurt am Main: Verlag der Autoren, 1990) 175.

Fear Eats the Soul, should again be understood in regard to his position toward Brechtianism. Brecht's radical anti-illusionism, which had first been taken up by Godard (most notably in *Tout va bien, La Chinoise, Vent d'est, One Plus One,* and *Weekend*) and Straub/Huillet (*History Lessons, Not Reconciled*), now became questionable. Both Godard and Straub/Huillet stressed Brecht's anti-Aristotelian thesis of distanciation, textural fissures, and multilayeredness, and used them to question the narrative closure and specular seduction of the image as the determinant features of Hollywood cinema.[21] Fassbinder's own early works such as *Katzelmacher* and *Die Niklashauser Fart* show the respective influence of Straub/Huillet and Godard, but now, in the aftermath of the failed student movement in France and Germany, this counter-cinema of nonpleasure became to appear elitist, dogmatic, and antidemocratic. As Fassbinder commented, "Films from the brain are all right, but if they don't reach the audience, it's no good . . . He [Straub] tried to be revolutionary and human in an inhuman way."[22] It has often been said, including by Fassbinder himself, that the "discovery" of the films of Douglas Sirk led him to realize the aporias of his previous filmmaking. Yet Fassbinder's desire to use melodrama as an instrument to reach larger audiences should be seen less in this personal context and more as shaped by the historical context of the early and mid-1970s, when many directors and writers redefined the ways in which to engage audiences, reacting in part to changed funding policies by German states and television stations, which now favored films that had more audience appeal and a higher potential for commercial success.

While historically Fassbinder's attempt to wed Hollywood melodrama with epic theater reacted to specific changes of cultural production and consumption, aesthetically it faced the difficulty of reconciling the very oppositions through which Brecht set off his epic theater from Aristotelian theater and Wagnerian opera. Like traditional bourgeois drama, Hollywood melodrama emphasizes emotional subjectivity and evolutionary development, whereas Brecht emphasizes nonindividual experiences. Epic theater provides knowledge and, by stressing the exemplary aspect of its material, encourages the audience to learn. Excessive emotional identification is avoided so that one can watch the experiment unfold. Yet there are also numerous aspects, overlooked by most critics, in which Brecht and melodrama display similar or related concerns. Drawing on Peter Brook's study of nineteenth-century French melodrama, Roswitha Mueller has pointed to the striking similarities between that genre and Brecht's epic theater, such as a shared focus on ordinary life and ordinary people, the emphasis on polarization between good and evil, and the frequent use of the form of the parable. Melodrama's tendency to exteriorize psychological conflict—in Sirk often underscored by music, setting, decors, and acting—can be compared to Brechtian *Gestus,*

---

21. Cf. Elsaesser, "From Anti-illusionism to Hyper-realism" 173ff.
22. Arthur Lubow, "Cinema's New Wunderkinder," *New Times,* 15 May 1975, 54.

which challenges the representation of things as unquestioned givens, with the important distinction that *Gestus* addresses the social nature of individuals whereas melodrama stresses the personal component of emotional dilemmas. Finally, because of its origins in the French Revolution and an example of early popular culture, melodrama shares much of Brecht's intention to democratize art through the use of the vernacular.[23]

It is the merit of Fassbinder's critical melodramas to have established an awareness for the compatibility of these two art forms, and *Ali* provides an excellent example of how to exploit the creative tension marked by the names of Sirk and Brecht. By rewriting the love story of *All That Heaven Allows* (1956) between a wealthy widow and her gardener, fifteen years her junior, as one of a widowed German cleaning woman and a young Moroccan car mechanic, Fassbinder creates a social parable about contemporary German society.[24] Yet an important question arises at this point: while there is ample evidence in *Ali* for the use of distancing devices (such as the framing of characters in doors, windows, and stairways, nonsequential shots, unconventional camera codes, odd juxtapositioning of establishing shots and subjective point-of-view shots, tableaux-like arrangement of characters, etc.), it is questionable whether the creation of a critical distance can be simply or exclusively seen as the result of infusing an apolitical, or "neutral," genre with political bite. In other words, is it really true, as Mueller and other critics have argued, that Fassbinder politicizes a genre that had "decline[d] into consumerist vicariousness,"[25] or does Sirkian melodrama not already contain a certain subversiveness by virtue of its gay camp sensitivity, which made the genre appealing for Fassbinder in the first place?

The notion of camp and its relation to cultural politics is much debated. Susan Sontag argued in her seminal essay "Notes on Camp" that "the camp sensibility is disengaged, depoliticized—or at least apolitical."[26] Eric Rentschler's dismissal of camp aspects of Fassbinder's work is based on Sontag's verdict, when he argues that camp is incompatible with Fassbinder's overt radicalism.[27] Yet more recent discussions of camp have refuted Sontag's view and pointed to camp's intrinsic relation to cultural power.[28] Most critics, however, agree that camp and its politics lie, at least to a certain

23. Mueller 128ff.

24. Fassbinder's use of Sirk has been analyzed in detail by numerous critics. See Judith Mayne, "Fassbinder and Spectatorship," *New German Critique* 12 (1977): 61–74; Thomas Elsaesser, *New German Cinema: A History* (New Brunswick: Rutgers UP, 1989); Eric Rentschler, *West German Film in the Course of Time* (Redgrave: New York, 1984); Robert Phillip Kolker, *The Altering Eye* (Oxford: Oxford UP, 1983); Timothy Corrigan, *New German Film: The Displaced Image* (Austin: U of Texas P, 1983); James Franklin, *New German Cinema* (London: Columbus, 1983).

25. Mueller 132.

26. Susan Sontag, "Notes on Camp," *Against Interpretation* 277.

27. Rentschler 83f.

28. Cf. Andrew Ross's chapter "Uses of Camp" in *No Respect: Intellectuals and Popular Culture* (New York: Routledge, 1989).

degree, in the eye of the beholder.[29] It is thus important to consider how Fassbinder read Sirk's films and, in particular, *All That Heaven Allows.*[30] The predicament of the love affair between Cary Scott (Jane Wyman) and her gardener Ron Kirby (Rock Hudson) is described by Fassbinder as follows:

> [Jane] has a motherly touch, she looks as though she might be able to soften at the right moment: we can understand what Rock sees in her. He is a tree trunk. He is quite right to want to be inside her. The world around is evil. The women all talk too much. There are no men in the film apart from Rock, in that respect arm chairs and glasses are more important. After seeing this film small town America is the last place in the world I want to go.[31]

What is remarkable about this passage—and the entire essay on Sirk—is the attempt to undermine the binarism of identification and distanciation. While Fassbinder's fan writing identifies with "Rock" and "Jane," it also, distanciated, points to the social implications of their relationship (small-town 1950s America being an awful place to live). Deliberately ignoring the boundary between actors and their roles, and thus refusing a crucial constituency of epic theater, Fassbinder revels in the star persona of Rock Hudson, whose telling first name and "tree trunk" appearance both undo and celebrate a masculinist mystique. Jane's unconventional longing for this man, which is tied to feelings of guilt, pain, and repression—the makings of melodrama— are turned into camp by articulating emotional despair as incongruities between him and her: the contrast between youth and old age,[32] upper-middle class and working class, country club civilization and nature man.

Gay camp articulates critique as subversion through irony, aestheticism, theatricality, and excess. Al LaValley has pointed to the particularity of camp's double bind: "Often celebrating as it deconstructs, camp can allow outmoded emotions to flourish not just for their sentimentality or kitschy

---

29. This view was first expressed by Sontag. It has been reiterated by Richard Dyer, "It's Being So Camp as Keeps Us Going," *Our Image* 36 (1977); and Jack Babuscio, "Camp and the Gay Sensibility," in *Gays and Films,* ed. Richard Dyer (New York: Zoetrope, 1984).

30. It should be noted that Fassbinder's discussion is limited to six films (*All That Heaven Allows, Written on the Wind, Interlude, The Tarnished Angels, Imitation of Life, A Time to Live and a Time to Die*), all of which were made by Douglas Sirk, not Detlef Sierk. The conspicuous absence of any discussion of Sirk's pre-Hollywood films raises the question of whether Fassbinder falls victim to the very kind of repression of the past that he condemns in so many of his films.

31. "Six Films by Douglas Sirk," trans. Thomas Elsaesser, *Douglas Sirk,* by Jon Halliday et al. (Edinburgh: Edinburgh Film Festival, 1972) 97.

32. The contrast between youth and old age is often exploited in camp and can be found in such examples of high camp as *Whatever Happened to Baby Jane* (1961) and *Sunset Boulevard* (1956)—the model for Fassbinder's *Veronika Voss* (1981)—in which aging, egocentric women are obsessed by the romantic illusion of youth and unable to reconcile themselves to the reality of old age (cf. Babuscio 31).

quality, but for their seeds of rebellion against a drier, more conformist modernity. In this respect, camp treasures an excessive theatricality and out-rageousness as an avenue to heightened emotion."[33] This kind of treasuring is ubiquitous in Fassbinder's homage to Sirk, the director whom "not one of us, Godard or Fuller or me or anybody else can touch." The repeated use of expressions such as "it's too much" to describe Sirk's use of lighting, camera angles, sets, decors, and handling of actors reflects a gay sensibility that val-ues intensity over content, style over subject matter, artifice over the "nat-ural" or realism. This too-much-ness, exaggeration, or excess can produce a distanciating effect on the viewer; yet, unlike Brecht's *Verfremdung,* it needn't dissolve the basic meaning of the gesture but can also enhance and celebrate it. At the end of *All That Heaven Allows,* when Jane is taking care of the injured Rock and the viewer is led to understand that there will be a happy end, a deer walks up to the window and looks upon the united lovers. The exaggeration and improbability of the scene seems to ridicule the improbable and imposed ending of the film, but the fact that the last close-up belongs to the animal and not the characters also celebrates the triumph of nature and the natural over a society that inflicted grief upon the lovers.

Fassbinder's understanding of Sirk/camp/stance investigates the ideo-logical implications of emotions, and, by redefining critique as hysteric or excessive force rather than cool or rational operation, aims at decentering the kind of critical activity found in Brecht. While Sirk's melodramas have been read as camp, they clearly differ from the kind of *intentional* camp recreated in some of Fassbinder's films. The best example here is certainly *The Bitter Tears of Petra von Kant,* with its overt histrionics and theatricality, calculated tableaux, and stylized performances, its incongruous juxtaposition of Verdi, the Platters, and the Walker Brothers, and the structuring use of costumes, wigs, and setting, which divide the action into five acts. Among Fassbinder's early films the performance of Hanna Schygulla in *Gods of the Plague* stands out as a conscious imitation of the camp aura of Marlene Dietrich. In *Ali* the camp aspects seem to be subordinated to the social parable. The contrast between Ali's youth and Emmi's age is much less foregrounded than the more politically overt contrast between foreigner and native (we never see the two making love but, instead, are shown Ali with Barbara, the owner of the bar), but even this aspect of the film is secondary to the one of sexual politics. As in *All That Heaven Allows,* the issue in *Ali* is sexual repression, here enhanced by the mystique of the black body, proudly shown off by Emmi to her friends. A camp reading could be constructed—by the knowing viewer—around how *Ali* is playing off the off-screen identities of Fassbinder's Warholian stars vis-à-vis those of the Hollywood celebrities of *All That Heaven Allows*—that is, how the sexuality of the star personas Rock Hudson and Jane Wyman is quoted by Fassbinder's homemade stars El Hedi ben Salem M'Barek

33. Al LaValley, "The Great Escape," *American Film* (April 1985): 31.

Mohammed Mustafa, his gay lover, who had no acting experience and was basically playing himself (using his real name in the film but being called Ali by everybody), and Brigitte Mira, a stage actress, dancer, and cabaret singer whose career began in the 1930s.[34] In Fassbinder's made-for-television personality show and homage to Mira, *Wie ein Vogel auf dem Draht* (*Like a Bird on the Wire* [1975]), we watch Mira surrounded by muscular men and talking about her five husbands, (the last one being twenty years her junior) while she sings "Die Männer sind alle Verbrecher" (All Men Are Scoundrels).

In *Ali,* as in most films, camp has less to do with the plot than with treasured great moments. One such moment begins the film, when Ali and Emmi dance in the bar. The scene contains two sets of opposing signals, which both stress its oddity *and* celebrate its transcending of the normal. Ali only asks Emmi to dance, who feels obviously out of place, because he is dared by one of the girls at the bar. To further mock the odd couple, the light is turned off, creating an atmosphere of unwanted romanticism, while the jukebox plays "Du schwarzer Zigeuner" (You Black Gypsy). We witness the inappropriateness of the scene, its characters, and its setting—an attractive young Arab with a "broken cock" (Ali's first words), a variation of the natural, *Walden*-reading treetrunk Rock, dancing with an elderly German woman in dress with loud colors to the tunes of a song with considerable racist undertones. But, besides being grotesque and a mockery, the scene is also endearing, because for the duration of the dance the difference of culture, race, and age is suspended. The unconventional sexual longing typical of melodrama is, for a brief moment, celebrated as a soaring beyond the limits imposed by society.

Brecht's influence on contemporary filmmakers is so pervasive, because his own notion of epic theater can be seen as drama's response to the cinematic production of the first two decades of the twentieth century. It had to be especially appealing to someone like Fassbinder, whose interest it was to make politically radical films that would still reach large audiences. What unites films like *The American Soldier, Ali: Fear Eats the Soul,* and almost all of Fassbinder's films is the high degree of artificiality, which serves as a strategy for forcing the audience to question its assumptions about society and its inhabitants. It is important to note, however, that Fassbinder does not merely stress this artificiality through the use of Brechtian aesthetics in order to politicize the genres, such as the gangster film or the melodrama, but he also draws on the inherent or potential subversiveness of the genres and particular films on which his "remakes" are based and thus forces German audiences to reconsider stereotypical perceptions of Hollywood film as apolitical and serving the status quo. The resulting films are hybrid and often messy constructions that provoke different and contradictory responses from the audience; by both offsetting and enhancing viewer identification, they often

---

34. In an interview Fassbinder stated that he originally had offered the part of Emmi to Lana Turner but couldn't meet her financial demands.

"Often celebrating as it deconstructs, camp can allow outmoded emotions to flourish not just for their sentimentality or kitschy quality, but for their seeds of rebellion against a drier, more conformist modernity. In this respect, camp treasures an excessive theatricality and outrageousness as an avenue to heightened emotion."—Al LaValley

Brigitte Mira and El Hedi ben Salem in *Ali: Fear Eats the Soul.* (Publicity still, Stiftung Deutsche Kinemathek Berlin.)

force us to identify with the characters against our better knowledge. The fact that many of Fassbinder's films met with a more enthusiastic reception in the United States than at home forced German critics to reconsider earlier dismissals of his work, but it also demonstrated that his reputation in Germany was largely determined by his appreciation abroad. In this sense Fassbinder has become a German Hollywood director after all.

CHAPTER 5

The *Indianerphantasien* of Herbert Achternbusch

Livin' with Comanches ain't bein' alive.
> —*John Wayne in* The Searchers

In order to become Comanches you first have to die.
> —*Herbert Achternbusch in* The Comanche

In Herbert Achternbusch's film *Der Komantsche* (*The Comanche* [1979]) we witness the unconscious hero of the title lying in an oxygen tent in a Bavarian hospital, while his wife tapes his dreams and sells them to television. In these dreams the Comanche has visions of a better world. One such dream shows him in search of *Stammesbrüder* (members of his tribe) at the *Stammtisch* of a restaurant (the specially designed table for the regulars) where he teaches the local beer drinkers how to become Comanches too. When called back to life, the protagonist panics; breathlessly, he runs through Munich, hurrying past a crowd in a soccer stadium until the camera zooms in on him, and, in the last shot, his red-eyed face fills almost the entire frame. Off-screen, we hear the Comanche's voice: "When I was still dreaming, I had an idea of how to live with people. But now that I'm awake and see the people, that idea is gone."[1]

Like so many representations of Native Americans in the German imagination since Karl May, Achternbusch's film could be read as an allegory of a vanished dream, offering a glimpse of harmony long lost in modern civilization only to affirm the inaccessibility of that harmony and the profundity of its loss. Yet, unlike May's Winnetou, Achternbusch's Comanche is a representation of a noble savage that does not try to eradicate the historical and political context that gave rise to its creation. In contrast to May's escapism and that of his many epigones, Achternbusch's representations rely on reductive narratives and stylistic incongruities that disturb rather than enhance audience identification; furthermore, his exotic fantasies of Bavarian Indians

---

1. Herbert Achternbusch, *Der Komantsche* (Heidelberg: Wunderhorn, 1979) 59.

"We're all Indians!" Postcard with drawing by Herbert Achternbusch. Reprinted by permission of the artist.

are at pains to foreground the postwar and post-Holocaust national identity that occasioned them and on which they comment—in some cases
through explicit parallel constructions of Indians and Jews. As I argue in
this chapter, this parallel should be not be seen as part of a defensive strategy common among many German leftists who compare the atrocities of
Nazi Germany to the genocide of American Indians in order to alleviate
the burden of their own history; nor are Achternbusch's works part of
what Hans M. Enzensberger once called a tourism of the revolution, that
is, an identification with the emancipatory struggles of repressed or marginalized people in faraway countries that remains blissfully ignorant of
conflicts closer to home.[2] Instead, Achternbusch's *Indianerphantasien* are
amplifications, not displacements, of problems of German cultural and
national identity; though not without contradiction or paradox, these
works attempt to challenge both the many traditional German depictions
of Native Americans and dominant postwar discourses of coming to terms
with the past, particularly the Holocaust. Before turning to Achternbusch's notion of anticolonial filmmaking and to an analysis of his
conflation of the Indian and the Jew, let me begin by sketching the "primitive aesthetics" through which Achternbusch's narratives are created and
articulated.

Primitive Aesthetics

If it was Rainer Werner Fassbinder's dream to create a German Hollywood
by exploiting genres of the classic American cinema, the films, writings, and
paintings of Herbert Achternbusch present a very different kind of relationship to U.S. cinema and to American mythology in general. As I argue in the
previous chapter, Fassbinder's strategy can perhaps be best described as a
Brechtian *Umfunktionierung,* in which genre conventions and spectator
expectations are playfully subverted, thereby creating parables of German
social reality in a film language understandable for an audience reared on
American models; his achievement lies not only in radicalizing mainstream
cinema but also in highlighting the subversive elements of that cinema, thus
challenging both bourgeois notions of entertainment and also leftist monolithic condemnations of Hollywood cinema as agents of cultural imperialism.
The films of Herbert Achternbusch, in contrast, show none of Fassbinder's
concerns for playfully subverting dominant modes of constructing narratives
or manipulating audience identification. Achternbusch's films, as well as his
writings, offer a frontal attack on seemingly everything handed down
through artistic and intellectual traditions, no matter whether of European or

---

2. Hans M. Enzensberger, "Tourists of the Revolution," in Enzensberger, *Critical Essays,*
ed. Reinhold Grimm and Bruce Armstrong (New York: Continuum, 1982).

American origin.[3] His narratives progress by leaps and bounds rather than by logic or character motivation; diegesis is interspersed with exegesis, as if characters need to explain what is going on in the film. Often a play on words (such as Comanche in a coma) or a wisecrack determines the turn of events (e.g., when the Comanche addresses a policeman: "Du bist vom Staat. Du bist ein Statist" [You're a federal employee—you're an extra]).[4]

His characters are not well rounded but sketchy; their behavior follows free association rather than psychological motivation; they speak a mixture of Bavarian dialect and pseudo high German, often exchanging long monologues that seem to leave no impression on those to them they are addressed. Achternbusch's films are mostly shot from a static camera; often the few cuts occur at rather unusual moments, as if to catch the spectators off-guard. The actors—or, rather, lay actors, for Achternbusch rarely works with professionals—play directly into the camera, apparently without much directorial guidance; the editing, finally, is often little more than the splicing together of the so-recorded shots and sequences. This intentional crudeness and rawness of his films is meant to preserve a personal vision, a stance that also governs Achternbusch's many writings. His published works include, and usually intermingle in one volume, short prose pieces, short novels (or what Achternbusch designates as such), dramas, poems, filmscripts, film reviews, letters, photos, autobiographical remarks, and, since the mid-1980s, also paintings and drawings. To make things even more confusing, much of his work has been reorganized and republished in seemingly chaotic fashion, only to form, according to Achternbusch, one big work called *Du hast keine Chance aber*

---

3. Despite his continued prolific output of films, writings, and paintings, Herbert Achternbusch has received little attention by scholars, particularly outside Germany. In the early 1980s several overviews were published, but since then interest in his work seems to have vanished. On his films, see Eric Rentschler, "Herbert Achternbusch: Celebrating the Power of Creation," in *New German Filmmakers: From Oberhausen through the 1970s*, ed. Klaus Phillips (New York: Ungar, 1984) 1–19; Thomas Elsaesser, "Achternbusch and the German Avant-Garde," *Discourse* 6 (1983): 92–112; the respective chapters in Eric Rentschler, *West German Film in the Course of Time: Reflections on the Twenty Years since Oberhausen* (Bedford Hills: Redgrave, 1984); Thomas Elsaesser, *New German Cinema: A History* (New Brunswick: Rutgers UP, 1989); Hans Günther Pflaum *Germany on Film: Theme and Content in the Cinema of the Federal Republic of Germany*, trans. Richrad C. Helt and Roland Richter (Detroit: Wayne State UP, 1990); and Hans Günther Pflaum, "Herbert Achternbusch: Bio- und Filmographie, Essay," in *Cinegraph*, ed. Hans-Michael Bock (Munich: Text + Kritik, 1987ff.); Wolfgang Jacobsen et al., *Herbert Achternbusch* (Munich: Hanser, 1984). On Achternbusch's writings, see Jörg Drews, ed., *Herbert Achternbusch* (Frankfurt am Main: Suhrkamp, 1982); Isabel Keilig, "Bemerkungen zu Herbert Achternbuschs Sublimierungsversuchen gestörter Kommunikation," in *Aufbrüche, Abschiede: Studien zur deutschen Literatur seit 1968*, ed. Michael Zeller (Stuttgart: Klett, 1979) 70–82; W. G. Sebald, "The Art of Transformations: Herbert Achternbusch's Theatrical Mission," in *A Radical Stage: Theatre in Germany in the 1970s and 1980s*, ed. W. G. Sebald (New York: Berg, 1988) 174–84. My following remarks summarize and extend some of the points made in these references.

4. *Der Komantsche* 34.

nutze sie ("You don't stand a chance but use it") after a famous line from his feature *Die Atlantikschwimmer* (*Atlantic Swimmers*).[5] The themes and topics of Achternbusch's literary and cinematic work encompass those found in most canonical works—love and death, the utopia of a better life, hope, anarchy, freedom—but their mode of articulation is entirely different. As Achternbusch puts it: "I always have a simple story, but I tell it so fanatically and wildly and tenderly and cursingly and on fire and in need of being loved that you'll find a slice of life in front of you."[6]

Works by Herbert Achternbusch are therefore always highly personal, almost to the point of egomania, and yet they never show any of the narcissism of which Peter Handke is frequently accused. While Handke (and Wenders) prefer the position of the spectator or the voyeur, Achternbusch is always on center stage, radically exposing himself while slipping into a multiplicity of roles, masks, and identities, only to document, time and again, how these alter egos have been shaped and misshaped by that which surrounds them.[7] The anxieties, deformations, and self-destructions of his soul and body thus become legible as the objectified effects of a malignant society.

If for Fassbinder the epithet "Made in Bavaria" aptly describes his fifteen-year development from a Munich avant-garde theater man and underground filmmaker to a high-paid star at Bavaria Studios, eventually directing international coproductions at Germany's most sophisticated film studio, Achternbusch's filmic output, from his debut feature *Das Andechser Gefühl* (*The Andechs Feeling* [1974]) to his recent *Hades* (1995) continually bears the signs of a Bavarian cottage industry. Virtually all of his twenty-five features to date are made on miniscule budgets by a small crew of professionals and amateurs, mostly shot near Munich and its suburbs—with notable contrastive scenes of exotic locales such as Sri Lanka, Greenland, Wyoming, and Tibet—and often set in beer gardens, public swimming pools, zoos, or amid the hills and lakes of the Bavarian countryside. No other German contemporary director embodies the principle of *Autorenfilm* as radically as Achternbusch: he always writes, directs, and produces his films and in some cases even distributes them; in most instances he also plays the lead, with his friends and beer hall buddies in supporting roles. He proudly proclaims that

---

5. On Achternbusch's strategies of continuous rearrangements of mobile texts, see Drews 15–16; and Sebald 174–75.

6. *Die Atlantikschwimmer: Schriften, 1973–79* (Frankfurt am Main: Suhrkamp, 1986) 265.

7. Elsaesser has pointed out how Achternbusch's *Der Neger Erwin* (*The Negro Erwin*) provides a parody of Wenders's notion of experience. In *Alice in the Cities* we hear Edda accuse her ex-boyfriend Philip of treating his experiences as if they were raw eggs; in *The Negro Erwin* the filmmaker (played by Achternbusch) stuffs himself with raw eggs at the beginning of the film: "A raw egg is the best means of self-control, especially after leaving prison. . . . A raw egg gives me dignity, bearing an upright walk an inner calm . . . with raw eggs in my pockets I have to treat myself as delicately as a raw egg" (cf. Elsaesser, "Achternbusch and the German Avant-Garde" 107).

his films are made "sloppily, quickly, and without content" (*schludrig, schnell und inhaltslos*)[8]—and yet this dilettantism clearly is an aesthetic program: unlike other directors, who also had to turn the handicap of inexperience and limited budgets of their first features into their stylistic virtue but who progressed as quickly as possible beyond that stage, Achternbusch, even after more than twenty years of filmmaking, refuses to adopt a more professional-looking style.[9]

The multiple idiosyncrasies that set Achternbusch apart from virtually all other directors of the New German Cinema are even more remarkable if we consider his early writings on film. Like Wenders, Achternbusch wrote about films before becoming a filmmaker in his own right; like Handke and the greatly admired Alexander Kluge, Achternbusch had critical success as a writer before becoming a *Filmautor;* and, like Fassbinder, he pursues parallel careers as filmmaker and playwright. As in Brinkmann, Fassbinder, Wenders, and Handke, one finds the same cinephilia, the same fascination for directors such as John Ford or Ozu, for genres such as the western, for certain periods such as the Hollywood cinema of the 1930s and 1940s. The following lines excerpted from a review show the same preference for paraphrase rather than analysis, the same celebratory stance of a cinema of duration, that one would find in Wenders, Handke, or the authors associated with *Filmkritik:*

Recently I saw John Ford's *The Grapes of Wrath* in a complete print. Henry Fonda has rightfully shot someone, and after four years in prison he is on his way home. He runs into a priest who has run out of ideas but who was once so inspired that he would preach while walking on his hands. How long it takes until they light a match in a dark, evicted house! How long it takes until a face emerges from the pitch black surrounding! You think they're all dead. And it is because of these films that one once started making films oneself.[10]

Yet, despite these many similarities, Achternbusch's cinema is decisively marked by that which sets it apart from that of his colleagues. First, what is different in Achternbusch from the other authors is the relation of filming and writing within his own oeuvre: they are not treated as two separate realms but as part of one *Gesamtkunstwerk* in progress, which also includes

---

8. Herbert Achternbusch, *Mixwix* (Cologne: Kiepenheuer and Wietsch, 1990) 192.
9. In *Was ich denke* Achternbusch writes: "Schnelle Filme machen andere so langsam. Und ich mache meine langsamen Filme so schnell" (102), which means not only that it takes others a long time to make their fast films (while Achternbusch makes his slow films very fast) but also that these fast films slow down the spectators' intellect by bombarding them with special effects, predictible plots, etc.
10. Herbert Achternbusch, *Die Atlantikschwimmer* 121.

his paintings and books of photography. Instead of turning novels or stories into scripts, as Kluge and Handke have done, Achternbusch designates his published scripts "novels," a term he also seeks to apply to a recent collection of plays.[11] Instead of considering writing about films, an ersatz occupation to be abandoned once he was able to direct them, Achternbusch has turned his life itself into a film: "Since I couldn't make a film without money I only wanted to live as if in a movie."[12] In their literariness and wordiness his films recall books, while his books appear "filmic" through their many brief shot-like descriptions and the frequent insertion of photographs and drawings.

More important still, the foreign cinema he writes about—the style of John Ford, Kurosawa, or Ozu, the acting of Charles Chaplin, Buster Keaton or Jerry Lewis—has left few direct traces in his own work; rarely does one find the kind of allusions or "quotes" so prominent in Wenders or Fassbinder. There is perhaps more of a presence of the German artists Achternbusch admires—most notably the dry wit and nonsensical sententiousness of Karl Valentin and the aggressiveness toward social outsiders depicted in the plays of Marieluise Fleisser—but I would argue that on the whole most critics' search for influences and inherited traditions have come up with little more than superficial connections and seem motivated by the difficulty to explain Achternbusch's singularity. This strategy is also true for the tendency to situate Achternbusch's challenge to mainstream cinema and literature within the tradition of the (historical) avant-garde.[13] Of course, one does find in Achternbusch's film and prose much of what I have discussed with regard to Brinkmann and Jelinek:[14] a militant aggression toward the various institutions responsible for funding, publishing, distributing, and exhibiting art as well as a critique of the discourses of academia and the feuilleton instrumental for their promotion; a refusal of the star cult of the directorial personality (in which Fassbinder, Herzog, or Syberberg revel); a questioning of the dividing line between reality and fiction, role and actor. Achternbusch's notion of quickly and cheaply produced films, of plays written in two days, of paintings painted on newspapers and paper napkins, does echo Warhol's attack on traditional notions of art and authenticity, as does Achternbusch's method of

---

11. In the preface to this collection he writes: "I'd be happy if someone would recognize a novel in these 17 plays. Its name would be 'Susn'" (*Die Einsicht der Einsicht: Theaterstücke* [Frankfurt am Main: Fischer, 1996] 5).

12. *Die Atlantikschwimmer* 149.

13. Cf. the cited works by Elsaesser and Rentschler; cf. also Peter von Becker's comparison between Achternbusch's theatrical works and those of Samuel Beckett: "Die Stadt, das Land und der Tod," *Theater Heute* 7 (1985): 22–27.

14. There seems to exist a mutual respect for one another's work among these authors. Achternbusch tells of how Jelinek has defended his play *Linz* in Austria (*Wohin: Schriften, 1985–88* [Frankfurt am Main: Suhrkamp, 1991] 268) and of his admiration for Brinkmann's *Rom Blicke;* according to Achternbusch, a volume of his own novel *Die Stunde des Todes* was found with Brinkmann when he was killed by a car in London (cf. *Die Atlantikschwimmer* 490f.).

working with a Warhol Factory-like group of collaborators and friends.[15] And one does find in his prose and films elements of "raw surrealism,"[16] of imitations of "écriture automatique, cut-up,"[17] of Joycean stream-of-consciousness. But these parallels seem less the result of Achternbusch's diligent reading than of having come up with his own, and very similar, responses to address the role of art and artist in modern or postmodern society. Nor does Achternbusch ever seek alliance or solidarity with other artists or political groups, an important trait of the historical avant-garde as well as the formation of the Young, and then New, German Cinema.[18] Furthermore, unlike the avant-gardism of Brinkmann's essays or poetry, Jelinek's early prose, Handke's *Sprechstücke,* or Wenders's shorts, Achternbusch's works never reflect the intellectual curiosity and formal rigor so evident in these other artists. His only formal desire is to leave form behind—an artistic illusion, to be sure, but one that Achternbusch has pursued with more radicalism, stubbornness, and staying power, if not "success," than anyone else before him.[19]

Achternbusch himself has always claimed to have worked "without role model and conceptualization" (*ohne Vorbild und ohne Begriffslehre*),[20] a gesture I am tempted to read at face value and not, as in Herzog or Fassbinder, as a strategic form of self-improvement. For the purpose of my argument I want to call this aesthetics a "primitivist aesthetics." What I mean by this is that Achternbusch's impersonations of Native Americans are supported by a style that, in its attempt to work without presuppositions and its reliance on

---

15. In a critique of Achternbusch's early novel *Hülle* (*Cover*)—note the Warhol-like title—Reinhold Grimm has attacked the author for a pretentiousness indebted to the then contemporary fad for Pop aesthetics and Pop criticism: "The whole thing is an inflated nothing . . . Achternbusch demonstrates in an embarassing way what happens when a diletant takes the newest literary theories seriously . . . All he proves is his inability; all he creates is boredom" (Reinhold Grimm, "Der Verfasser heißt Herbert Achternbusch," in Drews 61–62).

16. Rentschler, "Herbert Achternbusch" 18.

17. Wolfram Schütte, "Wo ein Film entsteht, da sind auch Menschen; oder 'Nur die verkommenste aller Künste, der Film, darf den Versuch wagen, unseren Nachkommen zu sagen, daß auch wir Menschen gewesen sind,'" in Drews 146–60; here 147.

18. For Achternbusch's frequent attacks on other writers and filmmakers, see, for example, "An die deutschen Filmbrüder," *Die Atlantikschwimmer* 459–60.

19. It seems to me that Achternbusch is also well aware of some of the aporias of the Pop-inspired literary avant-garde of the late 1960s. In *Die Alexanderschlacht* Achternbusch leaves a "free space for the opinion of the readers" ([Frankfurt am Main: Suhrkamp, 1971] 34) only to comment later that he has probably not left enough space and that he is actually not sure if he wants to hear their opinion anyhow—a much more honest reaction than the simulated call for reader participation found on the cover of Elfriede Jelinek's *wir sind lockvögel, baby,* which I discussed in chapter 3.

20. Herbert Achternbusch, *Es ist ein leichtes beim Gehen den Boden zu berühren* (Frankfurt am Main: Suhrkamp, 1980) 5. This statement is reiterated by Kuschwarda City, another important Bavarian Indian whom I will discuss later: "I am the writer of the future. Because humans can express themselves only as individuals. Without role model and conceptualization" (*Die Einsicht der Einsicht* 73).

anarchic and anachronistic modes of production, achieves a most direct and aggressive form of audience address that challenges his viewers' traditional notions of primitivism.

To use the term *primitive* or *primitivism* is, of course, not without problems. As Marianna Torgovnick has shown in *Gone Primitive: Savage Intellects, Modern Lives,* Western views of Third World, native, aboriginal, or tribal cultures are always forms of "othering" that are imbricated in strategies of domination, appropriation, and stereotyping; in these discourses the primitive invariably becomes a placeholder for the noble savage or the cannibal.[21] Like for so many before him, Achternbusch also uses primitivism as a concept because it is so docile and malleable, and certain qualities he attributes to his Bavarian Indians fit quite squarely into the long list of stereotypes established by modern Western tradition. But, even though Achternbusch cannot claim to be entirely outside the traditions he intends to attack, his hyper-self-conscious impersonations of Native Americans are careful to foreground the artificiality of their performance and the constructedness of their subjects. They claim no ethnographic authority, nor do they create the illusion to represent real others. In John Ford's film *The Searchers,* which he intensely admires,[22] Achternbusch identifies with Debbie, the woman who was kidnapped by the Comanches as a young girl and "became an Indian herself."[23] Achternbusch's own Indian fantasies are motivated by this dream and by the knowledge of the impossibility of "going native." Exploiting this fundamental incongruity propels the narrative of all his Indian fantasies.

Anti-Colonial Filmmaking

Writing about Achternbusch's early films, Eric Rentschler has argued that among the many personal visions of the New German Cinema "none is as personal as Herbert Achternbusch's,"[24] a description in which we must be careful not to equate the personal with the autobiographical. For, even though Achternbusch is everywhere in his films and written works, they are never about him. His many incarnations of himself—which include various forms of Bavarian Indians such as the Comanche, an Indio (a story included in *Das Kamel* [1969]), Kuschwarda City (of a 1980 play of that title), and Hick (of a trilogy composed of the unrealized script *Oceanstreet* [1990] and the films *Hick's Last Stand* [1990] and *Ab nach Tibet* [*Off to Tibet*] [1994])—are not premised on creating illusion but on a form of enactment that displays both

---

21. Cf. Marianna Torgovnick, *Gone Primitive: Savage Intellects, Modern Lives* (Chicago: Chicago UP, 1990).

22. In "Der Tag wird kommen" he writes: "*The Searchers* by John Ford, the best film and my most personal weakness . . . If I had made this film, I'd have nothing else to say" (*Die Atlantikschwimmer* 20f.).

23. Achternbusch, *Die Alexanderschlacht* 43.

24. Rentschler, "Herbert Achternbusch" 1.

Herbert Achternbusch as "Herbert, die Krücke" in *Heilt Hitler!* (1986).
(Publicity still, Stiftung Deutsche Kinemathek Berlin.)

Achternbusch's existential need for identification with the other *and* a fundamental incongruity between character and fiction. This form of identification produces narratives that rely on impersonation in the "primitive" sense that I have outlined here—not as a form of "ethnic drag" that stages and conceals its dominance over the other and that subsumes markers of difference under universal meanings but as an antinaturalist impersonation that foregrounds fundamental incompatibility and difference.[25]

Achternbusch's impersonations of Indians are therefore at pains to avoid being taken for the "real thing." Supported by the formal features I have outlined earlier in this chapter, they propel narratives that exploit incongruity and stress disparity, if not despair. *The Comanche,* as I indicated, is an allegory of a vanished dream of the community of all humans. Where the Comanche looks for *Stammesbrüder,* he finds only *Stammtischbrüder;* the *Wald* (forest) is gone—all that's left is *Wienerwald.* He paddles his canoe on the streets of Munich, as all water has turned into pavement. Where his feathers used to be, antennas indicate that his mind is being exploited by the cul-

25. Cf. Katrin Sieg, "Ethnic Drag and National Identity: Multicultural Crises, Crossings, and Interventions," in *The Imperialist Imagination: German Colonialism and Its Legacy,* ed. Sara Friedrichsmeyer, Sara Lennox, and Susanne Zantop (Ann Arbor: U of Michigan P, 1998) 295–319.

ture industry. His name contains his malaise—the coma into which he has fallen because his wife shot him and from which he's rudely awaken at the end of the film by a mysterious letter, only to be paralyzed once again by the fear of masses of humans around him. Yet, despite his incapacitation, the Comanche is the only one with a subjectivity, the only one who could lead others who in turn eagerly await his recovery. The 1980 play *Kuschwarda City,* fragments of which already appear in *Die Alexanderschlacht,* offers a similar apocalyptic vision of being an Indian in Bavaria. Partitioned into "four catastrophes," it chronicles in surrealist fashion the evermore violent fate of its title hero as a rebel out of control.

To be sure, these and other Indian fantasies by Achternbusch contain a good measure of the romantic imagery of Native Americans found in the novels of Karl May. They are also indebted to post-1968 notions of seeing Indians as the embodiment of an "alternative" lifestyle. Following broad trends toward environmentalism and antitechnology, during the 1970s North American Indians became symbols for a precapitalist social and economic model. *Stadtindianer,* hut dwellers and urban guerillas fought airport extensions, nuclear power plants, and other evils of the White Man's society.[26] The Göttinger *Stadtindianer* acquired fame in Germany's subculture when in a "Mescalero Letter" they expressed *klammheimliche Freude* (clandestine joy) after the killing of state attorney-general Siegfried Buback in 1977. But—and this is my point—Achternbusch's films and texts are always painfully aware of the naïveté of such identifications and projections. They never grant their audience the pleasure of escapism that made May so successful. Instead, they baffle through their refusal to explain—the psychology of the characters, the desires that propel the narrative, its many gaps and twists. Often the films contain nonsensical episodes. In *Niemandsland (No-Man's-Land* [1991]), a western set in the Alpine village of Mals about a "tribe that does not exist,"[27] we witness a competition in *Tauchsiederwefen* (throwing electric water heaters), a parody of one of May's many invented customs "typical" of the North American Indians. Ridicule and laughter dispel pathos and suspense. Interspersed within the outrageous fantasies of the director are historical facts that, in their oddity, further enhance the bizarreness of the representation. [28] In place of a captivating illusionism, a bold matter-of-fact-ness pre-

26. Cf. Rentschler, *West German Film in the Course of Time* 179f.

27. *Es ist niemand da* 60.

28. Achternbusch explains that the yellow feather worn by his Comanche is based on the fact that this tribe wore feathers only to poke fun at other tribes. He recalls a screening of the film in New York: "In the Museum of Modern Art, a man in a gray suit got up and asked what the film had to do with Comanches for he was a Comanche. I smiled at him and said: 'And the yellow feather? Didn't the Comanches wear yellow feathers to ridicule the other feather-wearing tribes?' And even though he had already degenerated into an engineer, he had great respect for me" (*Wind: Schriften, 1982–83* 409f.). In a conversation with me in June 1996 Herbert Achternbusch listed a series of works that he had consulted for his films, including anthropological studies, memoirs, historical accounts, and biographies.

vails. If Tom Ripley, in Wenders's *American Friend,* self-consciously asks what's wrong with a cowboy in Hamburg, Achternbusch sees absolutely nothing wrong with a Comanche in Munich.

With the exception of *Hick's Last Stand,* all of Achternbusch's Indian fantasies are set not in the United States but in Bavaria, which is made to look strange and bizarre, augmenting existing stereotypes and clichés of Germany's most mythologized and ridiculed region. As for so many Germans, for Achternbusch America is not a confederation of states but a state of mind—and yet, his America is still very different from that of the other authors considered in this study, a place where the dialectic of the strange and the familiar takes on a very succinct shape. Neither antagonist nor catalyst, the United States is not the site to set one's subjectivity in motion, to experience the self as other as in Handke's, Wenders's, or Treut's America; nor does it provide the chance to revel in the "authenticity of the inauthentic" so important for Brinkmann, Jelinek, or Fassbinder. Achternbusch's interest in this country therefore shows none of the symptoms of what Laura Mulvey has called "Americanitis," that is, the fascination of European intellectuals with "the new levels of articulation" they saw in Hollywood genre cinema.[29] Rather, Achternbusch's fascination with America is profoundly anti-intellectual: no attempt is made to differentiate geography, politics, or people, and there is little interest in its culture, be it "high" or "low." In its complete otherness America invites identification because it seems to have absolutely nothing to do with where he comes from—a *Heimat* away from home, a refuge from the oppressing rural communities where he grew up, more of a notion or a feeling really than a country and yet something with which Achternbusch seems to be on intimate terms. In *Die Alexanderschlacht* (1971) he associates America with his childhood in the Bavarian forest:

> When I chopped down a tree in the woods with my axe, I was in Wyoming, and when . . . I shot a deer with my shotgun, I was in Oregon. And when I pissed into the inkwell at school, I did this as an American . . . When I sat in church and heard the priest talk about America, I imagined America, and there were no stupid saints and popes standing around who always would have thumbscrews hidden under their gown for me. When a young calf stood in our barn, I patted it and I was in America. When I changed the spark plug of my father's motorbike and I started up the bike and went for a spin in the fields, I was in America.[30]

America is a place longed for but never reached. "In the distance glows America" is the promise given to Herbert, before, in the final scene of *The*

29. Laura Mulvey, "Americanitis: European Intellectuals and Hollywood Melodrama," *Fetishism and Curiosity* (London: BFI, 1996) 19–28; here 19.

30. Achternbusch, *Die Alexanderschlacht* 197f.

Atlantic Swimmers, he sets out on his cross-Atlantic swim to capture the prize of a department store. Achternbusch's own stays in the United States—the first one in 1979, when he spent a few weeks touring with his films in California,[31] and a later, more extended one in 1989 when filming *Hick's Last Stand* in the West—have done little to alter this vision. As if not to have the real America interfere with that of his imagination, Achternbusch made an effort to keep the country at a distance, intentionally misspelling names of people and places or mocking the exaggerated acculturation of Wim Wenders (who was then living in California while shooting *Hammett*) as someone who knows the United States better than the Americans do—except that "no American would want to know their country as well as a German."[32] For Achternbusch America is not a geographical or political reality but just one of the many exotic locales of his films. These places could all be called "No-Man's-Land"—sites where the poet's imagination may run wild but which he refuses to portray in realistic terms for fear of imposing a colonial attitude: "How am I supposed to create an image of Greenland [which we see in *Servus Bayern* (*Bye Bye Bavaria*)] or Sri Lanka [which we see in the dreams of the Comanche]? I can't do that . . . I will not subordinate these countries (*Ich mache mir diese Länder nicht untertan*)."[33]

This equation of antirealism with anticolonialism is a crucial element in Achternbusch's primitive aesthetics and one that we must now explore more closely. As a representational policy, it clearly sets his films off from mainstream Hollywood cinema, no matter whether we are talking about classic Hollywood cinema, which often portrays Indians through racist stereotypes (as do many of John Ford's westerns),[34] or about contemporary American cinema, which—seemingly politically correct—pretends to empathize with Native Americans by adopting the position of the benevolent white outsider but which still denies Native Americans their own voice (*Dances with Wolves*). Closer to home, Achternbusch's Indian fantasies could be read as polemic answers to films such as Harald Reinl's *Winnetou* sequels of the 1960s, the extremely popular action-packed adaptations of May's novels, or to the social realism of Hark Bohm's *Tschetan, der Indianerjunge* (1973) or the rock group BAP's song "Blonde Mohikaner"(1993), which both pleaded

---

31. Cf. "Amerika: Bericht ans Goethe-Institut," in *Die Alexanderschlacht* 483–89. This and a few other texts by Achternbusch available in English translation can be found in Eric Rentschler, ed., *West German Filmmakers on Film: Visions and Voices* (New York: Holmes and Meier, 1988).

32. *Die Atlantikschwimmer* 483.

33. Hans Günther Pflaum, "Interview," in Jacobsen et al., *Herbert Achternbusch* 59–120; here 81.

34. Apparently, this racist depiction of native Americans has not detracted from Achternbusch's admiration for Ford, even though Achternbusch is careful not to reiterate that racism in his own works.

for consideration toward the marginalized. No such gesture of "speaking on behalf of" can be found in his work.[35]

Among contemporary German filmmakers Achternbusch's anticolonial vision seems closest to that of Werner Herzog, with whom he is frequently compared, not least because of his own early admiration for Herzog and their collaboration on *Herz aus Glas* (*Heart of Glass* [1977]).[36] Like Achternbusch's Indian fantasies, Werner Herzog's films set in the Peruvian jungle can—or want to—be read as a critique of colonialism for the ways in which they portray the inadequacy of the colonial system of representation and understanding. *Aguirre, the Wrath of God* (1972) traces the deadly fate of a rebellious group of sixteenth-century Conquistadores in search of El Dorado. What leads to their demise is not so much the confrontation with the native population, which remains conspicuously absent from the film and which Herzog, in an antirealist gesture similar to Achternbusch, chooses to portray only through synecdochic extensions (their arrows, screams, drumming, the traps they set, their abandoned huts); rather, what proves deadly is the Spaniards' inability to understand what is in front of them, their refusal to accept a pattern of conceptualization other than the one they brought with them. In *Fitzcarraldo* (1982) the hero is more successful in imposing his Western geometry onto the Amazon forest in order to get access to a rubber plantation, yet he too fails, in the end, and ultimately recognizes the inadequacy of his enterprise. If these narratives seem to criticize the logic of colonialism, the making of the films, particularly the controversial shooting of *Fitzcarraldo,* which claimed the life of one Indian actor, relies on the very system of control the film criticizes. As Lutz P. Koepnick has argued, "Herzog at once comprehends the aporetic shortsightedness of the colonial gaze and yet in his role as an auteur director, he reproduces the instrumental logic of his hero."[37]

Herzog's depictions of North America and its Indians show an even greater difference to Achternbusch's. *Stroszek* (1977) traces the downward spiral of the life of Bruno, an ex-convict from Berlin who moves to Railroad Flats, Wisconsin, to better his lot. If life in Germany was bad for Bruno, in America things get only worse. At crucial points in the film the fate of Bruno the outcast, who doesn't understand the American way of life, is compared to that of Native Americans—the silent Indian mechanic he works with and the

---

35. In *Die Alexanderschlacht* the narrator mocks this plea for consideration, parodying once again the idiom of Karl May. Having a job in which he has to dress up as "Cheyenne-Indianer" in a "Cowboyklub," he tells visitors: "Ich kann machen Verständnis für roten Mann bei weißer Rasse" (I can create understanding for Red Man with White Race) (127).

36. On Achternbusch's admiration for and disenchantment with Herzog, see *Die Atlantikschwimmer*. See also Christopher Wickham, "Heart and Hole: Achternbusch, Herzog and the Concept of *Heimat,*" *Germanic Review* 64.3 (1989): 112–20.

37. Lutz P. Koepnick, "Colonial Forestry: Sylvan Politics in Werner Herzog's *Aguirre* and *Fitzcarraldo,*" *New German Critique* 60 (1993): 133–59; here 137. See also "Werner Herzog und die Indianer," *Kirche und Film* 35.4 (1982): a–e.

Indians performing tribal rituals on a reservation (outside of which no space
and context exists for their performance). It is here, where the last Native
Americans have become extras for the tourism industry, that Stroszek takes
his life, underscoring the dead end of both existences. *Stroszek* can be read as
a vicious attack on the American way of life as a new, and more sophisticated, form of colonialism. Just as the first settlers have eradicated and
domesticated the native population, contemporary society will not allow a
space for marginal figures like Bruno.

The comparison with Achternbusch's only film set in the United States,
Hick's Last Stand, shows the radical difference of the two directors' representation of Indians. Here we witness yet another incarnation of a Last
Bavarian Mohican, incoherently staggering across the badlands of South
Dakota and Wyoming in white cowboy boots, black leather jacket, and a
feather on his hat. Without dialogue, without other players besides Herbert
Achternbusch, and with the most minimal narrative progression, the film
consists only of an image track over which we hear Hick's extended monologue, a declaration of love to the absent Mary, occasionally interrupted by
songs by Judy Garland, Native American chants, and classical music. Here
Achternbusch's fear of filmically subjugating other countries or people finds
is most radical expression: a jerky camera captures endless images of passing
trucks, empty landscapes, abandoned houses; frequent zooms and out-of-
focus shots suggest the work of a hobby filmer, as does the grainy quality of
the image that appears to be blown-up super-eight material. (The credits list
Herbert Achternbusch as partly responsible for the camerawork.) This is
Indian territory, Hick's voice reminds us, but, except for a furtive look at a
Pow Wow, the natives are absent. "People who cannot endure injustice, will
not survive," he explains.[38]

The difference between Herzog's and Achternbusch's anticolonialism
revolves around their different notions of authenticity, which both directors
create not *in* but *through* their films. Despite his critique of traditional forms
of cinematic realism, Herzog's films rely on a notion of authenticity that
comes across as the talent of the *auteur*-director capable of capturing the
exoticism of foreign places and people—and Americans, as he once
remarked, "are the most exotic people in the world."[39] Authenticity in
Achternbusch, in contrast, comes not from the pretense of catching a glimpse
of the natives while they weren't watching. In that respect Achternbusch's
fear of imposing a colonial gaze is much more knowledgeable and self-critical
than Herzog's. Nor does it come from effacing the traces of the films' production in order to create a phantasmagoric spectacle, so important for Herzog.[40] In Achternbusch's primitivism the traces of faulty filmmaking do not

38. *Mixwix* 259.
39. Cf. Gene Walsh, *Images at the Horizon: A Workshop with Werner Herzog* (Chicago:
Facets, 1979) 10. See also Herzog's documentaries *God's Angry Man* and *Huie's Last Sermon*
(1980), which further exploit the alleged exoticism of the United States.
40. Cf. Koepnick, "Colonial Forestry" 157.

end up on the editing table but, rather, attest to the films' creation. Nor does authenticity arise, as in Herzog, from the various identifications between *auteur*-director, protagonist, and film(making). Free of such self-glorifications, Achternbusch's enactments show us the failures and wounds incurred in their productions, erasing the line between role and actor by making visible the risks it entails—it is the real Herbert Achternbusch who gets insulted, assaulted, and almost beaten up in *Bierkampf* (*Beer Battle* [1977]) when playing pranks on the beer drinkers at the Munich Oktoberfest. And, incidentally, the real Herbert Achternbusch was detained at O'Hare Airport when trying to pass customs with the two plastic bags he carries around as Hick in *Hick's Last Stand.*[41]

There can be no doubt that Achternbusch himself understands his primitive cinema as a form of anticolonialism. Repeatedly and with obvious pride, he has cited Heiner Müller, who once called Achternbusch "a classic of the anti-colonial struggle for liberation in the territory of the FRG."[42] But one must ask, of course, what *anticolonial* means in this context. For Müller, most likely, Achternbusch is an accomplice in the anticapitalist struggle against the West. For Achternbusch, who abhors political parties of both the Left and the Right, the term *anticolonialism* is not connected to one particular political system or one country of origin. Unlike so many writers and filmmakers of his generation, Achternbusch has resisted blaming American cultural imperialism for contemporary forms of colonization, even though one does find occasional references to the negative effects of *Amerikanisierung.*[43] Instead, *anticolonialism* seems to carry the broader meaning of a resistance against all forms of globalization or industrialization; in contrast to cultural imperialism, it is seen as a less purposeful and culturally directed process that will erase not *one* cultural identity at the expense of another but the coherence of all nations.[44] "This used to be Bavaria. Now the world rules here. Like the Congo or Canada, Bavaria has been subjected by the world, is being ruled by the world. Bavaria is a colony of the world. This piece of earth, too, has become world."[45] Seen in this context, the Bavarian Comanche and his various brothers become in Achterbusch's idiosyncratic performance

---

41. In a conversation with me in June 1996.

42. Herbert Achternbusch, "Autobahn," *Die Olympiasiegerin* (Frankfurt am Main: Suhrkamp, 1982) 15.

43. In "Das Andechser Gulasch" Achternbusch writes: "But what was I supposed to do in America since the whole world is being americanized. Someone's got to stay home, bite his teeth and bite off his tongue and spit it into someone's face in the hope that this other person will choke on it. I, for one, bulge out my hat and wear it like an Indian" (*Wohin: Schriften, 1985–88* [Frankfurt am Main: Suhrkamp, 1991] 22). See also the early story "Indio," in which the narrator says: "How difficult it is for Gerda [the name of Achternbusch's wife at the time] not to hate the Americans who are now about to destroy her people [the Germans] just as they destroyed mine" (*1969* 50).

44. On the difference between globalization and cultural imperialism, see John Tomlinson, *Cultural Imperialism* (Baltimore: Johns Hopkins UP, 1991).

45. Herbert Achternbusch, *Die Olympiasiegerin,* 11.

essential figures of resistance, metaphors of the artist's struggle and the struggle of art against the homogenizing and leveling effects of modernization and globalization.

Indians and Jews

It would be tempting to read Achternbusch's identification with the oppressed as an escapist strategy trying to shun the reality of one's own society.[46] And, indeed, there is a strong tendency in Achternbusch's work to cast himself time and again in the role of the victim and the marginalized, a tendency of which he himself is well aware. As he described his many roles in his films: "From a teacher in *The Andechs Feeling* to a lifeguard in *The Atlantic Swimmers,* to a lazybone in *Beer Battle* who steals a police uniform, to an insignificant writer in *Bye Bye Bavaria,* to a Zero in *The Young Monk* who stills dares to move a little, to an unconscious Comanche, to an ex-convict in *The Negro Erwin,* to a criminal in *The Last Hole,* to a decapitated person in *The Fool,* to a ghost in *The Ghost*—this is the development (*Werdegang*) in my films."[47] This awareness of self-victimization does not, of course, eliminate its naïveté. What does counter the escapist tendency of Achternbusch's impersonations is, as I have argued, the incongruity of their style and the antirealist narratives in which they are imbedded. What is more, if the roles he invents for himself can be seen as a form of exile, the means of oppression of the society that imposes this exile are depicted in no uncertain terms. If Achternbusch's alter egos and their locales appear exotic, the home soil that forces them out, oppresses, wounds, and kills is not. If we take this gesture of *Anti-Heimat* as the "real" referent of Achternbusch's antirealist cinema, it becomes clear that his Indian fantasies are not displacements but amplifications of problems of postwar German national identity. These become most visible when compared to the model that they most explicitly attempt to refute—the Indian fantasies of Karl May.[48]

Analyzing the reception of the annual "Karl-May-Festpiele" in the 1950s, Katrin Sieg has shown how the works of Karl May proved especially suitable to the needs of a West German audience plagued by guilt and eager to escape their social reality. She argues that the enormous popularity of the show stems from the ways in which it rehearses a disavowal of German nationalism as well as providing fantasies of restitution (*Wiedergut-*

---

46. Critics have repeatedly taken Achternbusch to task for what they perceive to be self-inflicted misery. As Hans-Horst Henschen, for example, writes: "How long will this author [Achternbusch] continue digging . . . until he will hit on what Kafka called the iron bars of one's own existence?" ("Meteorit, im Anflug: Herbert Achternbuschs Theater- und Kinokreuzzug," in Drews 84–94; here 94.

47. *Wind* 460.

48. It should be noted here that in May's strict dichotomy of "good Indians" and "bad Indians" the Comanches figure among the worst tribes.

machungsphantasien): "[Winnetou's] admiration for the 'good' whites (= Germans), and his refusal to hold them responsible for the atrocities of the 'bad' whites (= Yankees) register postwar Germans' fantasies of absolution and restitution: to be forgiven for the horrors perpetrated and to render them undone, a contradiction attesting to the processes of denial at work in postwar German culture."[49] The contrast to Achternbusch's Bavarian Indians could not be bigger: They do not entertain any such fantasies of restitution, nor do they try to blame a third party such as May's Yankees—in Achternbusch, the perpetrators and oppressors are the Germans of the Third Reich (among whom Achternbusch includes "meine Nazi-Eltern" [my Nazi parents][50]), and the guilt they have left behind for the generation(s) to come is insurmountable.[51] If for many leftists of Achternbusch's generation it became fashionable to talk about the genocide of the North American Indians to alleviate the burdens of their own history, for Achternbusch, in contrast, it is the Nazi Holocaust that needs to be addressed. Achternbusch leaves no doubt that his Indians are the victims of a genocide that took place on German soil. The grim social reality that the Comanche encounters in Germany, and which will cause him to panic after he has woken up from his coma, is explained to be a direct consequence of the Third Reich. As the nurse attending to him in the hospital says, "Germany has given all its love to Hitler, now it's got none left."[52]

If in the Karl-May-Festspiele, according to Sieg, the genocide of the Jews is absent and has been displaced by the genocide of the Native Americans, no such displacements occur in Achternbusch—in his Indian fantasies the Jew is everywhere, not as a physical reality but as an absence that demands recollection. "Uns fehlen die Juden!!! Niemand vermißt sie" (We're missing the Jews!!! Nobody misses them), writes Achternbush.[53] They are virtually extinct in Germany, and, according to Achternbusch, contemporary Germany has made no effort to preserve those traces of Jewish life the Nazis had not managed to eradicate, thus continuing the politics of the final solution. In his films real Jews are as absent as real Native Americans; for Achternbusch both are imaginary people who can be represented only by the void they have left in our cultures and whose remembrance is therefore a work of mourning. In *The Comanche* the protagonist goes to a Buddhist tem-

---

49. Sieg "Ethnic Drag and National Identity" 303.
50. *Hundstage* 162.
51. A fantasy of resitution seems to propell Wim Wenders's *State of Things.* Taking the search motif and not, like Achternbusch, the identification with Debbie as the essential feature of Ford's *The Searchers,* the director Munroe spends much of the film looking for the Jewish producer Gordon. When they finally meet up, they are shot together—communal victims at the hands of a nebuluous and never-seen perpetrator, the (Hollywood?) loan sharks; they die for their shared vision of art.
52. *Der Komantsche* 23.
53. *Wohin* 318.

ple to comfort God. "Hitler wanted to comfort him [God] with 6 million Jews, but that was a mistake."[54]

The impossibility of *Vergangenheitsbewältigung,* let alone *Wiedergut-machung,* is articulated most clearly in the film *Das letzte Loch* (*The Last Hole* [1981]). Here we follow the private detective Nil in his quest to uncover the murder of his Jewish friends. At night he is plagued by nightmares about the Holocaust, and he decides to go and see a doctor:

> *Doctor:* I'll prescribe you schnapps. With 2 cl you'll forget one Jew, with 6 million Jews—that makes 20 Jews per liter. . . . 6 million divided by 20 Jews, that makes 3,333—well, a third of a Jew remains, but for the rest you'll need 300000 liter schnapps . . .
> *Nil:* I would have to kill one more Jew to make it even.
> *Doctor:* But do you know one?
> *Nil:* None who's alive . . . Oh well, so I'll drink one bottle of schnapps for a thousand years. For someone's got to take care of justice![55]

The absurdity of the scene is determined by the incomprehensibility of the crime. If Auschwitz stands for a perfected rationalism void of humanism, for the postwar Achternbusch, to be human means to be necessarily irrational,[56] to insist on the idiosyncrasy of one's radical individualism.[57] The fate of the Jews is most closely connected to Achternbusch's image of the Indians in *Hick's Last Stand,* which has been read as a sequel to *The Last Hole.*[58] It is as if the Stromboli has spit out Nil onto the badlands of Wyoming, now appro-priately called Hick—as in hiccup—to indicate that a volcanic indigestion is the reason for his reincarnation.[59] Like Nil, Hick is an obsessive drinker and holds imaginary conversations with Yukon Jack, a brand of whiskey. Hick wears a hat like Native Americans, with paper towels hanging down at the sides that resemble the locks of an orthodox Jew. He states that he is a "racist

54. *Der Komantsche* 22. Significantly, this sentence was cut from a screening of the film by ZDF, a measure to which Achternbusch first agreed in order to have his film shown but which he protested afterward, comparing it to Nazi methods of censorship: "The first kick of the fascists was always in the balls. The first democratic grab for the balls is already happening. Let's fight back!" (*Die Atlantikschwimmer* 483).

55. *Das letzte Loch* 94ff.

56. In *Die Alexanderschlacht* he writes: "As long as something that concerns humans remains logical, it is superficial" (122).

57. In "Springtime" Achternbusch writes: "For many, my statements are too private. Pri-vate? In the country of past mass destructions one does not yet like the individual" (*Wohin* 134).

58. Cf. Helmut Schödel's review, "Indiana Herbert," *Die Zeit,* July 27, 1990. To my knowl-edge the only other literary attempt to connect the fate of the Jews with that of the Native Amer-icans is George Tabori's play *Weissman and Rotgesicht* (*Weissman and Copperface* [1990]).

59. The word *hick* always occurs at the end of Hick's lenghty monologues and can thus be seen as a parody of May's "Howgh, I have spoken," with which his Indian protagonists end their speeches.

Herbert Achternbusch as Hick in *Hick's Last Stand* (1991). (Publicity still, Stiftung Deutsche Kinemathek Berlin.)

against the Germans,"[60] a condition he explains to come from his German upbringing: "Germany has destroyed so much—why not me too?"[61]

As the Comanche, Kuschwarda City, Hick, and Nil make abundantly clear, Achternbusch's strategy to distance himself from the perpetrators is to cast himself, time and again, in the role of the victim. This victim status is further enhanced by the ways in which Achternbusch considers the Federal Republic of Germany to be little more than an extension of the Third Reich. As he says in a postface to *Heilt Hitler!* (*Heal Hitler!* [1986]): "As long as the CSU is in power, the Third Reich won't be over,"[62] a pessimistic view of history that permeates his works from early on. Living in what he believes to be a quasifascist state, Achternbusch feels imprisoned like an inmate of a concentration camp. "I heard about concentration camp prisoners who lived in their fantasies, who hardly realized the everyday, who fantasized themselves away in order to survive. I take the liberty to attempt

---

60. *Mixwix* 254.
61. Ibid. 251.
62. *Wohin* 82.

something similar."[63] Born in 1938, Achternbusch could claim what Chancellor Helmut Kohl called "die Gnade der späten Geburt"—the grace of being born late enough not be held responsible for the crimes of the Third Reich—but, instead, he feels, "I was not given the grace of an innocent death" (Mir ist die Gnade des einfachen Sterbens nicht gegeben).[64]

Death may not come easy for Achternbusch, but his Indian fantasies—as well as those of most of his films—are nevertheless almost always death fantasies. Unlike John Wayne in *The Searchers,* who claims that "livin' with Comanches aint bein' alive," Achternbusch insists that "you have to die first if you want to become a Comanche"[65]—death as the *entré billet* to savage nobility, the condition to reclaim innocence or victim status. As Nil writes in his farewell letter to Susn at the end of *The Last Hole:* "I commit suicide, for as a suicide I belong to the death mound of the victims. I do not want to belong to the death mound of the self-righteous Germans. Farewell . . . I'll jump into the volcano."[66] This explains Achternbusch's passion for his work, for art allows the one way out that the artist cannot or will not take in real life—death or suicide. Against Adorno, Achternbusch asserts that art offers the only possible mode of talking about the Holocaust: "It must have been then [during the early 1960s] that a German filosofer [*Filosof*] claimed that one could not write poetry after Auschwitz—which I thought was outrageous, and I replied that after Auschwitz one could only write poetry."[67] Achternbusch's compulsion to speak, write, paint, film, and act is a direct response to Adorno's call for artistic silence—and yet Achternbusch's thematic use of speechlessness, which is so prevalent throughout his writings and films, his fierce antirealism, and his notion of an autonomous art that nevertheless bears the scars of society at every turn is very close to Adorno's own aesthetic theory. Achternbusch may have marveled at the films of John Ford, but his artistic radicalism is clearly indebted to that of Adorno.[68]

It is the forte and the weakness of Achternbusch that his work of mourning knows only one strategy—identification and enactment. This primitivism makes his work more direct and more radical than that of any of his contem-

---

63. Ibid. 31. Elsewhere he writes: "I visited the concentration camp in Mauthausen and felt incredible back pain like never before . . . Artists should not be allowed to visit concentration camps—soon enough, they'll be sent there anyway!" (309).

64. Ibid. 277f.

65. *Der Komantsche* 41.

66. Herbert Achternbusch, *Das letzte Loch: Filmbuch* (Frankfurt am Main: Suhrkamp, 1982) 118. Achternbusch has repeated his intention not to belong to the death mound of self-righteous Germans on two other occasions (see *Wohin* 337; and *Was ich denke* 12).

67. Herbert Achternbusch, *Was ich denke* 27. In *The Last Hole* Nil describes Susn's hair as "brezenfarben" (having the color of pretzels), an allusion to Paul Celan's "Todesfuge" which is often considered the most famous attempt to poetically contradict Adorno's statement about the impossibility of poetry after Auschwitz (118).

68. As Hans-Horst Henschen has pointed out, Achternbusch's entire work echoes Adorno's statement from *Minima Moralia* that it is the task of art to introduce chaos into the existing order (89).

poraries, but it also makes it more intolerable as it eclipses, yet again, the real other. Casting himself, time and again, in the role of the oppressed does displace the victims of real genocides. But Achternbusch's most recent works contain indications that this outlook is changing, suggesting that he may have recognized to what extent his identification with the marginalized is based on mere victim envy. In his recent novel, *Hundstage,* he writes: "My sympathy for Jews is only sentimentality, only compassion. I don't want to be a Jew, and I have rid myself of their belief in one God without, however, being able to cope with the consequences."[69] And elsewhere he states: "Now that the era Kohl is coming to an end, my privileged status as a victim [*Opferbonus*], which I used, and for which I was glad, is about to expire."[70] German unification seems to have had a paradoxical effect on Achternbusch. The rise of neo-Nazism in the new Federal Republic has not been a confirmation of his view that the old one was a mere extension of the Third Reich but has led him to believe that it was indeed further away from Nazism than he previously believed, thus also forcing him to realize the naïveté of his own antifascism (which is, in fact, that of his entire generation). Now that there are again real victims of xenophobia and racism in Germany, Achternbusch can no longer claim to be one of them. And there are now reports that for his twenty-sixth feature, *Picasso in München* (*Picasso in Munich*), for the first time he will receive official financial support from the state of Bavaria; it looks indeed like the days of primitivism may be over.

---

69. *Hundstage* 171.
70. Ibid. 185.

Subjectivities in Motion

CHAPTER 6

The Specular America of
Peter Handke

Who's laughing now at the movies—the actors or the audience?
—Peter Handke

The works by Rolf Dieter Brinkmann, Elfriede Jelinek, Rainer Werner Fassbinder, and Herbert Achternbusch revolve around exploring the tension
between European avant-garde and contemporary American popular culture. The traditional disdain of European high art for mass culture and its
implicit elitism is challenged by the unorthodox leftist or anarchic cultural
politics of these artists in complex and contradictory terms. The writings and
films by Peter Handke, Wim Wenders, and Monika Treut can be seen as a
continuation but also an important variation of these concerns. Although
Handke and Wenders began their respective careers in the mid- and late
1960s with works often classified as avant-garde, their interest in popular culture is more developed in their works of the 1970s in which they employ popular culture to redefine traditional notions of subjectivity, authenticity, and
authority of the written word. (Like Rolf Dieter Brinkmann, Handke and
Wenders are fascinated with the surface art of contemporary America.) With
Monika Treut they also share a focus on the instability of traditional notions
of gender that are brought about through redefinitions of inwardness. While
Handke and Wenders depict the crisis of male subjectivity, Treut explores
how American popular culture can serve to erase a seemingly fixed binarism
of gender; in her work the United States emerges as the site for sexual liberation. Since Treut is about a decade younger than most artists discussed in this
study, her work also serves as a generational critique for the children of John
Ford and Theodor W. Adorno, pointing toward future developments of the
discourse of Americanization, which will be analyzed in the epilogue.

In Peter Handke's novel *Der kurze Brief zum langen Abschied* (*Short Letter, Long Farewell*) [1972]) the narrator relates to us an apparently everyday
scene of promenading people in New York City:

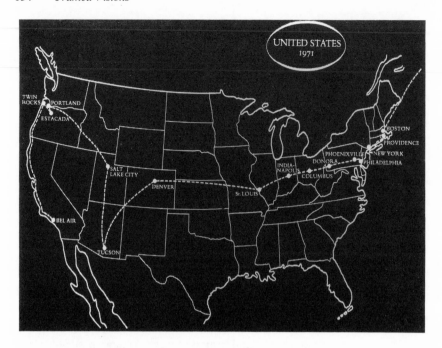

"A map for me is always also a film script."—Wim Wenders

Dustjacket for *Short Letter, Long Farewell* (Suhrkamp, 1972).

I got myself a bottle of beer and sat down again. Through the narrow curtained door I looked out at the street. The visible area was so small that the movements I saw in it took on a particular clarity; the people who traversed it seemed to move very slowly, as though displaying themselves; it was as if they were not passing the doorway but strolling back and forth in front of it. Women's breasts had never seemed so beautiful and so provocative. The sight of these women was almost painful and yet I was glad that I wanted only to watch them strolling back and forth, so pleased with themselves in the light of the big electric signs.[1]

Framed by the door and a curtain, the reality outside the bar becomes a pro-filmic event in relation to which the narrator assumes the role and experiences the pleasures of a voyeur who observes from his safe vantage point. Time and again the novel provides examples of how the I-narrator captures the world in a fashion similar to the lens of a camera, asserting himself as a veritable eye-narrator whose primary occupations consist in watching, watching him-

---

1. Peter Handke, *Short Letter, Long Farewell* in: *3 x Handke*, trans. Ralph Mannheim (New York: Macmillan, 1988) 103.

self, and watching himself watching—thus establishing a link between the inner world of the protagonist and the world viewed outside, between his subjectivity and the continuous flow of moving images.

The choice of New York by Handke's narrator as specular medium is neither random nor accidental. This city, and America in general, function in this novel as catalysts that set in motion not the exploration of a foreign country but of the person who enters it, "a playground for the imagination [and] a site where the subject comes to understand itself through a constant play and identifications with reflections of itself as an other."[2] These reflections are provided by an outside world that functions as a specular medium for a narrator who is primarily concerned with his self-image and a desire to change: "This is my second day in America . . . I wonder if I've already changed?"[3] While America's landscapes serve as the imagistic exteriority onto which he can project his imported preoccupations, its popular culture, especially film, provide him with an instance of the imaginary decisive in shaping human subjectivity.

Offending the Critics

When the novel was first published in 1972, it met with harsh criticism especially from the German Left. Next to the accusations of formalism and narcissism that had accompanied Handke's work from the beginning, one now reproached him for a political naïveté that falls for the glamour of America's second nature[4] and for his general refusal to acknowledge the country's troubled political situation. "Handke's United States do not want to conform to the country we read about in the newspaper. Hardly a trace of Vietnam, and the ghetto of Harlem flies by in eight lines . . . Handke's book reads as if [Herbert] Marcuse and not Richard Nixon had been elected president."[5] A novel that bypasses the question of ideology critique at the height of the Vietnam War had to be considered an affront to West German intellectuals. For Handke, however, the intense anti-Americanism of those days posed a personal attack on a country whose mass culture had had a significant impact on childhood experiences and on shaping his artistic imagination. His defense of America in *Short Letter, Long Farewell* thus constitutes a provocative reply to the fierce criticism of America by writers such as Hans Magnus Enzensberger, Reinhard Lettau, and Erich Fried.

In 1968 Hans Magnus Enzensberger wrote an open letter to the president of Wesleyan University, "On leaving America," in which he explained

---

2. Eric Rentschler, "How American Is It? The U.S. as Image and Imaginary in German Film," *Persistence of Vision* 2 (1985): 7.

3. *Short Letter, Long Farewell* 90.

4. Michael Schneider, "Das Innenleben des 'Grünen Handke,'" in *Über Peter Handke*, ed. Michael Scharang (Frankfurt am Main: Suhrkamp, 1972) 99.

5. Reinhard Baumgart, "Vorwärts, zurück in die Zukunft," in *Über Peter Handke* 91f.

his reasons for resigning from a fellowship. In an abrasive tone he stated, "I believe the class which rules the United States of America, and the government which implements its policies, to be the most dangerous body of men on earth."[6] In this harsh public statement Enzensberger compares the American situation of the late 1960s to that in Germany two generations earlier.[7] Reinhard Lettau followed up on this critique of an imperialist and fascist America in *Täglicher Faschismus: Amerikanische Evidenz aus 6 Monaten* (*Everyday Fascism: American Evidence of 6 Months* [1973]), a collection of newspaper articles from the *Los Angeles Times* and other national newspapers with pointed comments by Lettau, intended to document what he perceived as the country's rapid development toward fascism. Returning to the United States in 1967 after a three year absence and accepting a position at the University of California at San Diego (where Herbert Marcuse was teaching), Lettau encountered a changed and disturbing America: "Idle old men and women, dressed in tight clothes and bored stiff, who call themselves *senior citizens;* surfing, tanned hunks, gigantic blondes; stupefying, aggressive music—these are the hallmarks of California."[8] The political climate of police repression, racial violence, hatred of blacks and Mexicans, and poverty, which is largely ignored or distorted by the American press, create for Lettau the sensation of an everyday fascism uncannily similar—as for Enzensberger—to the Germany of the 1930s: "A policeman in a brown uniform and a black-and-brown steel helmet, which he doesn't take off even in his car, remind me of my childhood in Germany."[9] Being the reactions of two prominent literary figures, Enzensberger's letter and Lettau's "Evidence" are symptomatic of the way in which the German Left reacted to the America of the Vietnam War.[10] Their harsh indictments abandon literary genres in favor of more persuasive jour-

---

6. *New York Review of Books,* 29 February 1968, 31. The letter was published in Germany in *Die Zeit,* March 1, 1968, 16.

7. Of the German writers of this period Enzensberger's position is among the most critical and the most complex. Cf. Charlotte Melin, "A Look at Enzensberger's America before and after "On Leaving America," in *Amerika! New Images in German Literature,* ed. Heinz Osterle (New York: Peter Lang, 1989) 293–311. Cf. also Karla Lydia Schultz's analysis of pro- and anti-American sentiments in Enzensberger, Martin Walser, and Günter Kunert, " 'Think: You Could Become an American . . .' Three Contemporary German Poets Respond to America," *Yearbook of German-American Studies* 23 (1988): 153–63. See also her 1983 interview with Enzensberger, in which he explained "that he [Enzensberger] should have simply left [the United States] quietly, or better: thought twice about accepting the invitation and grant in the first place. He regrets having made a gesture—as gestures, Enzensberger says, don't make for good politics" (Schultz, "A Conversation with Hans Magnus Enzensberger," *Northwest Review* 21.1 [1983]: 145f.).

8. Reinhard Lettau, *Täglicher Faschismus: Amerikanische Evidenz aus 6 Monaten,* trans. Hanns Zischler and Reinhard Lettau (Reinbek: Rowohlt, 1973) 8.

9. Lettau 10f.

10. Cf. also Enzensberger's interview with Herbert Marcuse, "USA: Organisationsfrage und revolutionäres Subjekt - Fragen an Herbert Marcuse," special issue "Nordamerikanische Zustände," *Kursbuch* 22 (1970): 45–60.

nalistic or "objective" forms of communication, yet often their accusation of fascism through comparison with Germany's Nazi past unwittingly takes on the rhetoric that they set out to criticize.

In view of these indictments of America the polemical stance behind Handke's purely descriptive and apparently apolitical style becomes evident. When asked about Lettau's method Handke commented by saying that it yields a rather unproductive exactitude that obstructs, rather than serves, the perception of reality.[11] The following passage from the novel is clearly conceived to preempt the kind of criticism that informs Lettau's montage:

> Outside, a chubby-cheeked crew-cut student wearing sneakers and Bermuda shorts that revealed his fat thighs came toward me; I looked at him in horror, aghast at the thought that someone might still dare to make a general statement about this individual figure, that someone might classify him and set him down as a representative of something else. Involuntary I said hello and looked at him without embarrassment. He too said hello.[12]

As Handke went on to explain in the same interview, his narrator experiences incredible relief for not falling into the trap of generalizing about this individual student, thus securing himself a curiosity vital for the discovery of America and, by extension, of himself.

It should be stressed that Handke is not defending the politics of the United States but is reluctant to participate in a supposedly critical discourse that is equally coercive as the one being criticized. As he commented in a short essay, "Was soll ich dazu sagen?" (What Am I Supposed to Say to This?): "I wanted to say something about Vietnam that came from me, and I couldn't."[13] His critique is therefore primarily a critique of language. Since the intersubjective character of language fails to capture the individuality of the speaker, and since political opinions are largely based on and limited to the representation of political events in the media, every "personal" statement only reproduces its anonymous source and therefore precisely fails to express the personal. As a consequence, Handke first feels helpless and then angry about this apparent lack of power—an anger, however, that he cherishes as an authentic reaction and a moment of true feeling. In the second

---

11. Hellmuth Karasek, "Ohne zu verallgemeinern: Ein Gespräch mit Peter Handke," *Über Peter Handke* 89. Lettau later responded with a poem entitled "Interessante Begegnung": "Der Dramatiker Peter Handke / unterwegs nach einem Interesse / begegnet / der Sprache, / dann dem Senator Franz Burda aus / Offenburg, endlich / sich selbst. // 'Nach innen', seufzt er, 'geht/ der geheimnisvolle Weg'" (Interesting Encounter: The Playwright Peter Handke / on his way towards an interest / runs into / language / and then Senator Franz Burda from / Offenburg; finally / himself. // "Inwards," he sighs, "goes / the mysterious path").

12. *Short Letter, Long Farewell* 92.

13. "Was soll ich dazu sagen?" *Als das Wünschen noch geholfen hat* (Frankfurt am Main: Suhrkamp, 1975) 25

part of the essay Handke goes on to make an observation about the disappearing distinction between the reality of the war and its portrayal on TV. Here he argues that the media's coverage of the Paris peace talks is perceived by the spectators as following the suspense mechanisms of sports events or Hollywood films—as in these events, a solution will be reached and peace will eventually prevail because the viewing public has to be relieved from their feelings of suspense: "The armistice in Vietnam is not the result of the much talked-about human love of peace, nor of the exhaustion of materials; it is the result of the exhaustion of the minds of the Americans in combat and of their television audience. This exhaustion of the mind appears to be a longing for peace but should not be confused with love of peace. 'Thanks for joining us! Thanks for watching!'"[14]

Innerlichkeit and Popular Culture

Handke's refusal of leftist politics and his insistence on seeing the relationship to the United States as primarily an imaginary one can only be understood appropriately if situated in two important contexts of the early 1970s: the critical reception of the German literary tradition by young writers, a dialogue in which popular culture played an instrumental role in their approach to the canon of high art; and, second, the turn to the cinema as the art form most suited for experiencing a much-longed-for sensuality (*Sinnlichkeit*) and immediacy.

Many authors of the so-called New Subjectivity turned to the literature of the late eighteenth and early nineteenth centuries because they saw an affinity between the works of Goethe, Kleist, Karoline von Günderrode, and Büchner and their own times. Particularly Handke was often scolded as having retreated into a realm of the private in order to take refuge from a harsh and oppressive world. He wanted to rediscover a world of immediacy, experience, spontaneity, to revel in things and to explore that which was otherwise taken for granted. Central to the work of Handke, but also to his friend and collaborator Wim Wenders, is the project of redefining for themselves the concept of *Innerlichkeit* (inwardness), so important in the classic and Romantic authors they had turned to. For Handke and Wenders this redefinition of inwardness and the concomitant valorization of the private over the public sphere as the only space for the experience of one's individuality was decisively shaped by an appreciation of popular culture, in particular rock music, film, and "low" literature.

The importance for Handke of, for example, Raymond Chandler and Dashiell Hammett, the Beatles and the Rolling Stones, the Hollywood cinema of the 1950s and genre films like *Heimatfilme* (a German film genre that emphasizes love of the homeland and the value of country life and that flour-

---

14. Ibid. 27.

ished during the 1950s), "Fuzzyfilme," "Jerry-Cotton-Filme," etc.,[15] but also his interest in popular sports such as soccer cannot be overestimated.[16] From the beginning of his career Handke's works have displayed a profound knowledge and imaginative reception of detective fiction and cinema as well as Handke's own involvement in filmmaking. In 1969 Handke collaborated with Wim Wenders on a short, *Three American LPs,* which combines images of German urban life reminiscent of American films with rock music by Van Morrison, Creedence Clearwater Revival, and Harvey Mandel. Wenders went on to film Handke's novel *Die Angst des Tormanns beim Elfmeter (The Goalie's Anxiety at the Penalty Kick* [1971]), and Handke wrote the script for Wenders's *Falsche Bewegung (Wrong Move* [1974]). In 1987 Handke provided much of the dialogue for Wenders's *Der Himmel über Berlin (Wings of Desire).* Furthermore, Handke directed *Die Chronik der laufenden Ereignisse (The Chronic of Current Events* [(1970]) for television and made feature films of his novels *Die Linkshändige Frau (The Left-Handed Woman* [1977]) and *Die Abwesenheit (The Absence* [novel 1987; film 1994]), both produced by Wim Wenders. In 1980 Handke translated Walker Percy's novel *The Moviegoer,* whose cinephile protagonist Handke considered an elective affinity.[17] Handke's second novel, *Der Hausierer (The Peddler* [1966]), is exemplary for his interest in popular genres. Here he uses narrative patterns of the detective novel in order to dissect and reassemble genre conventions; while placing the reader in the detective's position of following traces and securing evidence, the novel repeatedly frustrates any attempt to get an overall picture. It is a suspense story with neither story nor suspense. In a deconstructive move typical for Handke's early work, well-known clichés are invoked in unfamiliar ways, stripping them of their worn-out and nonsignifying content and infusing them with new meaning. "What I wanted to do . . . was not to make obvious the clichés or the patterns but instead I wanted to use the patterns in such a way that they could describe real experiences."[18]

In contrast to Elfriede Jelinek, whose intention it is to unmask the mythmaking and therefore ideologically suspect products of popular culture,

---

15. Cf. Peter Handke, "Vorläufige Bemerkungen zu Landkinos und Heimatfilmen," *Ich bin ein Bewohner des Elfenbeinturms* (Frankfurt am Main: Suhrkamp, 1972) 147.

16. Despite the obvious importance of popular culture for Peter Handke, few critics have given this subject a serious treatment. A thorough analysis is found in Helmut Schmiedt, "Peter Handke, Franz Beckenbauer, John Lennon und andere Künstler: Zum Verhältnis von Popularkultur und Gegenwartsliteratur," *Text + Kritik* 24–24a (1978): 87–114. See also Handke, "Regeln für Schauspieler" ("Rules for Actors") from *Publikumsbeschimpfung (Offending the Audience),* in which he gives the following advice: "Listen to the cheers and boos at a soccer stadium . . . Listen to "Tell Me" by the Rolling Stones . . . Listen to Radio Luxemburg's Hit Parade . . . Watch Gary Cooper's face in *Man of the West*" ([Frankfurt am Main: Suhrkamp, 1966] 9).

17. Walker Percy, *Der Kinogeher,* trans. Peter Handke (Frankfurt am Main: Suhrkamp, 1980) 212.

18. From a conversation between Peter Handke and Manfred Durzak (Durzak, *Peter Handke und die deutsche Gegenwartsliteratur: Narziß auf Abwegen* [Stuttgart: Kohlhammer, 1982] 44).

Handke believes that, when used appropriately, the conventions, formulas, and genre of popular culture *do* give voice to authentic feelings and experiences. While a distinction has to be made between the analytical-critical enterprise of texts like *Der Hausierer* and Handke's open embrace of film in many of his earlier novels and his journals—most notably *Das Gewicht der Welt* (*The Weight of the World* [1979])—one can generally say that his interest in popular culture is neither that of Adorno and Horkheimer's critique of the culture industry nor that of an aesthetic legitimation of mass culture aimed at endowing it with the status of high culture. Handke is not out to close the gap, as were the literary critic Leslie Fiedler and many of the writers alluded to in chapter 2 and 3, whose projects were summed up neatly by Andy Warhol's famous slogan "All is pretty"—Handke, after all, is not designing comic books, directing soap operas, or writing thrillers. I consider it a telling detail that Handke first considered and then dismissed the idea of closing his 1990 *Versuch über die Jukebox* (*Essay on the Jukebox*) with a "Ballad of the Juke Box." Instead, he wrote a straightforward narrative, "completely serious,"[19] as the adequate stance for dealing with this machine and all it stands for. He neither wants to produce nor to parody mass culture but to point to the consequences of its rapid proliferation and growing importance. The inclusion of the lineup of a soccer team and the Japanese hit parade into a book of poetry, besides being a provocative gesture to the literary establishment, is first and foremost an acknowledgment that these "texts" exist and that they enjoy a much larger audience than most products of high culture.

The ways in which spectators actively participate in rock concerts and soccer games are an attractive model for a writer whose plays are searching for new ways of addressing the audience, even if this means offending them. When borrowing narrative patterns from genres such as the detective novel, Handke can count on the fact that most of his contemporary readers are familiar with them. "With the same gesture of self-assuredness with which Goethe's *Faust* or Wieland's novels relied on the fact that their audience were familiar with antiquity and its mythology, contemporary authors now present allusions to mass culture."[20] These allusions are most often used in a play of affirming or frustrating expectations. When Gerhard Roth, for instance, alludes to Raymond Chandler's detective hero Philip Marlowe in his America novel *Der große Horizont* (*The Great Horizon* [1974]) he creates for the reader the pleasant sensation of encountering a familiar friend in unexpected circumstances.[21] Handke's *Goalie's Anxiety at the Penalty Kick* is indeed

---

19. Peter Handke, *The Jukebox and Other Essays on Storytelling,* trans. Ralph Mannheim and Krishna Winston (New York: Farrar, 1994) 51.

20. Schmiedt 90.

21. See Gerhard Roth's *Der große Horizont* (Frankfurt am Main: Fischer, 1974), in which the protagonist constantly wonders what Chandler's detective would do in his situation. In many ways Roth's novel can be read as a reply to—and poor imitation of—Handke's *Short Letter, Long Farewell.*

The pop fan as cartoon character: "You poor poet! What did they do to you? You've got such beautiful long hair—why don't you be a little like the Beatles?"(*Märzheft,* 1972.)

about soccer but in a very different way than an unprepared reader would expect. The goalie Bloch inhabits the penalty box much like Handke dwells in the ivory tower. The soccer game takes place in front of him; for the most part he watches rather than participates. His tendency to position himself in the role of the spectator—he is also retired from the sport and a regular moviegoer—turns him into a metaphor for specularity. As Rainer Nägele has observed, the words *goalie* and *angst* of the novel's title map a tension between the realm of the popular and the existential,[22] a tension typical of

22. Rainer Nägele and Renate Voris, *Peter Handke* (Munich: Beck, 1978) 46.

Handke's artistic exploration of popular culture. The title of *Short Letter, Long Farewell* alludes to Chandler's *Long Goodbye,* borrowing less from Chandler's plot than from his creation of fear and paranoia against the backdrop of a bleak and depressing metropolis. In contrast to the great divide that marks modernism's anxiety of influence, Handke's sympathy and curiosity for popular culture points toward a creative though differentiated reception through the search of new ways of artistic expression and of representing the inner world of his protagonists.

A second important constitutive of the historical context of the late 1960s is the rising interest in the American cinema, which can be attributed, roughly, to two opposed sets of interests. By the end of this decade the terms *America* and *American mass culture* had virtually become synonymous for many Germans, particularly on the Left, and deriding its mass culture became the easiest way to get at the country's politics. It became popular to watch John Wayne "in order to shout, whistle and hoot. [Viewers] enjoyed what seemed to be the naivety of the ideology, naïvely displayed, and they enjoyed even more (perhaps without realizing it) the naivety of their own vocal protest."[23] For cinephiles like Handke, in contrast, the extracinematic reality did not interfere with their pleasure. Here is how Handke reacted to leftist moviegoers in a late show:

> Last night I watched [Sam] Peckinpah's *Ride the High Country* at the "Lupe" on Kurfürstendamm. To this immensely beautiful, quiet, and sad film in which you can breath again and watch, the Leftist late show audience, who had stumbled blindly and boisterously into the late show, reacted with intoxicated screaming, hooting, and hollering. They were no longer able to SEE anything; in their stupor, they only reacted to buzzwords. My wish—that they would lump them all together in a pile, the Leftist shit, the Rightist shit, and the Liberal shit and throw a bomb on them.[24]

This defense of cinema by Handke—reiterated by the protagonist of *Short Letter, Long Farewell*—is a symptomatic reaction and can be directly linked to the disenchanting experience of many after 1968. In his long essay *Erfahrungshunger* (Hunger for Experience) Michael Rutschky discusses the meaning of filmgoing as an attraction to direct sensual experience and a refusal of critical analysis and interpretation. After its commercial decline, in the 1960s, mostly due to the development of West German television, the cinema no longer represented a part of the culture industry so heavily criticized by the Frankfurt School. The opening of repertoire cinemas, often connected to a bar, offered a space where one could watch and discuss a daily changing

---

23. Elsaesser, "Germany's Imaginary America" 40.
24. Handke, "Dummheit und Unendlichkeit," *Ich bin ein Bewohner des Elfenbeinturms* 156.

program of films, mostly American classics of the 1940s and 1950s, and European art films.

Many German films of this time, from Werner Herzog's Kaspar Hauser film, *Everyman for Himself and God against All* (1974) to Wenders's *Kings of the Road* (1976), document this retreat from the political as manifestos of revulsion against words, celebrating instead the superiority of the image, often connected, as in these two examples, with an increasing importance of music. The cinema created a space "where one could live beyond general concepts, where one could satisfy the hunger for experience, where a confused searching around could calm down."[25] When Handke's narrator goes to see one of Johnny Weismuller's Tarzan pictures again, he experiences this exact sensation; although bored by the film, he is unable to leave because he enjoys how the rhythm of the film triggers the slow recollection of its previously seen images. The film provides him with a much-longed-for visual immediacy that is hard to come by outside the walls of the cinema; hence, the story becomes secondary to the images through which it is told. As Rutschky commented:

> The more meaning the stories in the cinema were supposed to transport, the less convincing the cinema became. If it convinces despite such stories then only because the images transcended the story—not into a more profound meaning, but into the indifference of the visible which absorbs our gaze. It was the landscape and not the message why we loved to watch the old Westerns; even if John Wayne was a pompous fascist—and we had no illusions about that—his bodily presence was not corrupted by his disgusting political convictions.[26]

Handke's addiction to the cinema shows the attitude of an intellectual anti-intellectualism.[27] Like the moviegoer of the Walker Percy novel that he translated, Handke is fascinated by the "peculiar reality"[28] of the cinema and its stars (be they William Holden or Henry Fonda). And it is only seemingly a contradiction that the same Handke who had said of himself that he could not stand literature with a story[29] indulges most in those Hollywood films with a strong storyline. What he and his narrator-spectator desire and what these films provide are a replacing of sense (*Sinn*) with sensuality (*Sinnlichkeit*) that renders irrelevant critical interpretation. In an odd Brechtian move Handke considers the Tarzan film, the Horror movie, the western,

25. Michael Rutschky, *Erfahrungshunger: Ein Essay über die siebziger Jahre* (Cologne: Kiepenheuer and Witsch, 1982) 197.

26. Rutschky 222f.

27. Peter Handke, *Das Gewicht der Welt: Ein Journal* (Frankfurt am Main: Suhrkamp, 1979) 249.

28. Walker Percy, *The Moviegoer* (New York: Avon, 1961) 21.

29. Handke, "Ich bin ein Bewohner des Elfenbeinturms," *Ich bin ein Bewohner des Elfenbeinturms* 23.

and the *Heimatfilm,* with their rigid genre conventions and their prescribed narrative patterns, the more realistic and therefore more honest works in comparison to what he calls the "problem film," that is, European art films by Bergman, Godard, Fellini, and Antonioni. "It is precisely the problem films which are the most dishonest genre film because in contrast to thrillers etc. they pretend to be real and natural, because they are using rules instead of making them visible."[30] For Handke the problem film is a sorry reincarnation of the aura of the theater, an institution that he had fiercely criticized with his experimental plays. Genre films, on the other hand, are accepted in their total falsity as the only adequate representation of a reality that is fabricated through and through (a strategy, as we saw, that also underlies Fassbinder's interest in gangster films). Consequently, the adequate reception of a film is not to search for the hidden meaning or to decipher its symbolism, as would be the challenge of serious film or literature. In its place steps pure specularity: "It is beautiful when I merely perceive [*wahrnehme*], when I only watch and look—that's when I feel the best."[31]

America as Image and Imaginary

As *Short Letter, Long Farewell* insists, America is first and foremost an imaginary America, prefabricated out of images, characters from novels and films, landscapes and buildings familiar from advertisements and billboards—a hyperreal America in which the narrator's stifled imagination struggles to distinguish reality from representation. Arriving in Tucson, he remarks: "It had already been inconceivable for me on the plane that I could be curious about anything in Tucson. I'd seen pictures of everything the place could possibly offer. And now, at the edge of the airfield, the first thing I saw was the agaves from the label of the tequila bottle in Providence!"[32] Like no other country, America has invented, processed, and disseminated images about itself; no country has been so successful in doing away with the distinction between reality and representation and in obliterating history. Movie stars such as Marilyn Monroe, Henry Fonda, and Buster Keaton have become exemplars of life, while the Pilgrims Fathers's landing with the *Mayflower* is but an imprint on a curtain in the narrator's hotel room. The very concept of nature has been displaced by a ubiquitous second nature; to the narrator unpeopled

---

30. Handke, "Theater und Film: Das Elend des Vergleichens," *Ich bin ein Bewohner des Elfenbeinturms* 74. This statement represents a further polemic against Brecht, since Godard, one of the most Brechtian of contemporary filmmakers, employs numerous techniques to distance the audience from his films.

31. Handke in an interview with Christian Linder (Linder, "Gespräch mit Peter Handke: Die Ausbeutung des Bewußtseins," *Schreiben und Leben* [Cologne: Kiepenheuer and Witsch, 1974] 36).

32. *Short Letter, Long Farewell* 170.

areas appear as *"imitations* of unspoiled nature,"[33] and the metropolis of
New York City is experienced as "a gentle panorama of nature"[34]—not a
naive confusion of first and second nature, as one German critic would have
it, but a deliberate deflation of Marx. As if to merge into this world of hyperreality, he says of himself: "I had no desire to be an original [*ein Original*]."[35]

Clearly, then, Handke's novel is not about the "real" America but about
the discourses and images that have constructed it and that it constructs of
itself. As he explained in an interview: "It's just very difficult to relate the
story to the real America . . . For me, America is a place which is a given
because of my knowledge of its signals—in fact, I only know the signals. So I
have an image, a dream world in which I must discover myself anew. Under
these circumstances one gains a certain distance to oneself."[36] While the novel
is not *about* America, its story can only take place *in* America, because, like
no other country, it provides the feature of complete exteriority that the narrator desires for projecting his interiority.

The phenomenon of specularity so important in Handke (and Wenders,
for that matter) is at the center of much contemporary film theory. Following
Saussure's linguistics and their revisions by contemporary French philoso-
phers, these theories are based on the assumption that signs (and therefore
films) create meaning without direct reference to the world. As instance of a
Lacanian imaginary film can be seen to produce the spectator as subject.
According to Lacan, the order of the imaginary is that part of the subject's
experience that precedes entry into the symbolic order and that is exemplified
by the mirror stage. During this phase the subject reaches a first understanding of him- or herself through its reflection in the mirror. As Lacan stresses,
this apprehension of the self is ambivalent; while the infant loves the coherent
identity of the mirror image, she or he also hates the image because it remains
external. Furthermore, since the subject is able to know itself only through this
external image, it is marked by a sense of self-alienation. Several critics have
argued that the same processes of identification and alienation experienced by
the infant during the mirror stage are induced through the perception of visual
images in the cinema. As Elsaesser writes: "The gaze is enough: The ability to
look turns the spectator into author and protagonist. Through the double, the
spectator experiences himself or herself as self-identical, as 'real' . . . The narrative feature film more and more becomes the paradigm of a society which
represents and defines itself through images. Seeing is knowing."[37]

33. Ibid. 120; emphasis mine.
34. Ibid. 107.
35. Ibid. 123.
36. Helmut Karasek 86f.
37. Thomas Elsaesser, "American Graffiti und Neuer Deutscher Film: Filmemacher zwischen Avantgarde und Postmoderne," in *Postmoderne: Zeichen eines kulturellen Wandels,* ed.
Andreas Huyssen and Klaus R. Scherpe (Reinbek: Rowohlt, 1986) 307f.

This notion of the imaginary renders problematic the project of ideology critique as put forth by Adorno and Horkheimer. As Jean Baudrillard writes: "It is no longer a question of a false representation of reality (ideology), but of concealing the fact that the real is no longer real."[38] Since no position outside of the imaginary is available, the imaginary itself is turned into a political category. The concern with politics is not absent from Handke's novel and, for that matter, from his prose in general—a common accusation—but it is formulated in ways that differ significantly from the sociological analyses indebted to the Frankfurt School, which dominated the discourse of literary criticism of the 1960s in West Germany and Austria. Thus, to read Handke's novel exclusively in terms of praising or indicting the United States would mean to miss the point. Rather, *Short Letter, Long Farewell* shifts the debate from a critique of ideology and false representation (the intention of Brechtian *Verfremdung*) to the analysis of specularity by foregrounding the ways in which the narrator experiences and appropriates America as a site for stabilizing and fashioning his identity.

At the center of Handke's work (be it prose or film) stands a specular subject: "Seeing is being for Handke's protagonists."[39] Looking, watching, observing, are their primary occupations; hence, they position themselves almost always in such a way that they can look on as spectators or pure outsiders. The peddler unmovingly witnesses how someone commits a murder. The goalie Bloch watches the game in front of him but for the most part remains unnoticed by the spectators. He explains: "It's very difficult to take your eyes off the forwards and the ball and watch the goalie . . . You have to tear yourself away from the ball; it's a completely unnatural thing to do."[40] In the novel *Der Chinese des Schmerzes* (*The Chinese of Pain* [1983]) the protagonist, Loser, explains his name to be a derivation of the dialect word *losen,* which in turn is derived from *lauschen,* that is, "to listen," and the novel is programmatically divided into three different stages of observation.[41] It would be easy to continue this list of examples up to Handke's most recent works. In *Short Letter, Long Farewell* the narrator employs a similar strategy; upon his arrival in Providence he programmatically explains America to be a place "where I had decided for once to observe rather than participate."[42] In New York City he witnesses the following scene:

It was a bright day and the wind made it seem even brighter; the clouds were racing across the sky. Out on the street I stopped and looked

---

38. Jean Baudrillard, "Simulacra and Simulations," in *Selected Writings,* ed. Mark Poster (Stanford: Stanford UP, 1988) 172.

39. Eric Rentschler, *West German Film in the Course of Time: Reflections on the Twenty Years since Oberhausen* (Bedford Hills: Redgrave, 1984) 167.

40. *Die Angst des Tormanns beim Elfmeter* (Frankfurt am Main: Suhrkamp, 1970) 123.

41. *Der Chinese des Schmerzes* (Frankfurt am Main: Suhrkamp, 1983) 32. The three stages are: "1. The observer is being distracted. 2. The observer acts. 3. The observer searches a witness."

42. *Short Letter, Long Farewell* 87.

around. Two girls were standing in a phone booth outside the hotel. One was talking into the phone; from time to time the other leaned over and took up the conversation, meanwhile pushing her hair back behind one ear. At first the sight of them merely arrested my attention, then it cheered me, and I took genuine pleasure in watching the two of them in the tiny booth, as one or the other kept pushing the door open with her foot, as they laughed, passed the receiver back and forth, exchanged whispers, inserted another coin, and continued to take turns in bending over the phone, while outside the steam from the sewer poured out of the street gratings and drifted across the asphalt. The sight relieved me of all burdens. I watched them in a paradisiacal state of lightness, a state in which one has no desire but to see, and in which to see is to know.[43]

I have quoted this passage at length because it demonstrates the core of the narrator's aesthetic experience abroad: an emphasis on randomness, a world waiting to be discovered where everything and everyone warrants equal and sustained attention, and a refusal to impose a narrative or psychological order that would "explain" or contextualize the events unfolding in front of the perceiving eye. The chance encounter with the girls in the phone booth and the ecstatic state of the voyeurlike holder of the gaze intersect at random, a randomness without which his "paradisiacal state of lightness" would not occur.

To be sure, there is a lot to be seen in America as the country presents itself to the narrator as total surface, where everything is visible. Here people are not immersed in things,[44] not because of their superficiality as the well-known stereotype would have it but because everything is immediately intelligible. This self-evidence stems from viewing the country as a set of meaningful signs that can be understood; through its repeated cinematic representation it has become a text that the narrator recognizes and where real nature, by definition, does not occur—in America there is no outside of signification. Hence, his attitude to consider everything as subject to reading: not only the books he carries along but also the landscape through which he travels and which alternately produces either a desire "to lie down in it and read a book"[45] or boredom, "when there was nothing but nature around me and I couldn't discover anything to read in it."[46] Even the acting of Henry Fonda, featured in many John Ford movies, assumes the quality of letters.[47] The autonomy of this surface is further underscored by the narrator's refusal "to interpret that which is enigmatic"—following the model of Heinrich Lee in Keller's novel *Grüner Heinrich*—an attitude that reiterates the refusal of a hermeneutics of suspicion that would necessitate some explanatory theory.

---

43. Ibid. 100f.
44. Ibid. 179.
45. Ibid. 107.
46. Ibid. 149.
47. *Das Gewicht der Welt* (Frankfurt am Main: Suhrkamp, 1979) 283.

Instead, the narrator puts complete trust in the surface of America, its land-scapes and its cinema. The paradox of Handke's America is that, in spite of its mediated and media-constituted reality, it becomes the site for an immediacy so desired by his narrator. As a foreign place and yet totally familiar, it provides the two poles between which his alienation and self-recognition can vacillate—a place of true feeling where he can watch himself become more alien to himself and at the same time feel more assured because he now knows better who he really is.

The Aura of the Jukebox

The instrumental role of American cinema in redefining traditional German inwardness is equally important for the narrator's reception of rock music—music, of course, being the cliché for how Germans ever since the late eighteenth century have fled from a world of hostility and political oppression. Although, strictly speaking, not a specular medium like film, music, too is inextricably bound up with the processes of fashioning the narrator's identity. Furthermore, like the genre film, the rock music of the 1960s is enjoyed by Handke because it opens up a space beyond interpretation and meaning (for the most part, the lyrics of these songs were secondary to their melodies) and beyond the detested "theory rituals of cultural critique."[48]

Like the heroes of the films of Wim Wenders, Handke's longtime friend and collaborator, Handke's narrator is infatuated with American rock music. He regularly frequents rhythm-and-blues bars and plays the jukebox, in one instance selecting the Otis Redding classic "Sitting on the Dock of the Bay." The song is about waiting and watching and in that respect similar to the filmgoing experience described earlier. A picture of Al Wilson on someone's T-shirt makes the narrator reminisce:

> Wilson was short and stocky. He had pimples that you could see clearly on TV, and wore glasses. A few months before, he had been found dead in his sleeping bag outside his house in Laurel Canyon near Los Angeles. In a delicate high voice he had sung "On the Road Again" and "Going up the Country." I felt differently about him than about Jimi Hendrix or Janis Joplin, who, like rock music in general, were beginning to leave me cold; I still ached with his death, and his short life, which I then thought I understood, often came back to me in painful half-waking thoughts.[49]

The sincere tone of these lines and their differentiated assessment of things past demonstrate a reluctance for the kind of nostalgia one commonly finds among many who were young in the 1960s and have since come of age. These

---

48. Handke, "Vorbemerkung," *Ich bin ein Bewohner des Elfenbeinturms* 7.
49. *Short Letter, Long Farewell* 93.

people are like the lovers in the novel that the narrator and Claire visit and who play old records only to evoke the memories of what they experienced when the records first came out: *I Want to Hold Your Hand:* "We were in that Mexican restaurant outside Los Angeles, drinking out of iced beer mugs." *Satisfaction:* "Remember the way the air mattresses skittered across the sand in the storm?" *Summer in the City:* "That was when we got our last money from home." *Wild Thing:* "We lived like Gypsies in those days."[50] This nostalgia is driven by the desire to relive their youth, now romanticized into a time of little money and lots of fun. It is also an attempt to perpetuate the lost reality of the late 1960s, which continues to have an effect only through its absence. Within the discussion of nostalgia film Jameson has identified a postmodernist "nostalgia" art language that is incompatible with genuine historicity, a distinction that can also be applied to the different stance taken toward rock music by the lovers and the narrator. According to Jameson, the nostalgia film is not interested in seriously engaging with issues of the past but contends itself with "approach[ing] the 'past' through stylistic connotation, conveying 'pastness' by the glossy qualities of the image."[51] The narrator's approach to (his own) history is closer to a Benjaminian concept in which the past flashes up and becomes intelligible at a moment of danger, thus asserting its relevance for the presence: "I said that memory hadn't transfigured [*verklärt*] the events of my own life, but that only by remembering them did they really happen to me."[52]

In August 1990, eighteen years after *Short Letter, Long Farewell,* Handke published a slim volume entitled *Versuch über die Jukebox* (*Essay on the Jukebox*), the second of (so far) three loosely connected essays that investigate concepts and aspects of the author's everyday.[53] I want to consider Handke's *Essay on the Jukebox* here as a kind of retrospective engagement with the issues of popular culture, especially rock music, which were articu-

---

50. Ibid. 162.

51. Fredric Jameson, *Postmodernism, or, The Cultural Logic of Late Capitalism* (Durham: Duke UP, 1991) 19.

52. *Short Letter, Long Farewell* 162.

53. Like the novel, the essay appeared during a time of intense political upheaval and debate: in November 1989 the Berlin Wall had come tumbling down. The ensuing period of national euphoria was soon to be followed by a sobriety about the implications and logistics of German unification, which took place later in October 1990. West German writers and intellectuals like Günter Grass and Jürgen Habermas were engaged in a heated and emotionally charged debate about the unification, and Christa Wolf came under attack for her publication of *Was bleibt,* which was read by West German critics as an attempt to dissociate herself form the GDR government by casting herself in the role of the victim. Although, as an Austrian, Handke was not directly involved with problems of German identity and nationality, the publication of a book on something as apolitical and seemingly irrelevant to the present situation as a jukebox confirmed for many writers the negative image they had already had of him. Like *Short Letter, Long Farewell,* then, *The Essay on the Jukebox* presents a certain polemic, even if not as calculated as in the case of the novel, and even if the subject matter of the jukebox is too unimportant to provoke any serious attacks.

lated in *Short Letter, Long Farewell.* Handke's narrative essay combines analysis and recollection (or what Handke elsewhere has called the gesture of *wieder-holen*), intending to reflect and grasp what the jukebox was to him and his generation—an archaeology of the imaginary. Told from the perspective of a "he," a thinly disguised stand-in for the author, *Essay on the Jukebox* is largely Handke's autobiographical attempt "to articulate the significance this object has had in the different phases of his life, now that he was no longer young."[54] As if to add to the temporal dimension a spatial distance, Handke chooses to write while traveling through northern Spain, carefully planning to embark on the project upon arrival in Soria, a remote and cold province town "almost bypassed by history."[55]

Just as in *Short Letter, Long Farewell,* the treatment of the subject matter in *Essay on the Jukebox* is organized according to the aesthetics of traveling, combining lengthy reflections about the appropriate genre and the seriousness of the topic ("Wasn't a small piece of writing like this more suitable for a newspaper, preferably for the weekend magazine, on the nostalgia pages, with color photographs of jukebox models from the earliest times to the present?")[56] intermixed with recurring descriptions of spaces traversed: Spanish cities, places, and streets. He thus establishes a poetic link between the travel back in time and forward in space. The questions of where to write, how to write, and if to write about the jukebox at all are of great importance and inseparably connected. The jukebox, this topic for "refugees from the world,"[57] requires a flight from familiar surroundings, an exposure to foreign or even strange environments that challenges the author's sensibility by denying the numbing comforts of the everyday. As Handke combs bar after bar in an increasingly futile search for one of the few remaining models of a Wurlitzer, it becomes clear that the impetus for writing is propelled by the feeling that both the jukebox and its historiograph seem to have come of age and that *its* and *his* memory is fading, if not sustained by recollection and writing. As Handke underscores, this recollection is not to be confused with a sentimental yearning or nostalgia: "Was that supposed to mean that he regretted the disappearance of his jukebox, these objects of yesteryear, unlikely to have a second future? No. He merely wanted to capture and acknowledge, before he even lost sight of it, what could emanate from a mere object."[58]

The importance of the jukebox for Handke is perhaps best understood in contrast to its significance for Wenders, whose many road movies display the jukebox as an ubiquitous and complex symbol for the director's ambivalent stance toward America, its music, and its mass culture. Typically, Wenders's protagonist is a taciturn and hypersensitive male whose inability to

---

54. *Jukebox* 49.
55. Ibid. 48.
56. Ibid. 62.
57. Ibid. 58.
58. Ibid. 103.

communicate with others, especially women, is compensated for by music. Often emanating from a jukebox, or, in private places, from a jukebox-like device such as the portable record player that Bruno in *Kings of the Road* carries in his cab of his truck (in back of which he stores a real jukebox), music provides Wenders's males with the means to relate to others. These others, of course, share the same taste, and thus no word needs to be spoken; a silent nod, a telling glance, a passing gesture, or, in a rare mood of exuberance, a singing along to the lyrics acknowledges a discrete understanding that stems from communal childhood memories, adolescent adventures, and mute rebellions. Yet, while American and English rock music has been for Wenders a "life-saver," it has also been part of the very American mass culture that colonized the subconscious of postwar Germans, manifesting itself as an uneasy infatuation that informs practically all of Wenders's work (as I will show in more detail in the next chapter).

For Handke, too, the jukebox and its music connote past experiences and experience of the past—however, not, as with Wenders, in the form of contemplation, compensation, or distraction but, on the contrary, as an experience of concentration and presence, of "presentness" or "enhanced presentness."[59] Instead of escape, Handke's jukebox provides the listener with an intensified perception of the present reality that takes on religious or mystical proportions:

> Suddenly, after the pause between records, which, along with those noises—clicking, a whirring sound of searching back and forth through the belly of the device, snapping, swinging into place, a crackle before the first measure—constituted the essence of the jukebox, as it were, a kind of music came swelling out of the depths that made him experience, for the first time in his life, as later only in moments of love, what is technically referred to a "levitation," and which he himself, more than a quarter of a century later, would call—what? "epiphany"? "ecstasy"? "fusing the world"?[60]

Thomas Elsaesser has argued that in Wenders playing the jukebox is always an attempt to communicate, to reach others, despite its solipsistic appearance. "It is as if the jukebox was the mediator, the zero degree even, of a certain subjectivity, inviting others to recognize themselves in the gesture of selecting this particular number, and thereby recognizing you."[61] In contrast, Handke's mystical overtones of his description of his jukebox experience is not directed at making even the most indirect contact. Rather, it is an experience of being contained and content with oneself. Consider the following passage of a child's experience:

---

59. Ibid. 98, 99.
60. Ibid. 91.
61. Elsaesser, "Germany's Imaginary America" 38.

A child was standing one time by such a jukebox (it was playing Madonna's "Like a Prayer," his own selection), the child still so small that the entire force of the loudspeaker down below was directed at his body. The child was listening, all ears, all solemn, all absorbed, while his parents had already reached the door, were ready to leave, calling to the child again and again, in between smiling at his behavior, as if to apologize for their offspring to the other patrons, until the song had died away and the child, still solemn and reverent, walked past his father and mother onto the street.[62]

Handke even separates the jukebox from the realm of American mass culture; although America remains for him the "home of the jukebox," he has no particular memory of a jukebox there.[63] It is a gesture that obliterates the sociohistorical background of the jukebox and its role in the reception of U.S. culture in West Germany and Austria during the 1950s and 1960s, creating a paradox: on the one hand defiantly naive, this strategy is also boldly radical, ascribing this mass-produced incarnation of mass production a ritualistic and thus auratic quality. In a reversal of Benjamin's belief that reproductions are lacking the aura of the original, Handke's jukebox contains an aura precisely because it is a copy. Furthermore, while there are certain designated jukebox songs ("Satisfaction" by the Rolling Stones being the most famous for Handke), the music itself is not the decisive part of this spectacle[64]—the same song playing at home on the radio would hardly have the same effect. Rather, it is only because of its setting in a public space that the box, in its mass-produced glamour, can become fetishized as the source of authentic experiences.

While Wenders stresses the complexity of American popular culture and links his enthusiastic reception of British and American rock music to an apprehension toward German *Kultur* tainted by a fascist past, Handke's *Essay on the Jukebox* considers the jukebox an autonomous object of art and source of mystical experience. In a strategy reminiscent of modernism's anxiety of influence vis-à-vis popular culture, the jukebox is elevated into the realm of the pure.

From *Bildungsroman* to Road Movie

Both *Essay on the Jukebox* and *Short Letter, Long Farewell* are organized around the extensive travels of their respective narrators. While *Essay on the*

---

62. *Jukebox* 87.
63. Ibid. 93.
64. In *Die Wiederholung* Handke writes: "The original Wurlitzer at the back wall was covered by a glass dome in which, bathed in bright light and held up by an arm, upright like a wheel, a black disk was turning; a sight so determining that the music, whatever it was, was only a backup" ([Frankfurt am Main: Suhrkamp, 1989] 261).

Jukebox parallels travel with recollection, in *Short Letter, Long Farewell* the notion of travel provides the intersection for the narrator's desire to see and his cinephilia. Travel is also the notion that underlies the bildungsroman, the psychological novel, the adventure novel, and the travelogue—genres from which *Short Letter, Long Farewell* freely borrows and which it combines with elements from the detective novel and the western. The rewriting of these diverse genres is intended to approximate the aesthetics of the road movie as the most adequate genre to give expression to Handke's cinematic imagination. Critics have given detailed analyses of Handke's use of these literary genres, pinpointing how elements from Gottfried Keller's *Der grüne Heinrich,* Karl Philip Moritz's *Anton Reiser,* and F. Scott Fitzgerald's *Great Gatsby* resurface in *Short Letter, Long Farewell.*[65] Theo Elm has compared Handke's use of aspects of the bildungsroman such as the experience of nature, the discourse on theater, and the *Bildungsgespräch* (the dialogue between the protagonist to be initiated and a wise and mature mentor, usually situated at the climax of the novel) with its traditional models. While novels such as *Wilhelm Meister, Heinrich von Ofterdingen,* and *Der grüne Heinrich* portray a harmony between protagonist and nature or show nature as a refuge from an oppressive society, Handke's narrator experiences nature as a place not of consolation but of alienation and horror. At one point he is threatened to drown in a swamp, and a short time later he has visions of a gently swaying cypress suddenly piercing his chest. With respect to theater, Elm contrasts Wilhelm Meister's passion for the stage and the significance of *Hamlet* with the passivity and indifference with which Handke's protagonist—a playwright himself, after all—observes the production of *Don Carlos* in St. Louis. Elm misses the point of Handke's polemic, however, when he argues that the narrator's preference for film actors over stage actors is guided by an ignorance about the technical apparatus governing film production. Rather, it is precisely because of film's lack of aura that acting can here assume its exemplary function for the narrator. It should be added that the discourse on theater in *Short Letter, Long Farewell* serves the function of refuting theater as institution because contemporary theater still relies on eighteenth-century ideas of a national theater that had hoped to bridge the gap between political groups and social classes and to serve as a moral institution. This critique, of course, was also the point made by Handke's experimental plays and by his essay "Theater und Film: Das Elend des Vergleichens" ("Theater and Film: The Misery of

---

65. Cf. Theo Elm,, "Die Fiktion eines Entwicklungsromans: Zur Erzählstrategie in Peter Handkes Roman *Der kurze Brief zum langen Abschied,*" *Poetica* 6 (1974): 353–77; Christoph Bartmann, "'Der Zusammenhang ist möglich': *Der kurze Brief zum langen Abschied* im Kontext," in *Peter Handke,* ed. Raimund Fellinger (Frankfurt am Main: Suhrkamp, 1985) 114–39; Sigrid Meyer, "Im 'Western' nichts Neues?: Zu den Modellen in *Der kurze Brief zum langen Abschied,*" in *Handke: Ansätze, Analysen, Anmerkungen,* ed. Manfred Jurgensen (Bern: Francke, 1979) 145–65; Baumgart, "Vorwärts, zurück in die Zukunft," *Über Peter Handke* 90–94.

Comparing"), which revolved around justifying the sentence: "I rather go to the movies than to the theater."[66] The third aspect of Elm's analysis is the *Bildungsgespräch,* a standard feature of the bildungsroman from *Agathon* to *The Magic Mountain.* Usually taking place at an elevated spot that symbolizes the superior values to be transmitted, in Handke's novel it is situated on a hill overlooking an orange grove and the house of John Ford, the wise old man telling stories to his foreign visitors. (I will return to a more detailed discussion of the role of John Ford.)

In a somewhat general fashion it could be said that *Short Letter, Long Farewell* invokes these all too apparent continuities with the bildungsroman and other canonic genres of high literature only in order to dismiss them: individual elements are used like a set piece or props, not really reworked but recycled.[67] Stripped of their aesthetic and historic context, they reappear as wornout elements, no longer able to grasp the imagistic reality experienced by the narrator. Handke's protagonist is not a "green" Heinrich but portrayed as artist-as-not-so-young-man (he celebrates his thirtieth birthday with his friend Claire). During his travels through the United States (which he had visited before) he discovers very little and seems already to know everything; the content of his moral and aesthetic education has been provided in his youth by Hollywood films and rock music and is now merely reiterated and perpetuated. The constant references to bildungsroman such as *Der grüne Heinrich* or *Wilhelm Meister* (the narrator at one points lies that his name is Wilhelm) are gratuitous and function as red herrings (in keeping with Handke's borrowing from the detective novel), which confuse rather than enlighten the reader. The defamiliarizing effect of this technique is to displace the canon of high German literature within the aesthetics of "low" genres, most notably the road movie.

The novel opens with a triple reference to the road. The first description—or, should I say, shot—is of Jefferson Street, a quiet street circling the business district of Providence, Rhode Island. The narrator's report is preceded by a motto from Karl Philip Moritz's *Anton Reiser* describing a setting that invites travel: "The weather seemed made for travel: the sky lay close to the earth and the objects round about were dark, as though to confine the traveler's attention to the road he was going to travel."[68] Finally, the dust jacket of the novel displays a map of the United States with the precise route and stops of the narrator's journey. The novel itself is littered with names of streets, places, and highways and with the paraphernalia of the road: gas stations, motels, restaurants, drive-in theaters, highway billboards, etc.

---

66. "Theater und Film: Das Elend des Vergleichens" 65.

67. Handke's script *Falsche Bewegung* (*Wrong Move*) can more appropriately be called a reworking of Goethe's *Wilhelm Meister* in terms of West-German cultural politics of the mid-1970s. See Richard McCormick, "The Writer in Film," in *The Cinema of Wim Wenders: Image, Narrative, and the Postmodern Condition,* ed. Roger Cook and Gerd Gemünden (Detroit: Wayne State UP, 1997) 89–109.

68. *Short Letter, Long Farewell* 83.

Interstate 76 from Philadelphia to Pittsburgh is known as the Pennsylvania Turnpike and is more than three hundred miles long. We entered it from State Route 100, near Downingtown, after the eighth toll station. On the seat beside her Claire had a box full of coins; at each toll station she would toss a few of them out the window into the hopper without coming to a full stop. From there to Donora we passed another fifteen toll stations.[69]

The actual descriptions of the roads are sparse and not meant to create an impression; they merely allow the reader to follow the protagonist through the big cities of New York, Philadelphia, St. Louis, and across the states of Pennsylvania, Ohio, Indiana, Missouri, Arizona, and Oregon.

The road movie and the bildungsroman share the feature of a traveling and predominantly male hero who is leaving behind the familiar and the family. Enticed by the unknown, the hero of the bildungsroman embarks on a learning experience. In the Goethean tradition the road leads eventually and inevitably to a wiser and more mature individual subject, turning it into a metaphor for progress and growth. In Keller's realist novel, too, Heinrich Lee returns after many years abroad (*in der Fremde*) as a socially responsible and psychologically more stable, but artistically disillusioned, young man. The genre of the road movie criticizes this notion of travel as leading to a more stable spiritual or social state, a critique that continues in cinematic form what twentieth-century novels such as *The Magic Mountain* or *The Tin Drum* had already shown—namely, that *Bildung* is no longer an unquestionable value in itself. Timothy Corrigan has outlined the distinctive characteristics of the road movie that can be readily identified—though with significant twists—in Handke's novel: a quest motif that propels the (usually) male character along the road of discovery; a focus on men and the absence of women that points to a crisis of gender and a threat to the male; a breaking apart of the family unit; a plot determined not by the protagonist but by the road itself, creating events and situations to which he only reacts and responds.[70]

While Handke's protagonist does leave behind his wife, she responds by not staying at home but following him across the North American continent. Having withdrawn the remaining funds from their bank account, she pursues him and stages attempts on his life; carrying a weapon, she is the more powerful and is always informed about his whereabouts, while he can only guess where she is. This reversal of roles points to an instability of the narrator's masculinity, which is most emphasized, within the logic of the road movie, by the fact that he cannot drive. As he tells his friend Claire, he cannot stand the thought of being examined (which makes him an elective affinity to the apron-wearing and unarmed James Stewart in the western *The Man Who*

---

69. Ibid. 121.

70. Timothy Corrigan, *A Cinema without Walls: Movies and Culture after Vietnam* (New Brunswick: Rutgers UP, 1991) 145.

Shot Liberty Valance).[71] Unlike most road heroes, Handke's narrator walks everywhere and thus arouses the suspicion of the Americans: "If you go walking in the country, people look at you" (Wer . . . nichts tut als gehen, den merkt man sich),[72] says Claire. Although he documents minutely every turn he makes, he still gets lost; his infatuation with orientation only points to his essential lack of orientation: not knowing where to go and why, he is a rebel without a clue.

The attraction of the road movie for Handke lies in the fact that this genre, more so than most other genres, caters to the hunger for images of a generation whose knowledge of reality is primarily a knowledge of the image of reality. Furthermore, the road movie is a genre that self-consciously reflects on cinema itself: "If the thriller makes the camera a weapon and the melodrama makes it a family member, in the road movie the camera adopts the framed perspective of the vehicle itself. In this genre, the perspective of the camera comes closest to the mechanical unrolling of images that defines the movie camera."[73] It is no coincidence, then, that the novel became, in Handke's own words, a "cult book"[74] of the 1970s—cult, of course, being an attribute nowadays usually reserved for films. If Handke wanted to *write* a film, then the road movie was the adequate genre because it is itself an allegory of the cinema: driving in a car creates the same sensation as sitting in a movie theater. When Handke's narrator rides across the Midwest, the landscape outside provides the same passing by of framed images as the movies do; this is why the first sensation of a European driving across the United States is often that of being in a film.

The manifest destiny of the travels across the States is John Ford (whose western *The Searchers* is the grandfather of all road movies). The road from Providence to Bel Air is guided, as these telling names indicate, by a quest or promise—namely, the quest for the origin of images. What awaits the narrator in California, however, is just another version of the celluloid reality that has engulfed his entire American experience: John Ford is just as "made" as his films.[75] His appearance in khaki pants and white shoes with thick rubber soles is the one known from publicity shots, and his anecdotes and observations are all familiar to the narrator: "John Ford repeated a good deal of

---

71. See the following entry to *Das Gewicht der Welt:* "It's much easier to wear an apron when you bear in mind that even Cary Grant appeared in the same costume in a movie" (131).

72. *Short Letter, Long Farewell* 132.

73. Corrigan 145f.

74. Peter Handke, *Aber ich lebe nur von den Zwischenräumen: Ein Gespräch, geführt von Herbert Gamper* (Frankfurt am Main: Suhrkamp, 1990) 125.

75. It would be easy, as Rainer Nägele has done, to point to the dicrepancies between the "real" John Ford and his image ("Die vermittelte Welt: Reflexionen zum Verhältnis von Fiktion und Wirklichkeit in Peter Handkes Roman *Der kurze Brief zum langen Abschied,*" *Jahrbuch der deutschen Schillergesellschaft* 19 [1975]: 406). The point bears repetition that this kind of ideology critique underestimates the very power of images that Handke's novel analyzes.

what I had heard about America."[76] Through the narrator's rendition of his visit we see where the role model character of this mythical father figure comes from: Ford's refusal to judge others, his reconciliation of the general and the singular, the peacefulness of his persona, and the encompassing nature of his subjectivity marked by his pronounced use of *we:* "We Americans always say 'we' even when we're talking about our private affairs . . . Maybe it's because we see everything we do as part of a common effort."[77] The topics discussed in this kind of *Bildungsgespräch* are no longer the traditional ones of reconciling art and life and of the place and responsibilities of the aspiring subject within a complex society. For John Ford everything is settled and resolved; there is no discrepancy between his films and real life ("Nothing is made up . . . It all really happened"),[78] between first and second nature ("'But those orange trees were planted,' said Judith. 'they are not nature.' 'When the sun shines through and plays in the leaves, I forget that,' said John Ford"),[79] between eternity and history ("When I see the leaves moving like that . . . I forget that there's such a thing a history").[80] It is as if the narrator and Judith, now reconciled, enter the movies themselves. "Expecting a story, we leaned forward a little; I realized that I was imitating the gesture of a character in one of his pictures who without shifting his positions cranes his long neck over a dying man to see if he's still alive."[81] With the same gesture with which Ford claimed that all his stories are true, Judith now assures him that everything she told him really happened. It seems only logical that in cinematic America—a country that has, in Ford's words, no paths but only roads[82]—all roads lead to John Ford. As Handke once commented: "In the most beautiful films you see a possibility how one could live. In fact, I really only like American films. The more films I see, the more I only want to see films by John Ford. Very attentive, concentrated, pathetic films, like John Ford makes them."[83] Peter Handke's novel *Short Letter, Long Farewell* is such a film.

---

76. *Short Letter, Long Farewell* 188. In her article "Im "Western" nichts Neues? Zu den Modellen in *Der kurze Brief zum langen Abschied"* Sigrid Mayer contrasts Handke's fictional description of the John Ford visit with Hans C. Blumenberg's obituary on Ford based on a real visit. The remarkable similarities between these two accounts show not only, as Mayer says, "that Handke's ficticious account of a visit with John Ford can stand the test of a news report" (157), but they also demonstrate how the image of Ford has overpowered any access to the "real" John Ford. Blumensberg's real encounter with the director is shaped by and caught up in the very logic of images that Handke's novel never tires of foregrounding.

77. *Short Letter, Long Farewell* 189.

78. Ibid. 192.

79. Ibid. 190.

80. Ibid.

81. Ibid. 193.

82. Ibid. 191.

83. Heiko Blum, "Chronik der laufenden Ereignisse: Gespräch mit Peter Handke," *Über Peter Handke* 81.

CHAPTER 7

The Oedi-Pal Cinema of
Wim Wenders

Wenn Männer unterwegs sind, kommt was ins Rollen. [When men get
going, things are bound to happen.]
—*Poster advertising,* Kings of the Road

The transition from Peter Handke to Wim Wenders is certainly the
smoothest among any of the artists discussed in this study. Their collaboration on a number of projects, extending from the late 1960s to the present, is
only possible because both agree in fundamental ways about questions of
aesthetics and the role of the artist in contemporary society and because both
are fascinated by similar topics and stories. Even when they disagree, as they
do perhaps in Wenders's more critical view toward contemporary American
cinema, they seem to argue like close friends do when they are basically in
agreement with each other.

Like much of Handke's prose, the films of Wim Wenders foreground the
pivotal role American mass media and popular culture play in shaping the
political, social, and psychological identity of the generation that grew up
after World War II. His films employ American genres such as the road
movie, the western, the thriller, and film noir, featuring as a constant ingredient the mostly diegetic use of American and British pop music and an abundance of mass media icons such as pinball machines, billboards, coke bottles,
and the ubiquitous jukebox. Typically, Wenders's protagonists are heavily
Americanized young men whose native language is German and whose identities are shaped in decisive yet contradictory terms by the American way of
life. Through these films Wenders's aesthetics emerge under the sign of a
love-hate relationship that vacillates between an admiration for the Hollywood cinema of the 1950s, with its technological proficiency, and a rejection
of its economic and ideological status. Like Handke, Wenders succeeds in
achieving a high level of self-reflexivity and ambiguity that informs all his
work and that serves to undermine any solely celebratory or condemning
stance.

This ambiguity is perhaps presented with the most sophistication in

Wenders's film *The American Friend* (1977), a thriller based on a novel by Patricia Highsmith that revolves around the relationship between the German craftsman Jonathan Zimmermann and the shady American art dealer Tom Ripley. While the film has often been read as an allegory on the German film industry, which is taken over by Mafiosi-like American corporations, on closer view it becomes clear that the film's formal and thematic antagonisms are not resolved but, instead, confront the viewer in all their paradoxical and contradictory force. Wenders himself has underscored that *The American Friend* "is really dialectical in its attitude to the American cinema: it's full of love and full of hatred, but it has not found a way out of this imagination."[1] The central metaphor of the film, the frame, is articulated in much the same way as I have used it in the introduction: while the frame maker Jonathan is framed by the faked blood analysis of Ripley and lured into committing a murder for money, ironically this setup initiates their friendship, in the course of which Ripley has Zimmermann restore and frame one of his paintings. If Ripley corrupts Jonathan, he also offers him freedom from deadening domesticity, and their relation becomes one in which rigid divisions of victim and seducer are dissolved into communal choices and commitments.

Since Wenders's cultural schizophrenia has been well documented,[2] and since it would make little sense to rehearse an argument that has been made in the previous chapter, let me instead focus on an important aspect of Wenders's work to which critics have paid little attention and which also pertains to a certain degree to Handke's *Short Letter, Long Farewell*—that is, the fact that in Wenders's films America and its mass culture appear as gendered constructs. Male protagonists and male stories are at the center of virtually each Wenders feature film (with the exception of *The Scarlet Letter,* a film from which the director now distances himself, and his more recent feature, *Until the End of the World*) and even most of his shorts and documentaries. The conspicuous absence of women may mislead us into believing that gender is not an issue in the cinematic universe of Wenders—it is. In what follows I want to explore how gender structures his approach to American mass cul-

---

1. Jan Dawson, "Wim Wenders: July–August 1977," *Sight and Sound* 47.1 (1977–78): 36.

2. Timothy Corrigan, *New German Film: The Displaced Image,* rev. ed. (Bloomington: Indiana UP, 1994); Dennis Mahoney, "'What's Wrong with a Cowboy in Hamburg?': Narcissism as Cultural Imperialism in Wim Wenders's *The American Friend,*" *Journal of Evolutionary Psychology* 7 (1986): 106–16; Kathe Geist, *The Cinema of Wim Wenders: From Paris, France to "Paris, Texas"* (Ann Arbor: UMI Research P, 1988); Thomas Elsaesser, "Germany's Imaginary America: Wim Wenders and Peter Handke," in *European Cinema Conference Papers,* ed. Susan Hayward (Aston: Aston UP, 1984) 31–52; Eric Rentschler, "How American Is It? The U.S. as Image and Imaginary in German Film," *Persistence of Vision* 2 (Fall 1985): 5–18; Gerd Gemünden, "On the Way to Language: Wenders' *Kings of the Road,*" *Film Criticism* 15.2 (1991): 13–28. One of the few critics who focuses on gender is Thomas Elsaesser ("American Graffiti und Neuer Deutscher Film: Filmemacher zwischen Avantgarde und Postmoderne," in *Postmoderne: Zeichen eines kulturellen Wandels,* ed. Andreas Huyssen and Klaus Scherpe [Hamburg: Rowohlt, 1986] 302–28).

Framing the framemaker: Dennis Hopper as Tom Ripley in *The American Friend* (1977). (Publicity still, Stiftung Deutsche Kinemathek Berlin.)

ture, to narrative, and to the logic of the image as the three areas that lie at the center of his filmmaking and his essayistic and theoretical work.

Between Lifesaver and Fatal Attraction

If one looks at Wenders's own statements about America, the United States seem to be portrayed as a kind of ersatz father; that is, as an alternative to a German fatherland tainted by a fascist past and unacceptable to the rebellious son. In an oft-quoted passage from a review of Joachim Fest's film, *Hitler—A Career,* Wenders notes:

> I don't think that any other country has had such a loss of faith in its own images, stories and myths as we have . . . There are good reasons for this distrust, for never before and in no other country have images and language been treated with such a complete lack of conscience as here; never before and in no other place have they been degraded to impart nothing but lies.[3]

3. Wim Wenders, "That's Entertainment: *Hitler,*" *Emotion Pictures: Reflections on the Cinema,* trans. Sean Whiteside (London: Faber and Faber, 1989) 94f.

Elsewhere he writes, "[Rock music] was for me the only alternative to Beethoven . . . because I was very insecure then about all culture that was offered to me, because I thought it was all fascism, pure fascism; and the only thing I was secure with from the beginning and felt had nothing to do with fascism was rock music."[4] While this characterization is admittedly exaggerated, the fact remains that Wenders and his generation were socialized into perceiving the mythic rather than the ideological propensities of the English-speaking world.[5] The heroes of the films of John Ford, Howard Hawks, and Nicholas Ray provided German adolescents with a much desired new mythology and served as models for European apprentices like Godard, Truffaut, and Wenders. Before becoming a filmmaker himself, Wenders reviewed films of Ford and Ray for *Filmkritik* and *Süddeutsche Zeitung,* praising them in a peculiar prose of positivistic description and paraphrase while intentionally imitating in his style the surface quality that he perceived to be their aesthetic forte.[6] Writing about Ford, Wenders marveled at "the friendliness, the care, the thoroughness, the seriousness, the peace, the humanity . . . those faces that are never forced into anything; those landscapes that aren't just backgrounds, those stories which, even if they are funny, are never foolish; those actors who are always playing different versions of themselves."[7] Together with Nicholas Ray, who also stars in *The American Friend,* Wenders made *Lightning over Water,* an experimental documentary about their friendship and Ray's dying of cancer. Clearly, this turn to U.S. filmmakers of an older generation is an attempt to rid himself of a cultural legacy that he repudiates yet dares not fully confront; like many of his characters, Wenders tries to escape the oedipal triangle rather than act it out, turning it into an oedi-pal relationship in which male bonding displaces patricide and, as I will show, heterosexual relationships.

One should be cautious, however, about seeing Wenders's attraction to American directors simply in terms of the father-son relationship that I've tenuously outlined. Wenders, for one, rejects any reading of his admiration

---

4. Jan Dawson, *Wim Wenders,* trans. Carla Wartenberg (New York: Zoetrope, 1976) 12.

5. In the same interview Wenders also notes: "My first memories of America were of a mythical country where everything was much better. It was chocolate and chewing gum. One of my cousins had an uncle in the United States and thanks to him I had a toy gun and an Indian headdress that I loved. In Germany at the time there weren't any toys and the only ones I knew were American toys, which were really marvelous . . . At three or four I didn't know my country was occupied. I had no idea . . . Certainly I saw troops, soldiers, tanks, but for me it was all spectacle" (12).

6. Wenders's aesthetics are in fact very close to the position of Siegfried Kracauer, who also claims that "the cinema seems to come into its own when it clings to the surface of things" (Kracauer, *Theory of Film: The Redemption of Physical Reality* [New York: Oxford UP, 1965] 285).

7. "Emotion Pictures: Slowly Rockin' On," *Emotion Pictures: Reflections on the Cinema* 49.

for Ford or Ray as the search for an ersatz father.[8] What is more, his films themselves invalidate the association of American cinema with typically male activities and characteristics. In Wenders's films rock music, billboards, the ever-present jukebox and pinball machine, and cinema itself are almost always associated with the female. In three of his films the girlfriend or woman in whom the protagonist is interested works in a movie theater—respectively, these are *The Goalie's Anxiety at the Penalty Kick, Wrong Move,* and *Kings of the Road,* but one may as well add Jane, the peep-show artist of *Paris, Texas* to the list, for hers is the most sophisticated form of spectacle. In *The Goalie's Anxiety at the Penalty Kick* we see Bloch playing the jukebox while escaping to the Hungarian border after committing a murder in Vienna. The song playing on the jukebox is "Gloria," the name of his female victim, who worked at the cinema. Philip, the journalist of *Alice in the Cities,* does not know how to deal with seven-year-old Alice, yet he is willing to accept his responsibilities after a visit to a Chuck Berry concert. Whereas previously he had turned Alice over to the police, he now takes her back to conclude the search for her mother. "King-of-the-road" Bruno Winter compensates for his inability to relate to women ("I always felt lonely inside a woman—lonely to the core")[9] with a truck replete with portable record player, jukebox, movie stills, and projection machines. The house of the androgynous Tom Ripley—he kisses his friends and confesses his attraction to Jonathan Zimmerman—displays a Canada Dry neon sign, a pool table, and a Wurlitzer jukebox. Their friendship is latently homoerotic, with Ripley assuming the role of the seducer who bestows pornographic gifts on Jonathan and who lures Jonathan away from wife and kid into a life of instability and adventure.[10] It would be easy to continue the list. In all these cases mass culture serves as a replacement for women; the imaginary femininity of mass culture leads to the real exclusion of women on the level of narrative. Thus, Wenders's imaginary America emerges not so much, as often asserted, as the land of the spiritual ersatz father, who is free of a tainted Nazi past, but as the mother figure.

This depiction of mass culture positions Wenders within a modernist tradition of the late nineteenth century, when "mass culture [became] associated with women while real, authentic culture remain[ed] the prerogative of

---

8. Cf. Wenders's voiceover in *Lightning over Water* (Wim Wenders and Chris Sievernich, *Nick'sFilm/ Lightning over Water* (Frankfurt am Main: Zweitausendeins, 1981); and Tom Farell, "Nick Ray's German Friend Wim Wenders," *Wide Angle* 5.4 (1983): 62. In the actual film Wenders tells Ray's wife, Susan, "I'm not his [Ray's] son." Susan then asks back, "Are you sure?" Wenders: "No, I'm not sure. Still, I'm not his son." The script does not contain this scene.

9. "Ich hab' mich immer nur einsam gefühlt in einer Frau. Einsam bis auf die Knochen" (Fritz Müller-Scherz, Wim Wenders, *Im Lauf der Zeit: Drehbuch* [Frankfurt am Main: Zweitausendeins, 1977] 330).

10. Significanctly, Wenders deviated from Highsmith's novel *Ripley's Game* by not casting the role of Ripley's wife, Helene.

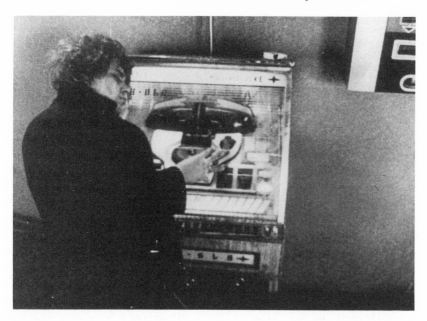

"For him a jukebox was a source of peace, or something that made one feel peaceful, made one sit still, in relative motionlessness or breathlessness, interrupted only by the measured, positively ceremonial act of 'going to push the buttons.'"—Peter Handke, *Essay on the Jukebox*

Scene from *Alabama* (1968) by Wim Wenders. (Publicity still, Stiftung Deutsche Kinemathek Berlin.)

men."[11] While Wenders's films can be seen as continuing this modernist tradition of gendering mass culture, they do deviate from it in significant and complex ways, placing them more within a postmodern sensibility. Like much of postmodern art, Wenders's films and their "heroes" are not obsessed with the anxiety of influence that defines high modernist art's volatile relationship with everyday life. On the contrary, these protagonists are infatuated with mass culture and its icons. Instead of the misogynist and masculinist undertones typical of modernism, the lure of mass culture is portrayed sympathetically, a welcome remedy or, in Wenders's own words, a "lifesaver."[12] It is through mass culture and (its) technological reproduction that the male protagonists first make contact. After Robert's involuntary swim in the Elbe, Bruno and Robert quite literally "warm up" to each other when

---

11. Andreas Huyssen, "Mass Culture as Woman: Modernism's Other," *After the Great Divide: Modernism, Mass Culture, Postmodernism* (Bloomington: Indiana UP, 1987) 47.

12. Cf. Wenders famous statement to Jan Dawson, "My life was saved by Rock'n Roll" (*Wim Wenders* 11).

Bruno wraps Robert in a blanket and plays the song "The More I See You" on the portable record player in his cab. Later in the film they loudly accompany the tune "Just like Eddy," a ritualistic act that marks the high point of their friendship. Travis, the estranged father in *Paris, Texas,* first meets with the sympathy of his son, Hunter, when together they watch a home movie of their earlier happy family life. I have already mentioned how a Chuck Berry concert transforms Philip Winter into accepting responsibility for young Alice.

The attraction with such a feminized America bears serious consequences, however, for Wenders's respective protagonists: Bruno Winter, the thoroughly Americanized movie equipment repairman remains a loner in his moving/movie truck, although the film's ending suggests that everything must, and indeed will, change. Jonathan Zimmermann's dangerous liaison with Tom Ripley turns into a fatal attraction when Zimmermann's dealings with his American friend lead him into the hands of the Mafia and to his early death. Friedrich Munro, the German director of the Hollywood-produced film *The Survivors,* in *The State of Things,* dies when loan sharks catch up with him and the producer, Gordon, in Los Angeles.

In all these cases mass culture and Americanization—employed by Wenders as two virtually synonymous terms—are overdetermined concepts that connote complex processes of political, cultural, and sexual repression and displacement in the young Americanized male protagonists. Robert and Bruno seem most at ease with each other when they are lip-synching rock music, thus revealing their inability to verbalize conflict—namely, the conflict between each other, between them and their parents, and between them and women. Their singing along to records acknowledges a common childhood of displaced rebelliousness; instead of confronting the father, these German youths embrace the escape offered by rock music: "Whenever I'm sad / Whenever I'm blue / Whenever my troubles are heavy / Beneath the stars / I play my guitar / Just like Eddy."[13]

The relation of gender to mass culture pertains not only to the way in which Wenders's protagonists associate icons of mass culture with the female. In terms of spectatorship mass culture has traditionally been considered to ascribe its user—or, better, consumer—a passive, uncritical, and complacent position, traits usually associated with the female. As Patrice Petro has shown, "it is remarkable how theoretical discussions of art and mass culture are almost always accompanied by gendered metaphors which link 'masculine' values of production, activity, and attention with art, and 'feminine' values of consumption, passivity, and distraction with mass culture."[14] This

13. *Im Lauf der Zeit* 323.

14. Patrice Petro, "Mass Culture and the Feminine: The 'Place' of Television in Film Studies," *Cinema Journal* 25.3 (1986): 6. Cf. also Patrice Petro's critique of Kracauer in her study on spectatorship and gender, *Joyless Streets: Women and Melodramatic Representation in Weimar Germany* (Princeton: Princeton UP, 1989); and Siegfried Kracauer's famous essay "Die kleinen Ladenmädchen gehen ins Kino," in *Das Ornament der Masse,* ed. Karsten Witte (Frankfurt am Main: Suhrkamp, 1977) 279–94.

A life saved by rock 'n' roll: Robert (Hanns Zischler) and Bruno (Rüdiger Vogler) in *Kings of the Road* (1976). (Publicity still, Stiftung Deutsche Kinemathek Berlin.)

"feminization" of those who consume mass culture can also be seen in Wenders's protagonists. Bruno and Robert (as well as Philip Winter, Joseph Bloch, and Friedrich Munro) are prime examples of the hypersensitive, hesitant, and insecure male—in Germany labeled with the derogatory term *Softie*—who are caught up in narcissistic introspection and struggle with their masculine roles. Travis, the inept father and husband of *Paris, Texas,* has to learn from his son and the Mexican maid what a responsible male looks like, checking his so acquired image and ego in the mirror. Unlike Wenders's other male protagonists, he does finally confront his wife, Jane, but the peep-show setting provides his monologue with the protection of invisibility and a voice estranged by the intercom system. His deeds accomplished, Travis flees the scene and rides into the Houston sunrise, as a billboard sign ironically comments: "Together we make it happen."

If the consumption of mass culture such as pulp fiction, movies, and television shows is gendered female, the production and distribution of these consumer goods has traditionally been a male prerogative. And, indeed, in Wenders the producers and distributors of films do not portray the gender trouble evident in his movie-consuming protagonists; for the most part they are tough, macho males who smoke cigars and don't question their identity as male: Sam Fuller and Minot in *The American Friend,* Gordon in *The State of Things,* Peter Falk in *Wings of Desire,* and to a lesser degree the Friedrich Munro of *Lisbon Story.* In a recent interview with filmmaker Edgar Reitz, Wenders has even underscored this view with an essentialist argument: "I believe making images is a masculine affair. This strange 'taking-possession,' stealing, and violating which is always part of producing images is not a female thing. It is no accident that there are so few woman photographers, camera women, and ultimately so few women directors in the history of film."[15]

Male Fantasies, Male Narratives

It is not only behind the camera but also in front of it that one notices the striking absence of women. Clearly, women stand in the way of Wenders's narratives, which typically begin with a disoriented young man emotionally at a loss, often because he has left his wife (Robert Lander in *Kings of the Road,* Travis in *Paris, Texas*), is about to do so (Jonathan Zimmermann in *The American Friend*), or is trying to shake off his female companion (as Philip is trying with young Alice in *Alice in the Cities* and, in a different vein, Bloch, who murders his one-night-stand in Vienna). Much of each film is then spent with the protagonist coming to terms with his problematic relationship to women, often in connection with some form of male bonding and performed as a search for the mother (*Alice in the Cities; Paris, Texas*). Love in Wenders's films is always the impossibility of love between a man and a woman, displaced onto mass culture and analyzed by a male buddy, the oedi-pal.

To be sure, Wenders's films are *Männerfilme*—they are films by a man, about men and male topics. Yet these films foreground this male-centeredness as problematic and, in fact, have been interpreted this way by German feminists. As Helke Sander and Margarethe von Trotta said in an interview:

> [Helke Sander:] "Maybe men should altogether refrain from using women as the projection of their own problems. They should deal with themselves. Women in films are always signs for something else. Wim Wenders has resisted that in his *Kings of the Road* by leaving them out altogether.
> [von Trotta:] "I agree. I don't understand the reproach that women are excluded. I think it is only logical if he says: "I know better how to speak about men because that's where my own experiences are."[16]

---

15. Edgar Reitz, *Bilder in Bewegung: Essays, Gespräche zum Kino* (Reinbek: Rowohlt, 1995) 189. The interview was recorded for Reitz's documentary, *Die Nacht der Filmemacher.* Ironically, Wenders's wife, Donata, is a photographer who made the still photographs of Wenders's recent collaboration with Michelangelo Antonioni in *Par delà les nuages.* Cf. Wim Wenders, *Meine Zeit mit Antonioni* (1996).

16. Christa Maerker, "Was ich sagen möchte, kann ich so billig sagen: Gespräch mit Margarethe von Trotta und Helke Sander," in *Jahrbuch Film 78/79,* ed. Hans Günther Pflaum (Munich: Hanser, 1978) 81.

Like classic Hollywood cinema, Wenders's cinema does not really avail the female viewer a position, yet it deviates from dominant cinema because it renders forms of masculine identification problematic. Wenders's employment of the road movie that, like its cousin the western, is traditionally considered a male domain, subverts the Hollywood convention in which women are excluded and relegated to the role of an object in the drama of male desire and conflict; while the focus is still on men, the issue becomes the male protagonist's uneasiness with women, an impetus that was also underlying Handke's merging of the bildungsroman and road movie in *Short Letter, Long Farewell.* Like Handke's narrator, Bruno and Robert in *Kings of the Road* are "weak" males, insecure about their masculine roles, and incapable of relating to a woman. It is significant that their fistfight in the abandoned army hut at the end of the film—Wenders's version of a classic showdown—is initiated because Bruno teases Robert about his continued halfhearted efforts to call up his estranged wife. Robert, in turn, accuses Bruno of cowardice and a solipsistic lifestyle. It seems that the master narrative that determines the dead end of their communal travels is not so much, as has usually been argued, American cultural imperialism but, rather, the protagonists' realization that their self-definition of masculinity needs to change—"Es muß alles anders werden," (Everything has to change) as Robert says in his farewell note to Bruno. If for Handke the presence of John Ford facilitates the reconciliation between the narrator and his wife (following a showdown in Oregon that, like Wenders's, can be seen as a parody of Hollywood), for Wenders, too, John Ford seems to show the way toward a future in which everything will change: one of the last shots of Robert shows him stepping out of a dark train station into the bright sunlight very much like John Wayne, in *The Searchers,* stands in the desert, framed by the dark doorway of the homestead.

Wenders himself has addressed the problem of the exclusion of women on the level of narrative and has considered *Paris, Texas* his last film that relies on such a constellation. As he commented in an interview: "[Travis's departure into the sunrise] was for me the only chance to have him exit from the scene, and together with him all my earlier male characters. All of them have now settled down in a suburb of Paris, Texas."[17] Obviously, my critique does not apply in equal measure to films such as *Wings of a Desire, Until the End of the World,* and *Lisbon Story,* all of which are love stories. A discussion of the function of gender in these films would transcend the parameters of my analysis. While Wenders explicitly understands these films as a corrective to his previous centering on the male, I would argue that his revisions do not go beyond the level of narrative. In *Wings of Desire,* for example, there remains something deeply disturbing and unsettling about a love story between an artist and an angel who, because of his apparently benevolent gaze, is not only able to see without being seen but who also invades the private sphere by going through walls and who knows the secret thoughts of the object of his desire.

---

17. Taja Gut, "Unterwegs zur Filmkunst von Wim Wenders," *Individualität* 19 (1988): 28.

Wenders's exclusion of women as narrative agents has also to be seen, I would argue, as part of his *general* problem with narrative and even his refusal to tell stories. His early short *Same Player Shoots Again* (1967) consists of five times repeating the same shot of the limping legs of a man holding a gun, each shot tinted in different black-and-white film stock—a structure that imitates, as the title explains, the five plays the pinball machine allows per game. The short *Silver City* (1968) is strung together from ten three-minute static shots of an immobile camera and depicts mundane and banal scenes of the Munich cityscape. The relation between image and story is generally perceived by Wenders as a threat to the image, which is constantly being molded and manipulated in order for a story to take place, "a vampire who tries to suck the blood out of the image."[18] This tension between showing and telling dominates not only the early shorts but virtually all of Wenders's feature films, especially *The Goalie's Anxiety at the Penalty Kick, Wrong Move, Kings of the Road* (the story of a friendship between a projectionist and a psycholinguist), and *Alice in the Cities* (in which the protagonist cannot write about America but obsessively takes pictures).

No film deals with this subject more self-consciously than *The State of Things.* Made at a moment of personal crisis and marking a turning point in Wenders's career, this film examines self-critically the state of stories and the relation of women to narrative. In many ways the film summarizes familiar stylistic elements and (non)narrative patterns of Wenders's previous oeuvre and, of course, his own biography as filmmaker. The German director Friedrich Munro is a representative of non-Hollywood filmmaking; his black-and-white science fiction film *The Survivors,* as well as the first half of *The State of Things* itself, is poor on plot and suspense and rich on incident and atmosphere, "infusing a Hollywood genre with modern music, slow pacing, a poetic camera, and a tendency towards silence."[19] The depiction of the stranded crew idle at a hotel in Portugal, which takes up the first hour of the film, only hints at a general storyline, while individual relationships remain vague and inconclusive. Sketches of character portrayals are interspersed with exquisitely framed shots of the Portugal seacoast and the desolate hotel, creating a mood of stagnation and suffocation. Although the last part of the film, with its faster pace, rock music, urban landscape, and road movie sequences, is in many ways the opposite of the Portugal scenes, it is only the other (i.e., American) side of the Wenders trademark. As with most of his films, we find familiar forms of plotting men and male plots and frustrated attempts at heterosexual interaction. Looking for Gordon in the jungle of Hollywood, Friedrich turns into the Fordian searcher that *The State of Things* time and again alludes to; after Gordon tells Friedrich that he loves him, they find their communal death. The search for the absent father(s)

---

18. Wim Wenders, "Impossible Stories," *Cinema of Wim Wenders* 33–40.
19. Geist 93.

encounters only traces they left behind: the billboard at the Nuart Cinema announcing the John Ford film, the memorial star of Fritz Lang on Hollywood Boulevard, the Murnau quote that Friedrich leaves on somebody's answering machine.[20]

What distinguishes *The State of Things*, however, from earlier projects is the analytical and self-critical rigor with which Wenders scrutinizes the obsessions and aporias of his own filmmaking. Friedrich explains to his crew that "stories only exist in stories, whereas life goes by in the course of time without the need to turn out stories"; his own skepticism toward original narratives leads him to do a remake of Allan Dwan's *Most Dangerous Man Alive*. But the film's end proves him wrong: when he and Gordon are shot by the loansharks, Friedrich is indeed experiencing what only a few hours earlier Gordon had called "the biggest story in the world," that is, death.

Women again have no part in the narrative; while there are several actresses among the crew in Portugal, the story does not develop until after Friedrich leaves his lover, Kate, and his other "dependents" to search for Gordon. This exclusion from the picture is questioned by Kate when she looks through Polaroids her daughter took and comments on her dictaphone:

What's really interesting are these Polaroids that Julia made. Here Friedrich is perfectly framed and I am only half in the picture. Here is a beautiful framing job of Friedrich, looking very dapper and I'm not visible at all. And Mark right in the middle of the picture with Anna totally out of the shot, just her head remains. Dennis and Robert couldn't be more beautifully framed—they have plenty of space all around, even the curtains look good here. Whereas Joan only seems to have her entire body in the photograph because Dennis is on one side of her and Joe is on the other side of her; and of course Julia had to get both of these men, so Joan wins by default.[21]

As the child of a director and an actress, Julia has internalized the dominant aesthetics of photography and filmmaking, which marginalizes women; what triggers Kate's comments is her surprise to see these aesthetics permeate the ways of seeing of her presumably still innocent daughter—especially since these Polaroids taken during dinner are free of the artistic framing and grouping of the film production and thus attest more authentically to the spontaneous perception of the photographer. Since the entire film has to be

---

20. In an obituary to Fritz Lang, Wenders significantly calls him "the lost, no, the missed father" ("Death Is No Solution: The German Film Director Fritz Lang," *Emotion Pictures* 107).

21. Kate is played by the actress Viva Auden, best known for her acting in films by Andy Warhol and Paul Morrissey. It is safe to assume that Viva wrote her own lines for this scene, which would also befit the general improvisational character of the film and its production history.

read as Wenders's coming to terms with his narrative strategies, marking both a dead end and a new beginning, it can be argued that this scene is a self-critique of Wenders, acknowledging that it is particularly the integration of women into the picture and the story that need revision in the future.

From Manipulation to Seduction

Wenders's refusal to tell stories and the concomitant value placed on pure visual representation resurface in his oeuvre in the form of a self-conscious preoccupation with the image and its modes of technological reproduction. Virtually every Wenders film revolves around the question of the status of the image—from the early short *Alabama: 2000 Light Years* (1968), an allegory on the death of the camera, and the philosophical reflections on video and film in the documentary *Notebooks on Clothes and Cities* (1989) to, more recently, his feature *Until the End of the World,* a monumental sci-fi road movie about the invention of a contraption that can make the blind see, and *Lisbon Story* (1995), a loose sequel to *The State of Things* that once again takes up the ethics of capturing images on film. All his films thematize more or less explicitly the defense and preservation of pure and transparent images vis-à-vis a multiplicity of threats to the image. These threats seem to fall into three categories: (1) a threat to the image by the story that deprives the image of its autonomy and forces it into the service of an imposed narrative logic; (2) a manipulation of the image that exploits it for specific ideological purposes (embodied, according to Wenders, by contemporary Hollywood films, television, and MTV); and (3) a proliferation of images that uproots the autonomy of the pure image, severs it from its referent, and seduces the viewer into a world of simulacra. This chapter has already described the relation of image to narrative; I will now focus on the threat of manipulation and the threat of seduction—both notions that, with their connotations of the feminine, again foreground the importance of gender in understanding the cinematic universe of Wenders.

In *Alice in the Cities* Philip Winter relates the following experience to his friend Edda:

> I'm totally stuck. That was a horrible trip. From the moment you leave New York, nothing changes, everything looks the same so that you cannot imagine any change anymore. I have become a stranger to myself [*Ich bin mir selbst fremd geworden*] . . . And yet I went on and listened to the loud-mouth radio, and in the evening I would watch the inhuman television in a motel that looked like the motel from the night before.

Echoing statements, at times verbatim, from Wenders's early film reviews, Philip indicts the manipulative powers of television and radio, its reification of art, and the homogenizing effect of mass media. In one scene Philip angrily kicks in the TV set because John Ford's *Young Mr. Lincoln*—employed here as an example of authentic art and uncoerced images—is mutilated by a commercial. The 1982 film diary *Reverse Angle* continues this critique, now also including contemporary American *film:* "Contemporary American films look more and more like their own trailers. So much here in America has this tendency to become its own publicity, leading to an inflation and invasion of mindless and despotic images. And television, as usual, the poison ivy of the eyes."[22] Wenders's vocabulary is that of Adorno and Horkheimer's *Dialectic of Enlightenment* and their analysis of a world in which the culture industry erases individual experience through homogenization and brainwashing. Consider the following passage from Adorno's "Transparencies on Film":

> One will have observed that it is difficult, initially, to distinguish the preview of "coming attractions" from the main film for which one is waiting. This may tell us something about the main attractions. Like the previews and like the pop hits, they are advertisements for themselves, bearing the commodity character like a mark of Cain on their foreheads. Every commercial film is actually only the preview of that which it promises and will never deliver.[23]

The long prose poem "The American Dream"—an extensive monologue from 1984 in which Wenders critically assesses his seven-year-experience of living in the United States—condemns television as an agent in the subjugation of people and in the destruction of language and holds it responsible for a hollowing out of the integrity of images. Underlying this notion of critique is the concept of false representation, epitomized for both Wenders and Adorno in television, for it willfully disguises, falsifies and distorts.[24] "On that [TV] screen," Wenders comments during a stay in New York "there was no longer the slightest connection between reality and its representation in images."[25] This connection *does* exist, Wenders maintains, in films like *Young Mr. Lincoln* and many of the westerns by Ford, Hawks, and Walsh, which follow an ethic of representation in which the images are authentic and "mean themselves"—an ethic that is now lost:

---

22. Voiceover by Wenders from *Reverse Angle;* reprinted in *Cinema of Wim Wenders* 42–44.

23. *The Culture Industry: Selected Essays on Mass Culture,* ed. J. M. Bernstein (London: Routledge, 1991) 160.

24. Cf. also *Chambre 666,* a documenatry in which fifteen filmmakers address Wenders's concern that a televison aesthetics is threatening to permeate and replace a cinema aesthetics. On the relation of television to cinema, see also the interview with Reinhold Rauh (in Rauh, *Wim Wenders und seine Filme* [Munich: Heyne, 1990] 237–64).

25. *Emotion Pictures* 128.

Once there was
the 'American Cinema'
and its language
was the legitimate narrative form of America
and, in its finest moments, a fitting expression of the American Dream.
That cinema no longer exists.[26]

The second serious threat to the image is the threat of seduction. According to Jean Baudrillard, the most prominent representative of the theory of simulation, the boundary between representation and reality implodes, and, as a result, the very experience and ground of the "real" disappear, depriving the critical subject of its foundation. Signs and modes of representation come to constitute reality; signs gain autonomy and, in interaction with other signs, form a new type of social order—Baudrillard's hyperreal, in which the distinction between media and reality has been erased. "Simulation . . . is the death sentence of every reference. Whereas representation tries to absorb simulation by interpreting it as false representation, simulation envelops the whole edifice of representation as itself a simulacrum."[27]

What unites Adorno's and Baudrillard's theory of media across their apparent differences is the melancholic undertone mourning the loss of origins and their communal strategy to perceive mass culture as woman. Andreas Huyssen has shown how *The Dialectics of Enlightenment* casts mass culture as the female threat. Huyssen cites these telling passages from Adorno and Horkheimer's study: "[Mass culture] cannot renounce the threat of castration . . . mass culture, in her mirror, is always the most beautiful in the land."[28] For Baudrillard the attraction—and the threat—of simulacra lie in their seductive force: artifice is more seductive than the real, or "natural." "It is no longer the subject which desires, it is the object which seduces,"[29] writes Baudrillard, and, indeed, the desire of Wenders's heroes, the search for their identity, is time and again replaced by seduction through landscape—a landscape, to be sure, that itself is a highly cinematic and cinema-constituted landscape: a second nature much rather than a first or real nature.

The threat of the seduction through images within a world of simulacra is most forcefully presented in *Paris, Texas* and *Until the End of the World.*

---

26. Ibid. 133.

27. Jean Baudrillard, *Simulations,* trans. Pauls Foss, Paul Patton, and Philip Beitchman (New York: Semiotext[e] 1983) 11. The quote continues: "This would be the successive phases of the image: (1) it is the reflection of a basic reality; (2) it masks and perverts a basic reality; (3) it masks the *absence* of a basic reality; (4) it bears no relation to any reality whatever: it is its own pure simulacrum. In the first case, the image is a *good* appearance—the representation is of the order of sacrament. In the second, it is an *evil* appearance—of the order of malefice. In the third, it *plays at being* an appearance—it is of the order of sorcery. In the fourth, it is no longer of the order of appearance at all, but of simulation."

28. Huyssen, *After the Great Divide* 48.

29. Jean Baudrillard, *Selected Writings,* ed. Mark Poster (Stanford: Stanford UP) 202.

The first shot of Walt in *Paris, Texas* shows him answering the phone at the corner in front of a skyscraper. When Walt walks away from the scene we realize that, in fact, the skyscraper is only a billboard. Later in the film this confusion between reality and its replica occurs again, when Travis shows Walt a photograph of his property in Paris, Texas. Walt then asks: "You bought the picture of a vacant lot in the mail?" "No! I bought the land."[30] The entire film is abundant with second nature: highway billboards, neon cowboys, motel signs, a Statue of Liberty spray-painted on the peep-show in Houston—yet, unlike earlier films, these images are presented with little or no irony, not meaning to be parodic or critical but as a message into the void: "eine Botschaft ins Leere."[31] As the propelling force for Travis's and Hunter's search for the mother and thus the film's narrative, Jane is reduced to the status of an image: a photo of her and Travis taken in a photomaton, a smiling face in a home movie, and ultimately a spectacle in a peep show, watched by others but unable to see herself.

The case for the seductive force of images is reiterated in the "The American Dream" (written at the time of *Paris, Texas*). Consider the following passage:

Pictures and signs everywhere,
on huge boards, photographed, painted, in neon lights.
Nowhere else has this become such an art.
Nowhere else such an inflation of signs and symbols.
Nowhere else the eyes so busy,
so used to working overtime.

Nowhere else is vision harnessed like this,
to the service of seduction.
Nowhere else, therefore, so many longings and needs
because nowhere else has vision become so addicted.[32]

Finally, *Until the End of the World* represents the strongest moral indictment of the use and abuse of images. The plot revolves around the invention of a contraption that makes the blind see and the serious consequences for all who are involved in this experiment. Edith, the blind wife of scientist Henry Far-

30. Wim Wenders and Sam Shepard, *Paris, Texas,* ed. Chris Sievernich (Greno: Road Movies, 1984) 26.

31. Wim Wenders, *Written in the West: Photographien aus dem amerikanischen Westen* (Munich: Schirmer/Mosel, 1987) 13.

32. "Bilder und Zeichen überall, / auf riesigen Tafeln, fotografiert, gemalt, in Neonlicht. / Nirgendwo sonst zu solch einer Kunst geworden. / Nirgendwo sonst eine solche Inflation von Zeichen. / Nirgendwo sonst das Auge so beschäftigt, / so überbeschäftigt. / Nirgendwo sonst das Sehenkönnen so in Anspruch genommen, / so im Dienste der Verführung. / Nirgendwo sonst daher so viele Sehnsüchte und Bedürfnisse, / weil nirgendwo sonst solche Seh-Süchte" (*Emotion Pictures* 121).

ber, dies from the images of a damaged world. After Henry Farber refurbishes the machine, enabling it to make visible one's own dreams, Sam and Claire become addicted to their dreams; originally conceived to make the blind see, the machine now blinds those who can see. "While originally the camera served to merchandise the dreams which it produced, now it dissolves the dreams by making them visible. Its images have become a drug which devours its victims."[33] Paradoxically, the evil spirit of images is exorcised by images. Ozu-actor Ryu Chishu, representing the healing powers of Ozu's cinema, heals Sam Farber from an eye disease inflicted by his machine. Later, when Sam has become addicted to his dream images, his therapy consists of drawing rocks and leaves of grass and painting aquarelles.[34]

Until the End of the World reiterates this paradox on the level of form as well. Equal in length to *Kings of the Road,* it consists of three to four times as many shots. This acceleration of images seems propelled by the director's interest to show more, but it creates the opposite effect: the cities of Paris, Berlin, Lisbon, Tokyo, and San Francisco all look alike, resembling in their gratuity the sets for James Bond thrillers. They are the mere backdrops for the speedy chase across countries and continents, leaving neither time nor space for the camera to discover: that is, to see. It seems that Wenders has taken Cézanne's motto "You've got to hurry up, if you still want to see things" too literally.[35]

The project of discriminating between good and bad images, between false and authentic representation, between autonomy and manipulation or seduction, is omnipresent in the cinema of Wim Wenders. Against the threat of seduction and manipulation Wenders heroically upholds the notion of the image as something pure, transparent, and autonomous—an image that does not derive its meaning through a network of signification but is meaningful in itself. (In this respect Wenders's trust in the surface of things is quite similar to that of Rolf Dieter Brinkmann.) About *Easy Rider* Wenders remarked that it is a political film not because of its plot, but "it is political because it is beautiful."[36] "The American Dream" celebrates the self-sufficiency of a motel sign advertising a Holiday Inn: "The sign was not there only / to be seen and to draw attention to / the hotel that stood behind it. / It was also there on its own account. / It was a sheer pleasure to see it."[37] Elsewhere in the poem he admonishes: "In German, the two words / PROJECT [*vor-führen*] and SEDUCE [*ver-führen*] have the same root. / SEDUCED BY PROJECTION / the passive form

---

33. Stefan Kolditz, "Kommentierte Filmographie," *Wim Wenders* 300.
34. From a conversation with Wenders in Berlin, March 1, 1994. The presently circulating version of the film, with 179 minutes, does not contain these scenes. To my knowledge the planned six-hour version of the film was never released.
35. The motto was suggested to Wenders by Handke. It is now the final sentence of the author's voiceover to *Reverse Angle*. Cf. *Cinema of Wim Wenders* 44.
36. *Emotion Pictures* 29.
37. Ibid. 126.

of the active verb TO SEE." Seeing is what his cinema teaches. His heroes (like those of Peter Handke) preferably assume the position of the spectator; they look on, they witness, they observe; sometimes, like the angels in *Wings of Desire,* they take notes. Their task, and that of Wenders's cinema, is *wahrnehmen,* that is, to perceive and at the same time to authenticate by ascribing truth and beauty—hence the preserving gesture of many of his films that seek to capture what is about to disappear (sometimes with remarkable foresight): the apartment buildings soon to be torn down in the Hamburg harbor (*The American Friend*), the last functioning cinemas in the provinces (many of which were closed by the time *Kings of the Road* was finished), the borders between the two Germanies and Austria and Hungary (*Kings of the Road* and *The Goalie's Anxiety at the Penalty Kick*), and, most dramatically, the Berlin Wall in *Wings of Desire.* Time and again his films pay homage to his role models, who taught him the art of seeing: the films of Ozu, John Ford, Howard Hawks, and Nicholas Ray, the paintings of Edward Hopper and Caspar David Friedrich, the photography of Walker Evans and August Sander. Time and again these films indict the forces that block vision. Yet, as *Paris, Texas* and *Until the End of the World* demonstrate, this enterprise becomes more problematic and ambiguous. His films increasingly become aware of the difficulty and, in fact, impossibility of combatting the power of images through cinema, bringing them closer to a position that Jameson has called the winner loses logic. As Richard Kearney comments in an analysis of *Paris, Texas:*

The more cinema strives to expose the world of pseudo-images, the more it seems to confirm the omnipotence of the very system it wishes to contest. The more striking the portrait of a totalizing system of false imitations, the more impotent the viewer feels. To the extent, therefore, that Wenders *wins* by successfully representing an omnivorous system of mass media representation, to that same extent he *loses*—"since the critical capacity of his work is thereby paralyzed; and the impulses of negation and revolt, not to speak of those of social transformation, are increasingly perceived as vain and trivial in the face of the model itself."[38]

This is the reason why Wenders's favorite genre is the road movie. Behind the windshield Wenders's male heroes are safe from the endless flow of images rolling by and from female seduction and manipulation. They are flaneurs—observing the world, women, themselves, but not interacting with that which is presented in front of them. The world outside constantly changes, but in

38. Richard Kearney, *The Wake of Imagination: Toward a Postmodern Culture* (Minneapolis: U of Minnesota P, 1988) 322. The quote within the quote is from Fredric Jameson, *Postmodernism, or, The Cultural Logic of Late Capitalism* (Durham: Duke UP, 1991) 5f.

their metal containers they enjoy a relative stability outside of time and space, just as the moviegoers do in the dark and air-conditioned theater. This is also the reason why so many of Wenders's male protagonists are involved in framing pictures: the frame maker Jonathan Zimmermann, the photographer Philip Winter, the billboard maker Walt, the painter Derwatt, the projectionist Bruno Winter, the movie director Friedrich Munro, the engineer Sam Farber, the producer Max (*The End of Violence,* 1997). Their job is the production of images, but in a more important way they are involved in stopping the uncontrolled flow of images and in arresting the proliferation of signs and messages. It is their paradox—and Wenders's—that in order to battle images they have to create them.

CHAPTER 8

The Queer Utopia of Monika Treut

> I think going to America was part of a common German dream. The
> "American Dream" was a dream for me years ago, but by now, especially
> with New York, I've recently started hating the city, walking around
> cursing it, and friends say, "Hey Monika, you sound like a real New
> Yorker now."
>
> —*Monika Treut*

At the end of Monika Treut's *Virgin Machine* (1988) we see how Dorothee, a
journalist researching romantic love, discards photographs of couples that
she took in Hamburg into the San Francisco Bay. At the end of *My Father Is
Coming* (1991) Vicky, an aspiring German actress living in New York, accidentally drops portrait shots from her acting portfolio onto the sidewalk, and
her agent comments, "I think you'll need new photos." For both Dorothee
and Vicky the encounter with American culture presents the need to change,
metaphorically linked in both cases to the changing of an image. They both
belong to a long list of protagonists of German films who experience the
United States. From Luis Trenker's Nazi features *The Prodigal Son* (1934)
and *The Emperor of California* (1936) through a wealth of films from the New
German Cinema, including Werner Herzog's *Stroszek* (1977), Walter Bock-
meyer's *Flaming Hearts* (1978), Herbert Vesely's *Short Letter, Long Farewell*
(1977) (based on Peter Handke's novel), Volker Vogeler's *Damn This America* (1973), Werner Schroeter's *Willow Springs* (1973), Herbert Achternbusch's *Hick's Last Stand* (1990), and Wim Wenders's *Alice in the Cities*
(1974) and *The State of Things* (1982), to Percy Adlon's more recent *Bagdad
Café* (1987), *Rosalie Goes Shopping* (1988), and *Salmonberries* (1991), the
theme of leaving home for America is a conspicuously popular one with German filmmakers—a fact that has Eric Rentschler wonder how much these
films have to do with the real America. His reading of *The Prodigal Son, Alice
in the Cities,* and *Stroszek* concludes that for the respective travelers of these
films "the U.S. plays the role of an imaginary (in the Lacanian sense), a set of
possibilities one contemplates and toys with, or put in another way, as a hall

Female to Male: *Monika Treut.* (Photograph © Elfi Mikesch, 1990.)

of mirrors one passes through while self-reflecting. Confused, inexperienced, and incomplete human subjects gain wisdom and insight in America."[1]

Like most of these films, Monika Treut's features *The Virgin Machine* and *My Father Is Coming* represent America as a country that provides an escape from social and psychological restrictions found at home while also initiating the identity-producing mirror stage Rentschler describes. As is typical for films belonging to this tradition, in Treut's features the foreign country serves as backdrop and catalyst for a professional or personal quest, and the fact that here this quest is for a lesbian sexuality rather than the usual heterosexual one only seems a variation of a familiar theme. After all, the topos of experiencing abroad the pleasures of a transgressive sexuality denied at home is familiar from travel accounts at least since Flaubert's sojourns in Egypt. Yet, unlike in most of the narratives listed here, the German protagonists of *The Virgin Machine* and *My Father Is Coming* do not return home. Thus, Rentschler's argument that in *The Prodigal Son, Stroszek,* and *Alice in the Cities* the entry into the symbolic that follows the mirror stage invariably involves exiting from America does not hold true for Treut. Her narratives are concerned with the process of assimilating into the United States and with

1. Eric Rentschler, "How American Is It? The U.S. as Image and Imaginary in German Film," *Persistence of Vision* 2 (1985): 13.

the ways national, cultural, and sexual identity is redefined in *this* symbolic order.

What *is* different in the films of Monika Treut, therefore, is not only that the theme of male heterosexual sexual conquest abroad has been transformed into a lesbian one but also the way in which sexuality is here linked to notions of personal and cultural identity in general—thus providing a significant variation from the works of Handke and Wenders discussed in the previous chapters. By insisting that the most "natural" identity, namely gender, is more of a performance than an essence, Treut's scenarios also call into question the stability of other binaries such as *us/them, home/abroad,* or *American popular culture / German high art* on which so many German literary and cinematic depictions of the United States rely. Treut's genderbending, cross-cultural scenarios advocate a postmodern collapsing of oppositions, forcing us to rethink identities to a much greater degree than other writers and filmmakers before her. Employing Eve Kosofsky Sedgwick's definition of queer as "the open mesh of possibilities, gaps, overlaps, dissonances and resonances, lapses and excesses of meaning [that can't be made] to signify monolithically"[2] and Alexander Doty's description of queerness as "a quality related to any expression that can be marked as contra-, non-, or anti-straight,"[3] we can understand America in Treut's films as a queer utopia—not as a (yet again) reified other but as a place that fosters the production of identity through its tolerance of difference. As Alice Kuzniar puts it, paradoxically it is the very queerness of this land that makes it fit for foreigners.[4] My analysis of Treut's notion of the queer will use as an itinerary three exemplary modes of rehearsing different forms of cross-cultural explorations—pornography, performance, and the work of Camille Paglia. I will conclude with some comments on the styles of this queer cinema and the ways it engages its audience.

Pornography

Unlike the oedipal, or oedi-pal, scenarios of Wim Wenders, whose explorations of German-American relations provide the most exhaustive account of the dialectics of friend and foe, Treut's narratives are lesbian coming-out stories and thus challenge the patriarchial plots and plottings of her male colleague. In *The Virgin Machine* Dorothee Müller, a young Hamburg journalist, comes to San Francisco, notepad in hand, to research romantic love and her long-lost mother, who once worked there as a stripper. Although her mother has long gone, this loss is quickly overcome as Dorothee makes the acquaintance of women's erotica activist Susie Sexpert (Susie Bright) and

---

2. Eve Kosofsky Sedgwick, *Tendencies* (Durham: Duke UP, 1993) 8.

3. Alexander Doty, *Making Things Perfectly Queer: Interpreting Mass Culture* (Minneapolis: U of Minnesota P, 1993) xv.

4. Cf. Alice Kuzniar, "Comparative Gender: Rosa von Praunheim's and Monika Treut's Cross-Cultural Studies," *Spectator* 15 (1994): 51–59.

male impersonator Ramona (Shelley Mars). Through them she is initiated into the city's lesbian sex industry, goes to all-women strip shows, and tries (unwittingly) a lesbian call-girl service. In *My Father Is Coming* Vicky, an aspiring German actress working in New York, is forced to cover up her lifestyle when her father, Hans, shows up for a surprise visit. While he thinks she is an actress and married, she is in fact a waitress and bisexual—a sort of coming-out story in reverse, when at least for the time of his visit she is forced to recreate the straight sexual identity her father knew in Germany. In the end the father proves more tolerant than expected and accepts his daughter's sexual orientation.

As these short plot summaries show, the displacement explored in Treut's films is not only one of continents and cultures but foremost one of genders, as her lesbian/bisexual protagonists Dorothee and Vicky move from Germany to San Francisco and New York City, respectively, to escape the heterosexual identities they had in Germany.[5] In both features the emphasis is hardly ever on what the protagonists left behind (even though half of *Virgin Machine* takes place in Hamburg) but on what they experience abroad, and this experience is commonly described as one of experimenting, of finding out, of choosing options previously not considered. As Chris Straayer has pointed out in regard to *Virgin Machine*—and her argument applies to a lesser degree also to *My Father Is Coming*—it is somewhat misleading to talk about a lesbian coming-out story, for the film has none of the makings typical of the genre. Lacking are the inner torment and suffering of the protagonist; the depictions of society's repressions and reprimands; the slow development from initial decision to come out to a dramatic climax, often followed by some tragic turn of events. In contrast, *Virgin Machine* opposes romantic sentiment—its plot revolves about the very impossibility of experiencing romantic love—and homosexual isolation; it is much more, as Straayer has it, "a coming-in story," as a vibrant and lively San Francisco lesbian community is receptive and supportive of Dorothee's eagerness to join.[6] Similarly, *My*

---

5. This kind of liberation is also chronicled in Rosa von Praunheim's documentary, *Über-leben in New York* (*Survival in New York* [1989]) about three German women whose lives, and particularly sex lives, changed after they moved to the Big Apple. Von Praunheim introduces us to Claudia, who dumped her German boyfriend for a lesbian relationship with Ryan; to Ulli, who abandoned her rural Swabian background for a life in the American metropolis, where we see her living with her lover in Harlem as the only white woman on the block or together with a Vietnam veteran on welfare; and to Anna, a struggling actress like Vicky, who couldn't afford tuition for acting school and began working as a go-go dancer, fell in love with one of the regulars, and later got involved with a lawyer, who changed careers to manage the establishment where Anna works. While their stories are indeed unusual (certainly by non–New York standards), the camera treats the three women with respect and a caring distance and thus refrains from turning them into larger-than-life figures or symbols of an achieved quest for the truth in life. They struggle, they have to make ends meet, but their willingness to take emotional, social, and financial risks in their same-sex, interracial relationships rewards them with unusual experiences.

6. Chris Straayer, "Lesbian Narratives and Queer Characters in Monika Treut's *Virgin Machine*," *Journal of Film and Video* 45.2–3 (1993): 33.

Father Is Coming introduces us to the genderbending counterculture of New York's East Village peopled with gays, lesbians, a female-to-male transsexual, a fakir practicing skin piercing, and the flamboyant "post porn" artist Annie Sprinkle, who is running a New Age sex salon—a community that, like the one in San Francisco, encourages everybody "to do their own thing" without apparent fear of oppression and homophobia.

In both films' positive and affirmative portrayal of experimenting with new sexual identities an important function is assumed by pornography. As I use the term here, I mean it to describe not only "written and graphic, or other forms of communication intended to excite lascivious feelings" (*American Heritage Dictionary*) but also such varied practices and visual pleasures as the S/M couple Dorothee witnesses in her hotel, erotica like Susie Sexpert's dildo collection, the strip shows, the call-girl service Dorothee uses, the video of a male stripper that Ben, Vicky's roommate, watches, as well as the sexual practices advocated by sex activists and performers Susie Sexpert, Ramona, and most notably Annie Sprinkle. As we witness how Susie Sexpert explains to Dorothee (and to the viewer, as she unabashedly looks into the camera) the advantages of her dildo collection, we are made to understand that the productive appropriation of pornography has a liberating effect on its consumers. "Penis-to-vagina sex is old-fashioned. Nowadays, there are so many ways to make love," she explains. Ironically, this liberating effect becomes especially clear in a scene in *Virgin Machine* that seems to be an affirmation of the quest for romantic love that determined Dorothee's life in Germany. When after a night of passionate lovemaking Ramona presents the bill for services rendered to a startled Dorothee, Dorothee realizes that she has mistaken business for love. Significantly, this disillusion does not cause her to despair but, rather, after being momentarily baffled, to burst out in laughter. Realizing her own naïveté, this is a liberating laughter that indicates that she has traded in the last remnants of her search for romantic love that dominated her life in Germany for a notion of sexuality that exercises choices, pursues various options, and is built on equal exchange—namely, money for pleasure. In the final scene of the film we witness Dorothee herself dancing as a stripper, while women from the audience slip money under her bra. She is now both consumer and producer in the exchange circuit of pleasure and cash.

Pornography is also shown to have this liberating effect in *My Father Is Coming.* While Hans initially rejects Vicky's auditioning for a part in Annie Sprinkle's film *Pornutopia,* a visit to Annie's salon, where he is introduced to Annie's peculiar brand of New Age sex, makes him accept his daughter's sexual orientation. On his way home we see him checking out the porn theaters and dropping in on a skin-piercing artist. It must be added, though, that, unlike the sexual experimentation of the prodigal daughters Vicky and Dorothee, Hans's foreign affair, a mixture of genuine character transformation and sex tourism, fits squarely into a long tradition of European travel narratives.

The questions of agency in pornography and sex spectacles, and of its effects on the consumers, which are foregrounded in Dorothee's transformation and in Annie Sprinkle's performances, have been, of course, at the forefront of the heated debate about pornography in the United States throughout the 1980s. Since *Virgin Machine* was made at the height of the *West German* debate about pornography, with *Annie,* a short on Annie Sprinkle's one-woman show "Post-Post Porn Modernist" being made one year later, in 1989, we may understand the films as a conscious intervention in this debate. I therefore want to digress here for a moment and chart the parameters of that debate in order to reveal the polemic dimension of Treut's sexual politics. The appropriation of pornography can be seen here as a further example of the creative consumption of popular culture explored in this study, and the arguments voiced by antiporn feminists indeed echo those attacking mass media and popular culture.

The development of the German debate about pornography is remarkably similar to the one in the United States. It was launched by Alice Schwarzer, editor of *Emma,* in October 1987, with the usual half-decade time lag that also marks the transatlantic transfer of discussions about poststructuralism, postmodernism, and, more recently, political correctness. The *Emma* campaign closely followed the argumentation developed by feminist-activist Andrea Dworkin and feminist legal expert Catharine MacKinnon; *Emma*-Verlag published the translation of Dworkin's book, *Pornography: Men Possessing Women* and sponsored her appearance in Cologne. The so-called *Emma*-Gesetz (law) discussed in the German parliament, which meant to introduce legislation for litigation to pornography victims (but was not approved), was modeled after Dworkin and MacKinnon's proposal for an antipornography civil rights ordinance for Minneapolis.[7] Both Schwarzer and Dworkin argue that pornography exploits women by turning them into objects of the male gaze, that it eroticizes violence and thus serves as a blueprint for rape. Dworkin writes, "The pornographers are the secret police of male supremacy: keeping women subordinate through intimidation and assault."[8] But in the United States, and to a lesser degree in Germany, there were also women's groups who defended pornography on the grounds of free speech. FACT, the Feminist Anti-Censorship Task Force, took issue with radical feminists by saying that they overemphasize women's victimization and that they oversimplify the connection between the consumption of pornography and the actual occurrence of violence against women.[9] Among the most outspoken opponents to the antiporn campaign was a group with

---

7. My remarks are based on Ulrich Struve's insightful essay "'Denouncing the Pornographic Subject': The American and the German Pornography Debate and Elfriede Jelinek's *Lust,"* in *Elfriede Jelinek: Framed by Language,* ed. Jorun B. Johns and Katherine Arens (Riverside, CA: Ariadne, 1995) 89–106.

8. Andrea Dworkin, "Against the Male Flood: Censorship, Pornography, and Equality," *Harvard Women's Law Journal* 8 (1985): 13.

9. An interesting anthology from Austria, *Frauen-Gewalt-Pornographie,* ed. Karin Rick and Sylvia Treudl (Vienna: Wiener Frauenverlag, 1989), gathers a variety of responses to the debate on pornography and violence.

which Monika Treut strongly identifies, the lesbian S/M community, because their sexual practices of dominance and subservience were accused of being an eroticizing of inequality.

Since pornography is part of today's mass media and popular culture, we should not be surprised to find reiterated in this debate about pornography some of the arguments made by mass culture critics outlined earlier in this study. Indeed, the antiporn feminists' arguments rehearse the same rhetoric of mass manipulation, systematic domination, and victimization, and they demonstrate the same attitude of the intellectual to "know what's good for the people" that also characterizes Adorno's description of the culture industry. As Andrew Ross has argued, the antiporn movement has shown no interest in the wide variety of uses of pornography, especially in the subcultures; antiporn is largely unfamiliar with the material it criticizes; it holds an ahistorical and essentialist view of sexual difference; and it fails to comprehend pornography as a form of representation and thus as subject to interpretation.[10]

It is not difficult to see this critique of antiporn reiterated in Treut's films. Treut's intervention into the pornography debate, with her defense of women both as producers and consumers of pornography in *Virgin Machine, My Father Is Coming* and *Annie,* as well as her earlier advocacy of S/M in her feature *Seduction: The Cruel Woman* (codirected with Elfi Mikesch in 1985 and based on her research on de Sade and Sacher-Masoch)[11] and in her video *Bondage* (1983; rereleased as part of *Female Misbehavior* [1992]), can be seen as calculated provocation to the antiporn movement that was increasingly perceived as a segment of feminist activism aligning itself with (male) reactionary forces. Against the depiction of pornography as degrading to women, Dorothee's adventures in San Francisco emphasize the productive and creative use of popular culture by its consumers. Moreover, and in contrast to Lizzie Borden's *Working Girls* (1986), an early and influential film on prostitution from a woman's perspective, Treut's films do not revolve around the physical and psychological struggle involving prostitution. In other words, they do not attempt to legitimize pornography and prostitution by depicting it as hard work (the prostitutes in Borden's film refer to one another as working girls) and thereby succumbing to a Protestant work ethic. In Treut the pleasure principle is at work not only in the users of pornography but also in the sex workers themselves, as Ramona and Annie Sprinkle make clear[12]—

10. Andrew Ross, *No Respect: Intellectuals and Popular Culture* (New York and London: Routledge, 1989) 188.

11. Cf. Monika Treut's published dissertation, *Die grausame Frau: Zum Frauenbild bei de Sade and Sacher-Masoch* (Basel and Frankfurt am Main: Stroemfeld / Roter Stern, 1984). Forthcoming in English from Routledge.

12. As Sprinkle said about her beginnings as a prostitute: "I was working in a massage parlor. For 3 months I worked and didn't even know I was a hooker—I was having such a good time . . . I just thought of myself as a horny masseuse. I liked having sex with the guys after I gave them a brief massage. When it finally occured to me that I was a hooker, and I got over the initial shock, I enjoyed the idea" (qtd. in Linda Williams, "A Provoking Agent: The Pornography

although it must be emphasized that with Ramona this issue remains more ambiguous than with Annie. While the latter (over)plays on her naïveté and innocence, the former is cunning and calculating and will not let the issue of money be bracketed from her performance.

Finally, the fact that both *Virgin Machine* and *My Father Is Coming* are comedies can be seen as a strategy to deflate some of the angry rhetoric that had polarized the opposing parties in this highly charged antiporn debate, and Treut tells us that *Virgin Machine* did indeed have this effect on some of its viewers: "Some really hard-boiled feminists came to see the film, ready to be angry; by the end, they were laughing and could not hold an anti-porn stance with regard to the film."[13]

Performance

As we have seen, Treut's emphasis on the uses of pornography and on the creativity of consumption deflates the essentialist argument that pornography is harmful per se. Once we entertain the possibility of pornography *by* women and *for* women (such as the all-women strip show or Susie Sexpert's dildo collection), monolithic condemnations of exploitation and reification of women no longer hold true. While it would probably be an oversimplification to call Treut's position one of anti-antiporn, her work urges us to differentiate according to who produces and uses pornography and how.

Significantly, all three of Treut's features as well as her documentary *Female Misbehavior* (a four-part compilation film including *Dr. Paglia* [1992], a portrait of Camille Paglia; *Max* [1992], a portrait of a female-to-male sex change; *Bondage,* a portrait of Carol, a member of a New York lesbian sadomasochist group; and *Annie,* a portrait of sex performance artist Annie Sprinkle) make it clear that, as a means to explore and alter sexual identities, pornography is closely connected to the notion of performance. *Seduction: The Cruel Woman* is a film about Wanda, a dominatrix running a gallery specializing in S/M performance art in Hamburg, and about the ways in which she exploits the three people who are in love with her: her ex-husband, Gregor; her live-in lover, Caren; and Justine, a woman visiting from the United States. Wanda's power over the three stems from the fact that for her everything is role-playing and performance, while they seek to have a real relationship with her. Their attempts to break out of the game only strengthen Wanda's position as master of ceremony: When Justine slaps Wanda in the face because she hates all role-playing or when Gregor shoots Wanda during a live performance but merely hurts her cheek, Wanda con-

---

and Performance Art of Annie Sprinkle," in *Dirty Looks: Women, Pornography, Power,* ed. Pamela Church Gibson and Roma Gibson [London: BFI, 1993] 179).

13. Monika Treut, quoted in Julia Knight, "Female Misbehavior: The Cinema of Monika Treut," in *Women and Film: A Sight and Sound Reader,* ed. Pam Cook and Philip Dodd (Philadelphia: Temple UP, 1993) 185.

siders these acts of revolt part of the performance. The halfheartedness of their attempts demonstrates that they did not really mean it and that Justine and Gregor are now willing to participate in the game. For Wanda there is no outside of role-playing, and her embrace of artifice gives her power over those who still seek the illusion of authenticity. For those using S/M to enact sexual fantasies, role-playing can have a liberating effect, as the example of Herr Mährsch shows who poses as a journalist but really wants to perform as Wanda's toilet. His pleasure comes from playing helplessness and subservience. As Treut commented, "I'm interested in the liberating possibilities of a play [*Spiel*] which appropriates the images and projections of cruel women to produce pleasure and sovereignty."[14] Interestingly, Treut first encountered this kind of role-playing in the New York group Lesbian Sex Mafia (LSM). Their practices of sadomasochistic role-playing are seen by Treut as a subversive strategy to make sense of a reality in which the lines between reality and illusion are increasingly blurred: "In the metropolis of New York City where like nowhere else reality has become hyper-real, they direct their play: controlled, imaginative, and self-directed."[15] If all authenticity is staged authenticity, the only possible control left is to direct the mise-en-scène of the staging.

Pornography and performance are also linked in *Virgin Machine,* most notably in the figure of Ramona, whose impersonation of a masturbating male amuses the all-female audience. Significantly, her simulation of ejaculation with a beer bottle ends with Ramona's boxer shorts open and empty, suggesting castration and female empowerment. When Dorothee arranges a date with Ramona, Ramona performs so well that Dorothee mistakes it for real love, even though she knows that Ramona is a professional sex performer. The fact that Dorothee laughs after her rude awakening in the scene described earlier shows her recognition and acceptance that everything is performance, and when we witness Dorothee dancing as a stripper at the end of the film the scene seems to imply that now for her, too, performance is everything.

My Father Is Coming abounds with performances of all kinds: Vicky is an aspiring but unsuccessful actress who even fails to perform for her father as married woman. The father, in turn, who has no ambition for acting, lands a role in a beer commercial. Beyond these more literal examples of performance there is evidence of the performance of ethnicity and gender: the Puerto Rican Lisa says she can pass as New Yorker, and Joe, the female-to-male transsexual, certainly passes as a "real" male, even though he longs to let Vicky in on his past. The most radical performer is perhaps Annie Sprinkle, featured as narrative agent in *My Father Is Coming* and as performance artist in the documentary *Annie,* and her example again demonstrates how

14. Monika Treut, "Die Zeremonie der blutenden Rose: Vorüberlegungen zu einem Filmprojekt," *Frauen und Film* 36 (1984): 35.

15. Ibid. 42.

pornography is tied to performance. In fact, Sprinkle's one-woman performances such as "Post-Post Porn Modernist" have thoroughly questioned the distinction between art and pornography. As she said in an interview, "my feminist mother used to come into my room and joke whether I would grow up to be a whore or an artist. She was exactly right!"[16] As Linda Williams has argued, Sprinkle's comment is indicative of a strategy of defusing or going beyond rather than directly confronting familiar oppositions: she is both whore and artist.[17] In *My Father Is Coming* Sprinkle also conflates two traditionally opposing views of women; when together with Hans she is as much of a prostitute as she is a mother, both seducing and reassuring and nurturing him. Chris Straayer describes Sprinkle's work as an affirmation of a "fluid identity" that engages a wide variety of discourses, including "pornography, feminism, art, spirituality, sex education, advertising, political activism, performance art, body play, and the self-help health, prostitutes' rights and safe sex movements."[18] For both Williams and Straayer, Sprinkle is an exemplary proponent of queer aesthetics, politics, and sexualities who radically challenges the essentialisms we live by. In the short *Annie* we see how Ellen Steinberg, an unattractive, pudgy woman in her late thirties turns into her alias Annie Sprinkle by putting on makeup, false eyelashes, black stockings, high heels. "Everybody can achieve this kind of transformation; it's fun and it's easy," she tells us. But in her *Anatomy of a Pin-up Photo* she reveals the more torturous, self-disciplining side of dressing up for sexiness. If these two examples blur the lines between "sexy" and "not sexy" people by showing that each person can be both if employing the devices demonstrated in the video and the photo, another example questions the strict division between male and female. When Hans accidentally enters the women's room after spilling Coke on his pants, Annie, unperturbed by his presence, goes about her business and tells him from the toilet seat: "I just love it when we all share the same bathroom. I mean we all have a male side and a female side anyway."

The three examples of Wanda, Ramona, and Annie Sprinkle connect sex to performance, to role-playing, to theater. But the implication here is not that when we're having sex we're putting on a show. Rather, Wanda's S/M show, Ramona's male impersonation, and Annie Sprinkle's performance art suggest that gender itself is a performance rather than an essence and that sexual identity is something we can experiment with, alter, and manipulate. What is at stake in these performances, therefore, is to show that gender is a persistent impersonation and construction and that those who insist on the naturalness of gender often use it to legitimize gender hierarchy and compul-

---

16. Quoted in Linda Williams, "Provoking Agent," 176.

17. Ibid. 177. It is interesting to note in this context that traditional definitions of pornography such as Webster's rely on the very possibility of separating it from art: "Pornography = obscene literature, art, or photography, esp. that having little or no artistic merit."

18. Chris Straayer, "The Seduction of Boundaries: Feminist Fluidity in Annie Sprinkle's Art/Education/Sex," *Dirty Looks* 156.

A Bavarian in the East Village: Annie Sprinkle introduces Hans (Alfred Edel) to the sights of the city in *My Father Is Coming* (1991). (Publicity still, Tara Releasing, San Rafael, CA.)

sive heterosexuality. The notion of gender as a performative act has been theorized by Judith Butler, who argues that sexual identity is something we institute through a stylized repetition of acts that create the *appearance* of substance.[19] As Butler makes clear, we should not understand gender as a role that we simply put on to express or disguise an interior self. The selves do not exist prior to the cultural conventions that prescribe the modes of reenactment, since the model of a private internal and a public external overlooks "that the ascription of interiority is itself a publicly regulated and sanctioned form of essence fabrication."[20] Hence—and this is where the comparison to theater roles breaks down—there is no real gender outside of performance: "Gender reality is performative which means, quite simply, that it is real only to the extent that it is performed."[21] Since the performances by Wanda, Ramona, and Annie Sprinkle draw our attention to the ways in which we construct our identities, they can be seen as performances of performances—

19. Cf. Judith Butler, *Gender Trouble: Feminism and the Subversion of Identity* (New York and London: Routledge, 1990).

20. Judith Butler, "Performative Acts and Gender Constitution: An Essay in Phenomenology and Feminist Theory," *Performing Feminisms: Feminist Critical Theory and Theatre,* ed. Sue-Ellen Case (Baltimore: Johns Hopkins UP, 1990) 279.

21. Ibid. 278.

strategies of defamiliarization that reveal as construction site something we believed to be a given. They thereby make visible distinctions such as natural/artificial, surface/depth, inner/outer, through which discourse about genders almost always operates, and they allow us to question these distinctions. Significantly, those performances in *My Father Is Coming* that attempt to cover up, rather than lay open, fail: Vicky cannot trick her father into believing that she is married to Ben, nor can Ben, who is encouraged by Vicky to play a "good butch," pull it off as a straight male. Nor can Vicky cut it as a porn performer at Annie's audition, presumably because she is only doing it, as she tells her father, to pay the rent. There is a reluctance on Vicky's part to give up the notion of separating natural/artificial; she believes in self-styled and self-controlled performances. When Joe asks her if she dresses for sex or for business, she replies: "I dress who I am." Ironically, when she bursts out in anger and tears up Ben's shirt because he's moving in with his lover, Ben compliments her: "You are an actress after all."[22]

Since acts of constituting gender intersect with other discursively constituted identities such as race, class, and ethnicity, gender cannot be considered separately from the political and cultural intersections in which it is invariably produced and maintained. Gender identities are therefore imminently political, and the earlier examples of subverting these identities have to be seen as political strategies that defy preestablished identities. The possibility of a queer sexuality, of being neither male nor female (or both), may well be the real issue at the core of the antipornography debate, and, not surprisingly, the gay and lesbian community has been the prime target of attack. Consider Sprinkle's experience of being raided by the Cleveland vice squad when giving her performance "Post-Post Porn Modernist" but never being bothered when she performed live sex shows in that same city.[23] As Butler says, "performing one's gender wrong initiates a set of punishments."[24]

Clearly, the question of punishment is almost completely bracketed in *Virgin Machine* and *My Father Is Coming,* except for the threat of the *non-du-père* to Vicky's bisexuality. As the double entendre of the title makes clear, the panic caused by the father's visit is deflected once he gets it on with Annie. Treut has been taken to task for downplaying the political stakes of gender-bending, but I think the politics of her queer cinema should be discussed in the larger context of how she engages her audience.

Camille Paglia

Let me therefore turn to the third *p*-word of my itinerary, Camille Paglia, who is featured in the twenty-minute sequence, *Dr. Paglia,* the first part of

---

22. Ben and Vicky's positions are similar to those of Wanda and Justine described earlier, which illustrate that there is no "outside" of role-playing.

23. Cf. Williams, "Provoking Agent," 176.

24. Butler, "Performative Acts" 279.

Treut's 1992 compilation documentary, *Female Misbehavior*. Author of the best-selling books *Sexual Personae* (1990), *Sex, Art, and American Culture* (1992) and *Vamps and Tramps: New Essays* (1994), Paglia is well-known for her attacks on American feminism (and on academia in general), which she promotes in her scholarly and journalistic writings and which she performs in numerous, nationwide lectures on college campuses and appearances on talk shows, news shows, and any other show willing to book her. Her argument is rather simple and tailored to the message-oriented workings of the media society on which she thrives. It can be summarized like this: the cultural elite, and American feminism in particular, have retreated into an ivory tower of French theory; their continuing loss of touch with reality has allowed conservative Christian organizations to set the terms for an overdue curricular reform of the humanities. We must revitalize the 1960s cosmic vision of sexual and artistic liberation; political radicalism may not be harnessed by political correctness. Paglia's language is one of paganism, of drives and tribes, that values Dionysian exuberance over "the Apollonian office persona"[25] and organicism and nature over what she calls social constructionism à la Foucault (not surprisingly, she is deeply opposed to Judith Butler's "unpersuasive and jargon-ridden" performance theory quoted earlier).[26]

Discussing Paglia as a further example of Treut's cross-cultural explorations gives a certain twist to the notion of queer here applied, for Paglia's writings on sexuality are very much at odds with scholarship on sexuality and gender of the last twenty years. Hence, queer can be read here to mean something like the German *quer stehen*. An antifeminist feminist who prides herself in her "general obnoxiousness,"[27] Paglia has become a persona-non-grata not only in the academic circles that she attacks but also among radical women activists such as Susie Bright (the Susie Sexpert of *Virgin Machine*) and Pat Califia, a San Francisco lesbian S/M activist, who calls Paglia "repetitious, hateful, and in the end dreadfully dull."[28] This raises the question of why Monika Treut became interested in Camille Paglia and why Paglia now lists Treut as "my most important ally in the international movement for a progressive pro-porn, anti-dogma feminism."[29] Was it the mutual experience of being a lesbian outsider with significant obstacles in the pursuit of their respective careers? (Treut tells us about her problems getting funding for her films in Germany as well as being ignored and attacked by critics, while Paglia struggled, without success, to find her place in American academia.) Was it Paglia's libertarian sexual politics and her endorsement of pornography? Was it her Davidian eagerness to take on the country's most established, Goliath-like feminist scholars? Or was it simply Camille Paglia's refusal to be p-c, understood by many as a provocative gesture to speak one's mind at a

25. Camille Paglia, *Vamps and Tramps* (New York: Vintage, 1994) xii.
26. Ibid. 475.
27. Ibid. 103.
28. Ibid. 465.
29. Ibid. 206f.

time when political correctness is increasingly experienced as a form of (self-) censorship?

Like *Seduction: The Cruel Woman, Virgin Machine,* and *My Father Is Coming, Female Misbehavior* focuses on the radical potential of pornography and its implication for gender performance, two subjects on which Paglia has a lot to say (in *Dr. Paglia* she describes herself as a "butch bottom" who "some weeks of the month . . . feel[s] very female, others very male. I feel I have a sex change every month").[30] Yet, despite the fact that Treut and Paglia agree on many issues, the main use the filmmaker makes of the writer is perhaps more strategic than argumentative. In fact, this is also how Paglia perceives of herself in the film: "The value of my work is not just what I am *saying* but rather that I am breaking up all these bunkered positions."[31] Just as *Virgin Machine* is a polemic response to German antiporn feminists such as Alice Schwarzer, the short *Dr. Paglia* is a polemic attack on a certain kind of feminism that in Paglia's view has become dogmatic and unwilling to learn from its mistakes. Treut herself describes the four pieces that make up *Female Misbehavior* as "a series of politically incorrect portraits of women in post-feminist times."[32] The notion of postfeminism implies for Treut neither that the goals of feminism have been achieved nor that they are irrelevant but that a new kind of feminism has to emerge that would be self-critical of the movement's failures and shortcomings during the 1970s and 1980s.[33] And, like her protagonists, Treut seems to suggest that, regarding these issues, there is more to be learned in the United States than at home because America's puritanical society creates stronger dissenting minorities than Germany.[34]

Hence, like in Treut's three feature films, there is a transatlantic filter implied in *Female Misbehavior* by virtue of the fact that a German director researches American sexual practices. The sexual experiences made by the American Justine in Hamburg, by Dorothee in San Francisco, by Vicky in New York, and the four people portrayed in *Female Misbehavior* "take on an aura of ethnography as we view the 'strange' events from a distance."[35] There is, then, a certain pedagogical or instructional dimension to Treut's films as she adroitly educates the less sexually sophisticated. This educational aspect is underscored both by the narrative (Dorothee's profession is that of a journalist doing research on romantic love) and by the use of real-life sex performers and activists such as Susie Bright, Shelley Mars, and Annie Sprinkle, whose agency in the narrative is often secondary to the message they relate to

30. Ibid. 247.

31. Ibid. 246.

32. Hollis Willis, "Bad Behavior: An Interview with Monika Treut," *Visions* 7 (1992): 12.

33. Cf. Gerd Gemünden, Alice Kuzniar, and Klaus Phillips, "From *Taboo Parlor* to Porn and Passing: An Interview with Monika Treut," *Film Quarterly* 50.3 (1997): 2–12; here 7f.

34. Cf. Fox, "Coming to America," 64.

35. Willis 11.

the viewers. As so often in documentaries of the New German Cinema and after, the lines between fiction and documentary are blurred. In Treut's films the instructional element is offset by humorous elements. *Virgin Machine* and *My Father Is Coming* are comedies that draw much of their laughter from the fact that sexual and cultural difference are explored in an off-hand, entertaining way.[36] Unlike many films on the subject, they completely lack violence; they fail to engage in the portrayal of punishment that for Butler is always connected to a deviant and defiant performance of gender; and they are not sexually very explicit—if they are about pornography, they are rarely pornographic (which has led to criticism from the lesbian community that Treut "doesn't deliver").

It seems to me that, regarding the combination of the educational and the entertaining, there indeed is something to be learned from Camille Paglia. Paglia has been extremely successful in working the media to get her message across, and this message itself consists of a hybrid concoction of art history and popular culture that explores and subverts how we have traditionally conceptualized high and low. We see an example of this in Treut's short in which she interviews Paglia in a museum shortly after having shown her wandering on Forty-second Street in Manhattan, where she is checking out the porn theaters and adult bookshops. In the museum we see Paglia standing next to a large black Egyptian tombstone bearing a hawk, while she explains how as a child she identified with these signs because they suggested a carnivorous and aggressive quality. She then goes on to say that there is an exact correlation between Egyptian signs and advertisement of the late 1940s and 1950s:

> I couldn't read as a child, but I would see images and people doing strange things—you know, people holding a box, or holding a box out like *this* (she demonstrates in the 1950s style of Betty Furness), which later I could read—TIDE SOAP. So I felt since earliest childhood that advertisements were never something that was just popular culture and not to be taken seriously. But rather right from the beginning I saw that there was a connection between ancient pagan culture and the popular culture all around . . . for me the Egyptian hieroglyphics and advertisements are in the same line. And its *true*. As I went on, I learned that the great pharaohs were *advertising* themselves. That's what they were

---

36. It must be added that, in contrast to Treut's explorations of gender, those of culture and nationality remain rather stereotypical, especially of her German characters. Hans is the quintessential Bavarian who comes to New York with a bag of *Weißwürste* smuggled through customs, a "dustbuster," and typical German prejudices about cleanliness and the questionable quality of drinking water abroad. Like many Germans of her generation, Vicky feels insecure about her German national heritage and is reluctant to tell her friend Lisa that she auditioned, and failed to get the part, to play a German tourist.

doing—"I am the greatest, I am the most fabulous." Which they've done now. Five thousand years later, we're still reading their signs.[37]

The connections and incongruities explored here between high art or serious intellectualism and popular culture are rehearsed throughout the film and most visibly indicated by the film's title, *Dr. Paglia,* a very German way to address a critic and writer that denotes learnedness, respect, and sincerity—as does the museum setting—only to witness how Paglia raps with breathtaking speed about lesbian and gay sexualities, pornography, sadomasochism, and the stupidity of American feminism. While much of what Paglia has to say is arrogant, wildly exaggerated, and even demagogic, her performance is funny and outrageous and very much aware of how to create and address an audience. Paglia here embodies her credo that "an elitist leftism is a contradiction in terms,"[38] and I would argue that this, and not Paglia's regressive antifeminism, is the lesson Treut considers most compatible with her own notion of filmmaking.[39] *Virgin Machine* and, especially, *My Father Is Coming* have been successful in crossing over into mainstream audiences through their combination of comedy, pop culture, and a radical sexual agenda—a form of postmodern bricolage that is not afraid to sacrifice aesthetic purity for a chance to reach larger audiences, even if that means drawing criticism from more radical groups that claim that Treut has gone mainstream and sold out. Treut's style can be seen as part of a queer aesthetics that B. Ruby Rich has recently described as "Homo Pomo: there are traces . . . of appropriation and pastiche, irony as well as reworking of history with social constructionism very much in mind. Definitely breaking with older humanist approaches and the films and tapes that accompanied identity politics, these works are irreverent, energetic, alternately minimalist and excessive. Above all, they're full of pleasure."[40] Indeed, the pleasure principle informs both Treut's narratives as well as their exuberant styles. Clearly, Treut's outrageous female characters are having fun, and they are fun to watch. The stories of *Seduction: The Cruel Woman, Virgin Machine,* and *My Father Is Coming* are all about the pleasure of finding out about different sexual orientations and practices, and even the most stereotypical German character, Vicky's father, Hans, is persuaded into some New Age sex with Annie Sprinkle—a rare depiction of sexual pleasure involving those over age sixty.[41] The point bears repetition that Treut's protagonists enjoy their sexu-

37. *Vamps and Tramps* 236f.

38. Ibid. 360.

39. It should be noted that, in her scholarly work on de Sade and Sacher-Masoch, Treut draws heavily on French critics such as Deleuze, Foucault, and Derrida whom Paglia despises.

40. B. Ruby Rich, "Homo Pomo: The New Queer Cinema," *Women and Film* 165f.

41. Even in Fassbinder's *Ali: Fear Eats the Soul,* which I discussed in chapter 4, in which an older cleaning woman falls in love with a young Moroccan car mechanic, Fassbinder spares the audience of showing their lovemaking. An exception is again Rosa von Praunheim, whose *Unsere Leichen leben noch* centers on the sexual and other pleasures of older women.

alities without fear of punishment; where punishment seems to be involved, as in the sadomasochistic sex of *Bondage,* the protagonist Carol makes it clear that bondage makes her feel "very safe."

A similar transgressive pleasure informs the mixed styles of Treut's films. I have already mentioned the intertwining of documentary and feature film elements and the mixed agenda of teaching and *divertissement.* Other intertextual references would include the underground film à la Warhol, which was pioneering in its depiction of gay sexuality and use of nonactors, Warhol's Factory superstars. Like Warhol's films, Treut's underground style often takes on the look of a home movie, defending a postmodern dilettantism of "everybody can do it" in which scenes with dead spots or poor use of nonprofessional actors do not end up on the editing room floor. This style transforms the private into the public, thereby insisting that the personal is political—a credo that is also central to the aesthetics of Rolf Dieter Brinkmann. And there are numerous references to Weimar cinema, with its important tradition of queer cinema, its unsurpassed comedies, and films with a strong social and political agenda—all of which are being taken up by both *My Father Is Coming* and *Virgin Machine.* At the end of *Virgin Machine,* for example, the scene of Dorothee racing on her bicycle offers a rewriting of the famous bike sequence in *Kuhle Wampe.* In Brecht and Dudow's left-wing classic we watched young Boenicke participate in the futile rat race for employment soon to be ended by his suicide. In homage to *Kuhle Wampe* Dorothee, on her bicycle, donning the very same kind of 1920s proletarian-looking hat and a similar black outfit, is filmed much in the same angled shots that focus on the spokes and the turning of the pedals as if to de-emphasize individuality—except that this dyke on a bike is indeed racing toward a better future *because* she has just given up her work as a journalist.

In conclusion, it becomes clear that the queer cinema of Monika Treut questions more than the rigid categories of male and female. As Treut defends the visual pleasures of pornography, as she foregrounds the performance of gender, and as she follows Paglia's anti-elitist collision and collusion of art and popular culture, all kinds of other oppositions start to crumble as well. This postmodern bricolage of multiculturalism and multisexuality can be seen as a striving for the proliferation of difference—yet it also implies the dissolution of a certain German identity. Indeed, her protagonists' eagerness to leave behind, and seemingly without problems, the confining fatherland can be seen as an effacement of national identity that is grafted onto a larger, international identity (a strategy that we encountered already in many of the authors under discussion and which will be analyzed in more detailed in the epilogue). Interestingly, Paglia calls Treut an ally in the "*international* movement for . . . anti-dogma feminism"[42] without specifying the scope of this movement any further. One may wonder if Paglia appeals to Treut pre-

---

42. *Vamps and Tramps* 206; emphasis mine.

New dyke on a bike: Dorothea (Ina Blum) in *The Virgin Machine* (1988).
(Publicity still, First Run Features, New York, NY.)

cisely *because* she is an American (and if Paglia likes Treut because she is *not*). On this issue of nationalities it is also important to note that the two main enablers of transformed identity and sexual discovery—Dominique in *Virgin Machine* and Lisa in *My Father Is Coming*—are both neither American nor German. Dominique is from Uruguay but of Hungarian descent and conveniently speaks German, and Lisa is Puerto Rican but passes as American. It seems that the blurring of nationality is the prerequisite for transforming one's cultural identity. As Treut says about her audience, no matter whether German, American, Australian, French, or Finish, "it is always the same kind of person who likes my films. It's like a big family. They read the same books, they like the same movies, they talk about the same things."[43] In this internationalist frame of reference an imagined community with America is built that has no room for the more troubling sides of urban life in this country. Treut's tales about coming to, coming in, and coming out in America show the utopian potential this country has had and continues to have, for Germans, but one may wonder if this insight does not represent a more accurate description of the country left behind than the one represented on the screen.

---

43. In a conversation with Alice Kuzniar and me in April 1995. This part is not included in the interview cited earlier.

Epilogue: National Identity and Americanization in the Unified Germany

Die schärfsten Kritiker der Elche
waren früher selber welche.

[The harshest critics of the elks
used to be elks themselves.]

—*F. K. Wächter*

A headline in *Der Wochenspiegel* from July 1993 read: "Wir sind wieder wer! Aber wer?" (We are somebody again! But who?). Indeed, the fall of the Wall in 1989 and German unification the following year have had a paradoxical effect on Germans, instilling in them a euphoric sense of national pride but also triggering a deep crisis about precisely what it is that one ought to be proud of. Clearly, the political and social constellation that gave rise to the cultural productions under discussion in this study—the literature and films of what I here call the generation of John Ford and Theodor W. Adorno— has dramatically changed. German unification has meant not only the disappearance of the German Democratic Republic but also of the Federal Republic of Germany as we knew it. In the new Germany questions such as "who is German?" "what is German?" and "where is Germany?" have suddenly become the subject of heated debate.

The sense of crisis is particularly visible in those discussions about national and cultural identity that have taken place during the last years among German intellectuals from both the East and the West. For many 1989 has come to signal yet another "Stunde Null" (Zero Hour), a kind of magical date that allows or calls for a taking stock of German history at the threshold of a new beginning. A generation calling itself the '89ers has risen to challenge those who in the wake of the student protests in 1968 had established themselves—at least in the eyes of the '89ers—as the dominant force in determining the moral and aesthetic concerns of the Federal Republic. With

German unification and the end of the Cold War, the political and cultural context that legitimized the '68ers has disappeared, and it is time, claim the '89ers, to take the country in a new direction.

Not surprisingly, the fight over Germany's future is fought across its past. What has taken place during the last five years is a fierce struggle among German intellectuals who are rewriting the history of the postwar West and East Germanies and the Nazi years. Recent writings by the filmmakers Hans Jürgen Syberberg and Wim Wenders and the playwright and novelist Botho Strauß offer an ambitious and comprehensive reassessment of postwar Germany in order to lay the groundwork for the future unified country—a country where what they perceive to be the ill effects of Westernization and Americanization can be reversed through a recovery of German art, culture, and language. The rhetoric of cultural imperialism, not heard this loudly since the Vietnam War, makes a baffling comeback as an American, or rather Americanized German, culture industry once again becomes a powerful *Feindbild* (projected image of the enemy) against which a German identity must be upheld and resurrected. Furthermore, as the following comparative analysis will show, the generational difference that I have asserted throughout this study between, on the one hand, Syberberg and, on the other, Wenders and Strauss is starting to be erased; now that the '89ers are setting out to replace the '68ers, all those "over thirty," as it were, seem to form one age group fighting for inclusion in the newly emerging group of dominant intellectuals and ideologues.

Contested Memory

Let me begin by saying a few words about nation and nationhood in the German context. After all, these are notions that for several decades had not only been anathema to German intellectuals (with some important exceptions in the late 1980s, such as Martin Walser)[1] but have also been carefully avoided in the official discourse of Bonn, no matter whether the Social Democrats or the Christian Democratic Union were in power. The antinationalist consensus had long been a condition for the successful Westernization of the Federal Republic, and it has also been a driving force for Chancellor Helmut Kohl's advancement of the European Community. Most Germans born during or immediately after the war—those who grew up in the 1950s and early 1960s—were at pains to dissociate themselves from a nation that had organized and executed the Holocaust. The open embrace of American popular culture, for example, was one way to displace a tradition considered complicitous with, or at the very least tainted by, Nazism. As we saw with regard to Wim Wenders, this could even take on the form of replacing Beethoven with the Kinks.

---

1. Cf. Martin Walser, *Über Deutschland reden* (Frankfurt am Main: Suhrkamp, 1988).

Of course, these problems with nationhood and nationality are not exclusively a phenomenon of postwar Germany. After all, Germany did not become a nation in the modern sense until 1871, and throughout the last centuries numerous conflicts in religion, tribal roots, culture, and literature indicate that Germany has always been a much more diverse place than later proponents of a German "race," or *Volk,* would have us believe (which may explain the attraction of such an ideology in the first place). Yet the antinationalist sentiment is a particularly post–World War II phenomenon, and it is especially widespread among intellectuals of the generation that came of age in the late 1960s. Time and again, one finds among them two related strategies intended to dissociate themselves from the fatherland: one is to identify with a foreign minority, very often blacks and Native Americans, and the other is to think of oneself as a European or citizen of the world who in some sense is "beyond" the notion of nationhood. The writer Hans Christoph Buch, for example, prides himself on his multilingual internationalism, for being a "nomadic writer" and an "uprooted cosmopolitan," and even calls himself "ein weißer Neger" (a white Negro) because his grandfather's second marriage was to a Haitian.[2] The filmmaker Herbert Achternbusch, as I have noted, has repeatedly depicted himself as Native American in *Der Komantsche, Heilt Hitler,* and *Hick's Last Stand* and as "the Negro Erwin" in a film of that title. East German playwright Heiner Müller shows a similar gesture of self-marginalization by calling himself a "a perpetual Negro." And rock star and actor Marius Müller-Westernhagen addressed a cheering concert crowd: "I have never believed I am German. We are beyond that. We are citizens of the world."[3] This eagerness to efface the self by identifying with the other is perhaps best summed up in a scene from Percy Adlon's film *Salmonberries* (1993), in which a native from Kotzebue, Alaska, standing in a Berlin pub tries to explain in her rudimentary German that she is an Eskimo—to which the Berliners reply, "We're all Eskimos."

Yet, contrary to what these intellectuals seek, recent events in East and West Germany, as well as in other European countries, show that nationalism is not at all passé. Since unification the long-absent topic has returned with a vengeance.[4] For a brief period after the fall of the Berlin Wall the ques-

---

2. Hans Christoph Buch, *An alle! Reden, Essays und Briefe zur Lage der Nation* (Frankfurt am Main: Suhrkamp, 1994) 130–31.

3. Quoted in Marc Fischer, *After the Wall: Germany, Germans, and the Burdens of History* (New York: Simon and Schuster, 1995) 66.

4. Among the wealth of publications on the issue of Germany and nation, see especially the following: Hans Christoph Buch, *An alle! Reden Essays und Briefe zur Lage der Nation* (Frankfurt am Main: Suhrkamp, 1994); Friedrich Dieckmann, "Die Deutschen und die Nation," *Vom Einbringen: Vaterländische Beiträge* (Frankfurt am Main: Suhrkamp, 1992) 150–69; Françoise Bathélemy and Lutz Winckler, eds., *Mein Deutschland findet sich in keinem Atlas: Schriftsteller aus beiden deutschen Staaten über ihr nationales Selbstverständnis* (Frankfurt am Main: Luchterhand, 1990); Peter Schneider, *Extreme Mittellage: Eine Reise durch das deutsche Nationalgefühl* (Reinbeck: Rowohlt, 1990); Heiner Müller, *Zur Lage der Nation* (Reinbeck: Rowohlt, 1990); and

tion of Germany's future shape seemed to be up for public debate—what would be the name of the new country, its anthem, its capital, its national holiday?—but the Kohl government's rush to unity created a nation that preserved as much of the old Federal Republic as possible. A new nation has been established, but its sense of self remains problematic. This is particularly obvious if we look at the issues out of which a national identity is now being forged: What role will the German military play in and outside of NATO? How should former members of the SED, the East German Communist Party, be treated? How is Germany to deal with problems of immigration and citizenship? What roles will the history of the Third Reich and the memory of the Holocaust play in a future Germany?

The debate about Westernization—and especially Germany's relation to the culture, politics, and economy of the United States—is primarily a displaced discussion about nation and national identity. After World War II the Federal Republic had willingly accepted its position as a buffer zone against the Soviet empire's westward expansion. West Germans quickly learned to take their ideological and political cues from the United States; since Germans wanted nothing more than to forget and to rebuild, American consumerism and the United States' amnesic approach to history were readily emulated. With the end of the Cold War and German unification, Westernization has ceased to be a given. East German intellectuals are apprehensive about the impending import of American consumer culture, which for them seems new and threatening. Some have come to see unification as a takeover in which Americanization will displace a "genuine" (East) German culture. As Heiner Müller stated in 1990: "We'll be submerged by American mass culture, and true culture will suffer. The GDR's old ideological kitsch, which people just ignored, will be replaced by commercial kitsch, which gets much larger and more eager audiences. That's dangerous."[5] Yet also in the West, unification has led to a profound questioning among intellectuals about what role the culture of the United States is to play in a German national identity yet to be molded. Three texts that undertake a revision of Westernization are Hans Jürgen Syberberg's *Vom Unglück und Glück der Kunst in Deutschland nach dem letzten Kriege* (*On the Distress and Fortune of Art in Germany after the Last War* [1990]), Wim Wenders's "Reden über Deutschland" ("Talking about Germany" [1991]), and Botho Strauß's "Anschwellender Bocksge-

---

Jenseits der Nation (Reinbeck: Rowohlt, 1991); Jürgen Habermas, *Die nachholende Revolution* (Frankfurt am Main: Suhrkamp, 1990); Ralf Dahrendorf, "Die Sache mit der Nation," *Merkur* 500 (1990): 823–34; Peter Sloterdijk, *Versprechen auf Deutsch: Rede über das eigene Land* (Frankfurt am Main: Suhrkamp, 1990). In the United States, see Fischer, *After the Wall;* Jeff Peck, "Rac(e)ing the Nation: Is There a German 'Home'?" in *Becoming National,* ed. Geoff Eley and Ronald Grigor Suny (New York: Oxford UP, 1996) 481–92; and also the special issue of *New German Critique* (52 [1991]) on German unification.

5. Quoted in John Ardagh, *Germany and the Germans: After Unification* (London: Penguin, 1991) 482.

sang" (Increasing Tragedy [1993]). They can be seen as examples of what Andreas Huyssen has described as a "contested reorganization of cultural capital and realignment of national memory" in the aftermath of German unification.[6]

Nostalgia for the Nation

Even though the three texts differ significantly in form of address, adopted tone of voice, implied audience, and public response, they share strategies in intertwining history, memory, and a utopian vision: they are all birth-(or rebirth)-of-a-nation narratives in which key operative terms such as *loss* (in Syberberg), *vacuum* (in Wenders), and *retreat from the mainstream* (in Strauß) are linked to a nostalgia that longs for a past while desiring to belong to a better future. We witness in these essays the attempt to rewrite the postwar years and, to some extent, even the history of the Third Reich; in Syberberg and Wenders this is done through personal recollection, which imbues their voices with authenticity at the same time that it justifies selectivity. The nostalgia that motivates these acts of memory operates through sets of binary oppositions that can be found in all three essays—the opposition between own (*eigen*) and foreign (*fremd*); high art and mass culture; and tradition and the hubris of being up-to-date, or what Botho Strauß calls the "hybride Überschätzung der Zeitgenossenschaft."[7]

Hans Jürgen Syberberg's *Vom Unglück und Glück in Deutschland nach dem letzten Kriege,* completed between the fall of the Wall in November 1989 and German unification in October 1990, is the earliest and longest of the three essays to react to German unification. To Syberberg 1990 presents a historic chance to correct the mistakes of the last forty-five years of German history. In his reading the loss of World War II and the defeat of Hitler cleared the way for a modernization and Americanization (two terms that for Syberberg are virtually synonymous) that subsequently led to a degradation of West German art and culture, turning it into a copy of Hollywood superficiality. True German art was diluted, displaced, and driven out. The art of the Federal Republic revels in "the low, the crippled, the sick, the dirty; . . . it praises cowardice, betrayal, crime, prostitution, hatred, lies, vulgarism"[8] and is epitomized by Oskar Mazerath, the self-inflicted dwarf of Günter Grass's novel *The Tin Drum.* Having lost its true art, the country lacks a

---

6. Andreas Huyssen, *Twilight Memories: Marking Time in a Culture of Amnesia* (New York: Routledge, 1995) 4.

7. Botho Strauß, "Anschwellender Bocksgesang," *Der Spiegel* 6 (1993): 202–7; here 207. Reprinted in a longer version in: Heimo Schwilk and Ulrich Schacht, eds., *Die selbstbewußte Nation: "Anschwellender Bocksgesang" und weitere Beiträge zu einer deutschen Debatte* (Berlin: Ullstein, 1995).

8. Hans Jürgen Syberberg, *Vom Unglück und Glück der Kunst in Deutschland nach dem letzten Kriege* (Munich: Matthes and Seitz, 1990) 38.

sense of national and cultural identity, of pride, integrity, and morals. It is marked by a multiple loss: "Natur-Verlust . . . Weltverlust . . . Gottesverlust . . . Ich-Verlust" (loss of nature, universe, God, and self-identity).[9] Now, with the fall of the Wall, West Germany is suddenly given the chance to recover its lost heritage, for in the GDR German culture was preserved in a Stalinist deep-freeze; it is like a sleeping beauty that has risen from its slumber. German unification, Syberberg hopes, will undo American postwar reeducation—"the real separation from which we suffer"[10]—and reinstate Germany as a *Kulturnation* (cultural nation) in Central Europe.

The belief that East Germans are somehow the preservers of a more authentic or intact German identity was shared by many intellectuals in the West—thus their indignation when it became clear that what the majority of Easterners wanted was to participate as quickly as possible in an affluent Western lifestyle. But Syberberg does not really have the GDR in mind when he talks about the rebirth of the German cultural nation; he is thinking of Prussia, the land of Kleist and Kant, and the province of Pommerania, where Syberberg grew up. This Prussia must be conjured up in our imagination as "a counter-image to the accomplished corruption in the West and the bankruptcy in the East."[11] If it is true, as Syberberg already claimed in 1978, that "we live in a country without homeland [*Heimat*],"[12] then the only available *Heimat* is an imaginary one, and the reclaiming of East Germany means tapping into an imagination that can (still) perform this task.

Syberberg's essay is about the redemptive power of art and imagination in service of a national and cultural identity yet to be molded, but art assumes a very disturbing role in Syberberg's argument. In his deeply pessimistic account the postwar German malaise all but eclipses the horrors of the Third Reich and the Holocaust; the real tragedy for Syberberg is not Hitler but what came after him. What is even more disturbing is that he blames Jews for capitalizing on German guilt after the war and for turning guilt into a "business that kills artistic imagination."[13] For Syberberg art—and only art—is the true victim of the Holocaust.

Syberberg's shocking remarks raise the question of to what extent his essay continues or deviates from positions put forth in films such as *Ludwig—Requiem for a Virgin King* (1972), *Karl May* (1974), and *Our Hitler* (1977). Did those who praised him then (which includes the likes of Michel Foucault, Susan Sontag, Russell A. Berman, Leon Wieseltier, Francis Ford Coppola) simply not see the racism and nationalistic hubris, or was it absent? Eric Santner, who has written with admiration on the work of mourning performed in

9. Ibid. 28.
10. Ibid. 128.
11. Ibid. 158.
12. Hans Jürgen Syberberg, *Hitler, ein Film aus Deutschland* (Reinbek: Rowohlt, 1978) 15.
13. Syberberg, *Vom Unglück* 14.

Our Hitler,[14] argues that in his 1990 essay "Syberberg ends up recanting much of his own work."[15] But already in 1981 Fredric Jameson described Syberberg's aesthetics and aestheticism that blames not right-wing nationalists but the leftist critiques of irrationalism for the survival of fascist temptation in the 1960s and 1970s, because, as Syberberg claims, these critiques kept alive the demons of the German psyche by repressing them as a "perverse counter-position."[16] In an insightful recent essay Stephen Brockmann has argued that *Our Hitler* clearly prefigures *Vom Unglück.* What has changed is not so much Syberberg but the political context of Germany:

> While Syberberg's critique of Americanization and pop culture in 1977, in the context of a seemingly permanent German division and almost a decade of social-liberal government under Willy Brandt and Helmut Schmidt, appeared at least to sympathetic foreign critics as a positive and even potentially leftist reclaiming of German national tradition, by 1990, after almost a decade of conservative government under Kohl and the sudden collapse of the Cold War system in Europe, the same positions now meant something entirely different. This time, Syberberg's ideas were condemned at home as cryptofascist while they were largely ignored abroad.[17]

What has changed, according to Brockmann—and what gives Syberberg's essay a different meaning from his films—is the historical position from which he speaks. This question has also been raised with regard to Wenders and Strauß, for their post-Wall essays seem to be significant deviations from their positions in the 1970s and 1980s.

Among the three artists' work discussed here Wim Wenders's plea for a German national identity through an attack on American popular culture is perhaps the most surprising. Whereas Hans Jürgen Syberberg and Botho Strauß have never denied their abhorrence of Hollywood cinema, television, and most other forms of popular culture, Wenders's work has always reflected an ambiguous and highly self-conscious love-hate relationship with the United States that celebrates, rather than obliterates, the creative tensions out of which it arises. Yet his more recent films, *Until the End of the World* (1991), *Faraway, so Close!* (1994), and *Lisbon Story* (1995), as well as his

---

14. Cf. Eric Santner, *Stranded Objects: Mourning, Memory, and Film in Postwar Germany* (Ithaca: Cornell UP, 1990).

15. Eric Santner, "The Trouble with Hitler: Postwar German Aesthetics and the Legacy of Fascism," *New German Critique* 57 (1992): 5–24; here 12.

16. Fredric Jameson, "'In the Destructive Element Immerse': Hans-Jürgen Syberberg and Cultural Revolution," *October* 17 (1981): 99–118; here 99.

17. Stephen Brockmann, "Syberberg's Germany," *German Quarterly* 69.1 (1996): 48–62; here 54.

interviews and writings of the last five years take leave of that tension—a departure that Wenders credits to a changed understanding of his own identity as a "German at heart and a European filmmaker."[18] While Wenders's preoccupation with (his) German identity can be traced back to the mid-1980s, when he returned to Berlin after having spent seven years in the United States, it did not become the center of his work until German unification. In a speech, "Reden über Deutschland" ("Talking about Germany") given on November 10, 1991, the second anniversary of the opening of the Wall, Wenders outlines these changes as an intersection of a personal and national narrative.[19]

Wenders tells us the tale of his adolescent infatuation with American film and comics, his seven-year stay in the United States, and his decision to return to Germany. He tells us of his difficulty of being a German; of his early desire to be someone and somewhere else; of the cultural void left after fascism; of his suspicion of German national culture. For those who know Wenders's films and interviews of the 1970s and early 1980s, none of this is new. What is new, however, is the way in which this autobiography is now tied into the narrative of a newly emerging national identity in post-Wall Germany. What is new, in other words, is how Wenders rewrites the memories that construct his own identity according to events that took place long after he had these experiences. Wenders's narrative is basically one of personal and national loss—and of a possible recovery. The trope most often invoked in Wenders's elegiac speech is that of Germany as a vacuum. For him Germany is a country and nation marked by the repression of history and a failure to come to terms with the past; an absence of a genuine German culture; and a loss of authenticity, especially of authentic images *from* and *about* Germany. While Wenders has always been aware of Germans' troubled self-identity, the vacuum, as he now perceives it, has become apparent only since unification. To fill this vacuum, Wenders claims, one must construct a national identity based on what is genuinely German and has remained unchanged over the last centuries: the German language and particularly German literature.

According to Wenders, the vacuum owes its existence to two important factors: the legacy of the Third Reich and American popular culture. In both cases Germans are seen as the victims; while, during the Third Reich, Germany became "the first country in modern history that has been seduced in

---

18. Wim Wenders, "Talking about Germany," in *The Cinema of Wim Wenders: Image, Narrative, and the Postmodern Condition,* ed. Roger F. Cook and Gerd Gemünden (Detroit: Wayne State UP, 1997) 51–59; here 52.

19. Wenders's speech is part of a series organized by the Kammerspiele Munich and entitled "Über unser Land reden" [Talking about Our Country], which also includes Martin Walser's speech "Über Deutschland reden: Ein Bericht" [Talking about Germany: A Report], first given in 1988. Walser's speech is one of the few examples in which the notion of a unified Germany was addressed *before* the fall of the Wall.

such a horrible fashion by false images and lies,"[20] in the postwar years Wenders and his generation became an "easy prey for . . . American myths."[21] Fascism had discredited much of German culture and almost all sense of national pride and thus created a situation that was easily exploited by American popular culture. As an adolescent, Wenders was infatuated with Mickey Mouse and American films and rock music, which let "your senses extend further and further,"[22] but spending time in the United States led him to realize that the dream was in fact a nightmare. Wenders's experience of feeling the threat of losing his own language while in the United States seems to anticipate the loss of (German) language that marks contemporary Germany. Now that Germany has been united, Wenders seems to imply, it is time that the *Fremdbebilderung* (the state of being totally engulfed by foreign images)[23] and the subsequent "German way of life that is second-, third-, or even fourth-hand" come to an end.[24] The crux of the problem for Wenders is that identity is still being imported and not produced from within, and what matters, therefore, is a return to the German language as the country's most natural resource.

Wenders's speech calls into question much of the postmodern aspect of his earlier work—the effort to work *within* the aporias of high culture and popular culture; the creative use of an aesthetics of displacement; a celebration of the nomadic and fragmented subject.[25] In the 1970s Wenders's films challenged the authority of the written word, yet by the 1990s he "no longer trusts the narrative power of images," and he feels that today images have to be protected by words and stories.[26] My contention is not that Wenders's notion of the *Feindbild(er)*, the inflation of foreign images on German television screens and film theaters, is entirely inaccurate; it is not. In recent years American films have accounted for 75 percent to 85 percent of the German market, whereas German films make up about 10 percent of the domestic exhibition market. As in the United States, more and more people are seeing fewer and fewer films, and only titles by American distributors show real

---

20. Wenders, "Talking about Germany" 57.

21. Ibid. 55.

22. Wim Wenders, *Emotion Pictures: Reflections on the Cinema*, trans. Sean Whiteside (London: Faber and Faber, 1989) 54.

23. Wenders, "Talking about Germany" 59.

24. Ibid. 58.

25. It could be argued that Wenders's turn away from American culture has deprived him of his main artistic topic and has created in his oeuvre the very vaccum that he feels has befallen Germany. His latest features, *Until the End of the World, Faraway, So Close!* and *Lisbon Stories* can be seen as remakes of, or sequels to, *Wrong Move, Wings of Desire,* and *The State of Things* and have had only marginal success with audiences both in Germany and abroad. Particularly *Faraway, So Close!* has been vehemently attacked in the German press and was subsequently pulled from distribution by Wenders.

26. Cook and Gemünden, *Cinema of Wim Wenders* 86.

profits, the only exception being German popular comedies. Since the introduction of cable television in the mid-1980s more and more American programs have been imported to fill the greatly expanded time slots, and the most successful German television programs seem to be the ones that most closely follow the style and genre conventions set by American television. What *is* troublesome in Wenders's account is the way in which he defines German culture exclusively in terms of an opposition to American popular culture. This forces him to describe a German cultural identity in terms of rootedness, authenticity, and purity, qualities that are all, as it were, located outside of history. The eighteenth-century notion of *Kulturnation*—that is, the idea of a shared literature, music, art, and philosophy—that provides a certain cultural identity in lieu of nationhood, is invoked by Wenders with all its cliché-ridden, elitist, and racist implications. As in the past, so now for Wenders, culture becomes the ground on which political battles are (to be) fought.[27] Wenders's notion of *Kulturnation* is problematic because it assumes a homogeneity that does not exist in a de facto way and that becomes especially troublesome when instrumentalized against an overcommitment to Westernization and Americanization. In an ironic rewriting of Wenders's famous statement that his life was saved by rock 'n' roll,[28] Goethe and Kafka have now replaced the Velvet Underground as the real *Subkultur* (counterculture). Wenders may lament that identification is not produced from within but imported from outside, but it becomes obvious that only by creating an outside enemy—American popular culture—can he sustain his search for an inside remedy.

The portrayal of popular culture as an attack on "authentic," "genuine" art and the portrayal of media culture and medialization as an attack on memory are not new in Wenders's work, but the argument has never before been stated in such unambiguous and apodictic terms. The point bears repetition: what I am criticizing here is less Wenders's depiction of the state of things than the remedy he offers. A naive return to the language of the German Romantics as a recuperation of logocentrism is a highly suspect answer to the problem of remembering in postmodern society. What is even more disturbing is the way in which this logocentrism is tied into a new nationalism that wants to undo the effects of Western integration and democracy of the last forty years.

---

27. A further example for the present significance of the *Kulturnation* is that, while the GDR and the FRG hardly ever openly discussed reunification during the last twenty years of their coexistence, there was considerable debate about the question of whether there existed one or two German literatures. With unification the notion of "cultural nation" has been invoked to provide cultural ties across the deep rifts that separate East and West Germans in terms of politics, economics, and history. See, for example, Günter de Bruyn, "Über die deutsche Kulturnation," first published in the *Frankfurter Allgemeine Zeitung,* February 3, 1990; English translation in *New German Critique* 52 (1991): 60–66.

28. Jan Dawson, *Wim Wenders,* trans. Carla Wartenberg (Toronto: Festival of Festivals, 1976) 28.

Both Syberberg's and Wenders's essays about nation and national identity are troublesome and to some extent even ludicrous. One could ask why one should even bother with them, apart from the fact that the authors are internationally respected artists. And, indeed, their publications have gone mostly unnoticed. But the public outcry and heated debate that followed Botho Strauß's essay "Anschwellender Bocksgesang," which presents arguments similar to Wenders and Syberberg, has retrospectively amplified Syberberg's and Wenders's pronouncements. Clearly, Strauß hit a nerve.

It is not easy to summarize what "Anschwellender Bocksgesang" is really about (which further explains the variety of responses it has provoked); rather than being a coherently presented argument, the essay offers a series of observations on what Strauß finds wrong with the politics and culture of contemporary Germany, written in a reflective and convoluted language reminiscent of Heidegger and Rilke and in obvious contrast to the easily consumed pseudorational language of mass media that Strauß despises. Among the three authors Strauß is the one who is most outspoken in his criticism of the generation of 1968 (with which he, Syberberg, and Wenders once identified) and of the general leftist tradition that, in Strauß's view, has shaped postwar Germany. German history after 1945 is "the history of the hatred towards the fathers and a psychopathic anti-fascism."[29] The legacy of the '68ers is a discourse of enlightenment and rationality bereft of moral integrity and artistic ambition: "All the Left will do in the future is participate in the organization of social decay in form of political correctness."[30] According to Strauß, contemporary society is stifled by a "deception of the senses"[31]—the result of the society of spectacle, of mass media, infotainment, television, and so forth. These forms of (non)communication have made dialogue and exchange impossible; they have streamlined the conditions under which discourses are produced, transmitted, and understood. Only a tragedy yet to come—and this is what the title of Strauß's essay (literally, "increasing tragedy") refers to—will bring an end to this situation: "Modernity will not peter out into its postmodern extremities, but rather break off with a culture shock."[32] If Syberberg invokes Kleist and Wagner and Wenders relies on Goethe and Kafka, Strauß conjures up the image of a counterrevolution from the Right in the tradition of Novalis or Rudolf Borchardt to halt the "total dominance of the present."[33] This revolution will not be shown on television, since for the television audience any shock is just another form of entertainment; instead, it will occur at the "magic places of retreat" and through "Abkehr vom Mainstream" (turning one's back on the mainstream).[34]

---

29. Strauß, "Anschwellender Bocksgesang" 204.
30. Strauß, "Der eigentliche Skandal," *Der Spiegel* 16 (1994): 168–69; here 169.
31. Strauß, "Anschwellender Bocksgesang" 206.
32. Ibid. 204.
33. Ibid.
34. Ibid. 206.

The implications for the question of national identity are not as obvious in Strauß as in the two other authors. Strauß, after all, advocates *Einzelgängertum* (the cult of the loner), not national unity. Unlike Syberberg and Wenders, Strauß avoids the tendency to cast the Germans in the role of the victim, emphasizing that the crimes of the Nazis cannot be atoned (*abgearbeitet werden*) in two or three generations. (All those—and there were many—who accused Strauß of paving the way for the neo-Nazis clearly overlooked this important point.) Nor does he see contemporary media culture as merely an American imposition; rather, the media are only the logical consequence of a critical rationalism that lacks imagination and loss of utopian vision. Strauß, like Syberberg and Wenders, does seek "a reconnection to a long tradition," but this tradition is couched in less nationalist terms. Nevertheless, Strauß's essay has become—perhaps against or beyond his intentions—the pièce de résistance of resurgent German nationalism, culminating in the anthology *Die selbstbewußte Nation: "Anschwellender Bocksgesang" und weitere Beiträge zu einer deutschen Debatte* (1994), now in its third edition, which includes essays by Syberberg, Brigitte Seebacher-Brandt, Ernst Nolte, Rainer Zitelmann, Michael Wolffsohn, Alfred Mechtersheimer, and other neoconservatives.

I have argued that it is particularly the issue of Westernization (or an alleged Americanization) across which national identity is now being debated. Syberberg, Wenders, and Strauß all favor a return to German high culture in order to ward off what they perceive as the increasing loss of German identity in the late twentieth century. The *Kulturnation* is invoked once more to provide a sense of belonging and to stem the tide against "imported identification" (Wenders), "the international arbitrariness of multi-cultural media charisma" (Syberberg),[35] and "the inhuman moderation of tragedy through television" (Strauß).[36] Theirs is a nostalgia that is deeply problematic because it invokes a unity that never existed and that has outlived its usefulness as a model for the twenty-first century. The demon of American cultural imperialism conjured up by the three authors has little to do with reality. As Michael Ermarth has argued, for the Germans "Americanization has functioned as one of the indispensable tropes of the 20th century," a "last and still lasting *Lebenslüge.*"[37] The way Syberberg, Strauß, and Wenders employ the term displays the very lack of differentiation and homogenization of which they accuse American mass media. Americanization, to the extent that it is more than a German invention, has always been a complex and reciprocal process, more voluntary and indigenous than usually acknowledged.[38] There is no outside of modernity—a simple truth made obvious by the fact that had

---

35. Syberberg, *Vom Unglück* 14.
36. Strauß, "Anschwellender Bocksgesang" 206.
37. Michael Ermarth, "German Reunification as Self-Inflicted Americanization: Critical Views on the Course of Contemporary German Development," forthcoming.
38. Cf. Dan Diner, *Verkehrte Welten: Antiamerikanismus in Deutschland* (Frankfurt am Main: Eichborn, 1993).

Strauß not published his article in *Der Spiegel*—an instrument of the mass media that he so despises—it would have gone completely unnoticed (which in fact it did when it was published earlier the same year in the literary journal *Der Pfahl*).

In a rather perverse way Americanization as the alleged cause for an instability or even absence of national identity has been linked to the outbreak of xenophobia and violence after 1990. The rhetoric of the lack of identity has been instrumentalized in problematic ways to "explain" xenophobia and violence against foreigners in the unified Germany. As Wenders put it:

> How can we be surprised that there is so much hatred towards foreigners when the residents cannot even define their own country for themselves; when they do not know what their own place in this country is; when in their blind aggression they are not actually defending territory but rather fighting for inclusion in their own country? It seems to me that we are all foreigners here trying to settle an unknown country named Germany.[39]

Not only for Wenders but for many Germans the tendency to empathize with foreigners and to portray oneself as a foreigner has been a popular response after the violent attacks on asylum seekers and Turkish families. On television one could see celebrities wearing T-shirts that said, "Ich bin ein Ausländer" (I'm a foreigner), or wearing buttons that announced, "Mein Freund ist Ausländer" (My friend is a foreigner). Although well intentioned, this show of solidarity attests to a profound uncertainty about how to handle the problem of xenophobia and racism. While empathy and identification are necessary, they harbor the danger of glossing over the real differences between Germans and foreigners without doing anything to diminish them. More important, they can be read as a pretext to excuse xenophobia or at least render it understandable. I am not suggesting that this is Wenders's intention, but his formulations are less than felicitous.

Botho Strauß reads xenophobia somewhat differently from Wenders. For him the many intellectuals who put on a show of solidarity with foreigners after an arson attack are either hypocrites or examples of a repressed German self-hatred (which for him is typical of the '68ers): "Intellectuals are friendly towards what is foreign not because it is foreign but because they are angry against all that is ours, and because they welcome anything that will destroy it."[40] For Strauß racism and xenophobia are " 'sunken' cult passions which originally were sacred and produced order and meaning."[41] If Wenders suggests that we are xenophobic because we don't know who we are, Strauß seems to argue that the problem between Germans and foreigners is that we

---

39. Wenders, "Talking about Germany" 53.
40. Strauß, "Anschwellender Bocksgesang" 203.
41. Ibid. 205.

tend to de-emphasize difference when we should insist on it.[42] In the end Strauß and Wenders are two sides of the same dictum that explains xenophobia as the outcome of an insufficiently developed sense of German identity.

What should be learned from the texts discussed here? Clearly, the antinationalist legacy of the 1970s and 1980s has left the Left totally unprepared to get involved in a discourse about nationhood after 1989 and has thus allowed the Right to set the terms of the discussion. It is simply not possible to claim *Sonderstatus* any more: Germans are not all "Comanches," "Negroes," or "Eskimos." Similarly, statements like Klaus Theweleit's recent plea—"One should allow foreigners into the country only to escape the hell which Germans create when they're by themselves . . . we must achieve the de-Germanization [*Entdeutschung*] of our own *flesh*"[43]—do indeed show the signs of self-hatred Strauß attacks. The image of the German as a heel-clicking fascistoid pater familias that Theweleit paints is just as outmoded as that of Syberberg and Wenders. The German Left continues to underestimate the meaning of national identity for the population at large, a shortcoming that also applies to a certain degree to Jürgen Habermas's plea for a *Verfassungspatriotismus* (constitutional patriotism). One could indeed read Wenders's and Strauß's tales of conversion and revision as strategies for inclusion within the generation of the '89ers, now that the '68ers will apparently have to abdicate leadership. If we do not want to follow them down the path of the *Kulturnation,* we must find alternative models to talk about nation and nationhood. I must confess that a German who claims to be a patriot but not a nationalist reminds me of an alcoholic who promises to have only one drink. But the topic of national identity should no longer be determined by neoconservatives such as Strauß, Syberberg, and Wenders nor by old Leftists like Theweleit who continue to be haunted by the ghosts of the past. What needs to be emphasized contra Strauss *and* Theweleit is the heterogeneity that *already* exists within Germany—both as a consequence of forty years of Western integration but also because the alleged cultural and ethnic homogeneity has always been a fictional construct.

Toward a New German Hollywood?

So far I have portrayed the debate about national identity after 1989 as a decisive turning point for the way in which the generation under discussion here has considered its relationship to the cultural hegemony of the United States in Germany. For someone like Wenders this has meant recanting some of the most interesting aspects of his work. The phenomenon that I am trying

---

42. While I would not go so far as to agree with Ignatz Bubis that Strauß advocates neo-Nazism and anti-Semitism—a charge thar Strauß denies—his desire to shock and provoke has discredited him. Cf. Strauß, "Der eigentliche Skandal," 168–70.

43. Klaus Theweleit, *Das Land, das Ausland heißt: Essays, Reden, Interviews zu Politik und Kunst* (Munich: Deutscher Taschenbuchverlag, 1995) 156.

to describe—discourses of Westernization in contemporary Germany—is characterized, however, not only by the differences I have outlined so far but also by important continuities. Nor have these changes occurred as suddenly as the rhetoric of the "Zero Hour" of 1989 may suggest. To begin with the second point, Wenders's 1985 move from California to Berlin was already understood as a conscious effort to reconnect with German history and culture. *Wings of Desire* (1987), his film about an angel in Berlin who decides to become a human when he falls in love with a circus artist, celebrates Wenders's own version of *Menschwerdung* as *Deutschwerdung,* for the transformation of an astral onlooker into someone who wants to find his own history can easily be read as the homecoming of the prodigal son who in his years abroad has found out where he really belongs. Similarly, Peter Handke's 1984 novel *Langsame Heimkehr* (*Slow Homecoming*) also reflects the diminished fascination with American popular culture noticeable in *Wings of Desire* and which Wenders describes in his 1991 speech. (Incidentally, in this speech Wenders invokes Handke's novel—"the first [German book] after years of only reading in English"[44]—to have initiated his own homecoming to the German language.) The America portrayed in this novel differs significantly from that of *Short Letter, Long Farewell.* For the most part the events of *Slow Homecoming* take place in Alaska, a state Handke considers *not* to be part of the United States, one that is devoid of the paraphernalia of popular culture that litter the earlier novel. When Sorger, the geologist protagonist, spends a few days in New York before returning to Europe, the city is described in terms that bear hardly any resemblance to the semiotic puzzle of *Short Letter;* instead, in keeping with the protagonist's profession, images of nature, rock formations, and geographic patterns determine the look of the metropolis, creating the image of a city outside of human history. In the last scene, on board the airplane to Europe, the novel even bids farewell to its author's greatest passion, the (American) cinema: "The empty screen, which moments ago was glimmering in the sunrise, turned dark."[45] Between Wenders's image of the *Weisse Wand* (white screen) that concludes *Kings of the Road,* a gesture of new beginnings toward a German appropriation of the American cinema,[46] and Handke's black screen, which concludes *Langsame Heimkehr,* we have come full circle.

Yet, just because Handke and Wenders, two of my main witnesses for a creative exploration of cultural imperialism in the 1970s and early 1980s, have turned their back on the United States, this does not mean that the country has lost its significance for the German imagination. Novels continue to be published and films released that attest to an ongoing fascination with

---

44. Wenders, "Talking about Germany" 54.
45. Peter Handke, *Langsame Heimkehr* (Frankfurt am Main: Suhrkamp) 208.
46. Cf. Gerd Gemünden, "On the Way to Language: Wenders's *Kings of the Road*," *Film Quarterly* 15.2 (1991): 13–28.

U.S. culture, history, and geography.[47] American products such as films, television programs, music CDs, fashion, and sports equipment continue to find German consumers and audiences. In fact, the cultural hegemony of the United States was perhaps never as dominant as it is now, but—and this is my point—it is not perceived as such. For West German artists and intellectuals in their twenties and thirties, the import of American culture is not part of a cultural imperialism or an unwanted Americanization but, rather, an accepted part of life. (Interestingly, young East Germans today express the same kind of curiosity and openness for the United States that one found in the West two decades ago,[48] while older Easterners such as Heiner Müller fear an impending American takeover.) For a generation that grew up with the United States at the fingertips of their remote control, that wore Levis and drank Coke, and that will eventually inherit their parents' rock albums, the United States has always been second nature. For many of them American culture never had the sense of being foreign and imposed; its ubiquity and ever-presentness has made it into the uncontested mainstream in music, film, fashion, and fast-food dining. There is evidence that American mass culture has had a homogenizing effect on those age thirty or younger living in Europe and other industrialized countries. As Godfrey Carr and Georgina Paul put it: "Young people in Germany have less to differentiate them from their peers in other industrialized countries than their counterparts of a generation ago. In more general terms, culture is becoming ever more a matter of lifestyle in a manner which transcends national boundaries."[49]

This alleged homogenizing effect of the American way of consuming is somewhat challenged in a 1993 *New York Times* article by William E. Schmidt, "In Europe, America's Grip on Pop Culture Is Fading," who claims that, since the end of the Cold War, American popular culture has lost its stronghold over European youths. According to the report, "America's hegemony over pop culture is being challenged, for the first time in decades, by the emergence of a rival European consciousness among young people, reflected in a very separate sense of music and fashion and even style."[50] Soliciting opinions from young people in Germany, France, Italy, and England, the article portrays Europeans between fifteen and twenty-five as being more fascinated with the diverse cultures of their various European neighbors than

---

47. Some recent writings in this vain include Bodo Morshäuser, *Tod in New York City* (Frankfurt am Main: Suhrkamp, 1995); Franz Böni, *Amerika* (Bern: Erpf, 1992); Michael Scharrang, *Auf nach Amerika!* (Hamburg: Luchterhand, 1992); Jürgen Lodemann, *Amerika überm Abgrund* (Eggingen: Isele, 1992); among recent films, Jan Schütte's, *Auf Wiedersehen, Amerika* (*Bye Bye America* [1995]) deserves to be mentioned.

48. Cf., for example, Christoph Dieckmann, *Oh! Great! Wonderful! Anfänger in Amerika* (Berlin: Links, 1992).

49. Godfrey Carr and Georgina Paul, "Unification and Its Aftermath," in *German Cultural Studies: An Introduction,* ed. Rob Burns (Oxford: Oxford UP, 1995) 325–48; here 345.

50. William E. Schmidt, "In Europe, America's Grip on Pop Culture Is Fading," *New York Times,* 28 March 1993, 3.

with an American culture that by virtue of its ubiquity has become all too familiar and somewhat stale. Even though American culture may continue to determine markets and minds, a fusion of styles has taken place that makes European culture look more diverse and varied. According to Schmidt, MTV Europe is a case in point: modeled after the successful American television channel, it offers its European teenage viewers music and fashion that their American counterparts would hardly recognize.

While I would agree with Schmidt that an interesting blend of American and European styles has taken place during the last ten years, I would insist that American popular culture has not ceased to be the single most important influence. Sometimes the fusion of styles has led to very interesting developments such the emergence of German hiphop and rap music; at others it has produced merely bad copies, such as the creation of Felix, a European film award modeled after its famous cousin Oscar. On the whole, the issue of American cultural hegemony in Europe is more complex than Schmidt describes. The development of German film from the mid-1980s onward is one example that shows how U.S. culture has penetrated on a much deeper level. What happened then in Germany was the disappearance of the *Autorenfilm* and the concomitant rise of European art film and German genre film. For the former kind of cinema I will again use Wenders as my witness, but recent films by Bernardo Bertolucci and the Tavianni brothers in Italy, Bertrand Tavenier in France, Krzysztoff Kieslowski and Agnieska Holland in Poland, and Volker Schlöndorff in Germany would serve equally well to make my point. Even though Wenders understood his return to Berlin on a personal level as a search for the lost German in him, professionally he sought to inscribe himself within a European tradition of filmmaking. For him a European identity—not a German identity—could be the only viable resistance to an impending American takeover of Germany and Europe:

> Only the European cinema can today still uphold a certain dignity and ethics in the midst of the wild cacophony of images; only this cinema can stop the avalanche threatening to smother us in this age of electronic images, of satellite and cable communication. Against this avalanche, which will bestow on us the same loss of reality and identity that dominates American TV, we have one remedy—our European images, our communal art and language, the European cinema which needs to be preserved and protected.[51]

Beyond tapping into a European tradition of filmmaking, *Euro-Film* means for Wenders a form of film production and distribution in which several national cinemas pool their resources in order to be able to compete, at least to a certain extent, with the technical sophistication of American big budget

---

51. Wenders, *Act of Seeing* 181.

films. Yet, as the financial failure and mixed critical reviews of his own French-German-Australian coproduction *Until the End of the World* showed, it was not enough to offer audiences a hodgepodge, science fiction, road movie, thriller dressed up as a European art film with an international cast. The yet unresolved problem that this film spells out is how to tap into the rich but very diverse traditions of European filmmaking without erasing specific national charms and styles—something that international coproductions too often seem to demand.

On the German market Euro-Films have not had much of an impact. The more significant displacement of the *Autorenfilm* came through the revival of genre film, a development that was inaugurated by the surprise success of Doris Dörrie's *Männer . . .* (*Men* [1985]) and that has climaxed in the recent boom of German comedies from Munich. At first sight tremendously popular films such as *Abgeschminkt* (1993), *Keiner liebt mich* (*Nobody Loves Me* [1995]), *Der bewegte Mann* (*Maybe, Maybe Not* [1994]), *Das Stadtgespräch* (1995), *Männerpension* (1996), *Das Superweib* (1996) or *Knocking on Heaven's Door* (1997), and several others seem to have less to do with the American cinema than Wenders's road movies or Fassbinder's gangster films or melodramas. These are films, after all, that almost exclusively take place in Germany (many of them in Munich) and that have as their protagonists middle-class women or men in their thirties who suffer through some relationship crisis (or what in Germany is referred to as *Beziehungskistendrama*). Many of these films draw their humor from exploiting the effects of the women's liberation movement on the male psyche, seemingly a particularly German predicament (or how else are we to explain the ubiquity of the topic?). While Wenders and Fassbinder were at pains to foreground the problematic tension between the *Autorenfilm* and American culture industry through plot, acting, mise-en-scène, stylization, music, etc., the contemporary Munich comedies strike the viewer as "purely" German. But in important ways the directors and producers of these films were willing to learn from Hollywood to a degree that the *Autorenfilmer* never were. Filmmakers such as Sönke Wortmann, Doris Dörrie, Katharina von Garnier, and Sherry Hormann have stayed clear of a mode of filmmaking in which the director's responsibilities would also include writing and producing and sometimes even editing, acting, and promoting. Instead, following the model of the American film industry, there has been a clear division of labor between directors, writers, and producers, and the filmmakers have been careful not to eclipse the actors and actresses as the real stars of the film (such as the emerging starlets Katja Riemann and Jenny Elvers). More credit is now given to high professional standards in filming and editing, and particularly to scriptwriting, a specialization virtually nonexistent among *Autorenfilmer*. With their fast editing, stylized interiors, witty dialogues, well-paced plot development, and a strong emphasis on entertainment rather than consciousness-raising, these German comedies do indeed come very close to the Hollywood cinema they seek to emulate. Their surprising and enormous success with German audiences confirms that they speak a film language with which German viewers are very familiar. Yet, while these films give their audiences the comforting feeling of watching a "well-made and entertaining German film" (long believed to be an oxymoron), they are in many ways more American than *Paris, Texas.* It is an irony that makes perfect sense that these "Americanized" films have so far not fared well with American audiences—not because humor doesn't travel but because they do not offer Americans anything that could not also be found at home. In fact, the attraction of the *Autorenfilm* was that it showed American viewers what their country looks like in the skewed perspective of those Germans who believed themselves to have grown up in the fifty-first state of the nation. This tension is completely absent in most German films from the 1990s. The German Hollywood of Munich comedies is a far cry from what Fassbinder had in mind when he first coined the term.

The example of the contemporary German cinema illustrates a point that goes also for literature and other fields of creative production: the discourse of colonization and cultural imperialism—no matter how accurate these terms really are—which shaped German cinema and literature from the late 1960s to the mid 1980s, has largely disappeared. Wenders's, Strauß's, and Syberberg's recent indictment of Westernization and the (American) culture industry are an exception that confirms this rule. Their outcry may have been loud, but it had little echo. Strauß may have created a media scandal, but it has afforded him little more than the proverbial fifteen minutes in the limelight. Indeed, the scandal may have only furthered the (self-)marginalization so valued by him and Syberberg. The fact that a huge public response to "Anschwellender Bocksgesang" became possible *only* because Strauß (re)published it in *Der Spiegel* clearly establishes the irony of the situation: it confirms Strauß's argument that media culture determines the rules of public debate, but it also demonstrates the inescapability from the rules.

As we approach the new millennium, it remains to be seen what future changes the discourse of cultural imperialism will undergo. Is the development of the last decade yet another swing of the pendulum of pro- and anti-American sentiment that has been so persistent throughout the twentieth century, or does it mark the disappearance of the pendulum altogether? Has the end of the Cold War also terminated the German self-perception as colony of the United States, or has the U.S. cultural hegemony in Germany and Austria entered a phase of near invisibility and therefore heightened performance, a state of "mission accomplished"? As new writers and filmmakers are emerging—the children of the children of Ford and Adorno—it will be well worth our time to follow their position within an increasingly internationalized world of cultural production.

Bibliography

Achternbusch, Herbert. *Die Alexanderschlacht.* Frankfurt am Main: Suhrkamp, 1971.

———. *Der Komantsche.* Heidelberg: Wunderhorn, 1977.

———. *Die Olympiasiegerin.* Frankfurt am Main: Suhrkamp, 1982.

———. *Das letzte Loch.* Frankfurt am Main: Suhrkamp, 1984.

———. *Die Atlantikschwimmer.* Frankfurt am Main: Suhrkamp, 1986.

———. *Mixwix.* Cologne: Kiepenheuer and Witsch, 1990.

———. *Wohin.* Frankfurt am Main: Suhrkamp, 1991.

———. *Es ist niemand da.* Frankfurt am Main: Fischer, 1992.

———. *Das Buch Arschi.* Stuttgart: Hatje, 1994.

———. *Hundstage.* Frankfurt am Main: Fischer, 1995.

———. *Die Einsicht der Einsicht: Theaterstücke.* Frankfurt am Main: Fischer, 1996.

Adelson, Leslie. "Subjectivity Reconsidered: Botho Strauss and Contemporary West German Prose." *New German Critique* 30 (1983): 3–59.

Adorno, Theodor W. "Fernsehen als Ideologie." *Eingriffe.* Frankfurt am Main: Suhrkamp, 1963. 81–98.

———. "Kann das Publikum wollen?" In *Vierzehn Mutmaßungen über das Fernsehen: Beiträge zu einem aktuellen Thema.* Ed. Anne Rose Katz. Munich: Deutscher Taschenbuch Verlag, 1963. 55–60.

———. "Prolog zum Fernsehen." *Eingriffe.* Frankfurt am Main: Suhrkamp, 1963. 69–80.

———. "The Culture Industry Reconsidered." Trans. Anson G. Rabinbach. *New German Critique* 6 (1975): 12–19.

———. "Television and the Patterns of Mass Culture." In *Television: The Critical View.* Ed. Horace Newcomb. New York: Oxford UP, 1976. 239–59.

———. *The Culture Industry: Selected Essays on Mass Culture.* Ed. J. M. Bernstein. London: Routledge, 1991.

Adorno, Theodor W., and Max Horkheimer. *The Dialectics of Enlightenment.* Trans. John Cumming. London: Allen Lane, 1973.

Alms, Barbara. "Triviale Muster—'hohe' Literatur: Elfriede Jelineks frühe Schriften." *Umbruch* 1 (1987): 31–35.

Attali, Jacques. *Noise: The Political Economy of Music.* Trans. Brian Massumi. Minneapolis: U of Minnesota P, 1985.

Barthes, Roland. *Mythologies.* Trans. Annette Lavers. New York: Farrar, 1972.

———. "That Old Thing, Art . . ." In *Post-Pop Art.* Ed. Paul Taylor. Cambridge, MA: MIT P, 1989. 21–31.

Bartmann, Christoph. "'Der Zusammenhang ist möglich': *Der kurze Brief zum langen Abschied* im Kontext." In *Peter Handke.* Ed. Raimund Fellinger. Frankfurt am Main: Suhrkamp, 1985. 114–39.

Bathrick, David. "Inscribing History, Prohibiting and Producing Desire: Fassbinder's *Lili Marleen.*" *New German Critique* 63 (1994): 35–53.

Baudrillard, Jean. *Simulations.* Trans. Paul Foss, Paul Patton, and Philip Beitchman. New York: Semiotext(e), 1983.

———. *Selected Writings.* Ed. Mark Poster. Stanford: Stanford UP, 1988.

———. *America.* Trans. Chris Turner. New York: Verso, 1988.

Baumgart, Reinhard. "Vorwärts, zurück in die Zukunft." In *Über Peter Handke.* Ed. Michael Scharang. Frankfurt am Main: Suhrkamp, 1972.

Bauschinger, Sigrid, Horst Denkler, and Wilfried Malsch, eds. *Amerika in der deutschen Literatur: Neue Welt—Nordamerika—USA.* Stuttgart: Kohlhammer, 1975.

Beicken, Peter. "'Neue Subjektivität': Zur Prosa der siebziger Jahre." In *Deutsche Literatur in der Bundesrepublik seit 1965.* Ed. Paul Michael Lützeler and Egon Schwarz. Königstein: Athenäum, 1980. 164–81.

Bengel, Michael, ed. *Johnsons Jahrestage.* Frankfurt am Main: Suhrkamp, 1985.

Benz, Wolfgang, ed. *Die Geschichte der Bundesrepublik Deutschland.* Vol. 4: *Kultur.* Frankfurt am Main: Fischer, 1989.

Berg, Gretchen. "Nothing to Lose: An Interview with Andy Warhol." In *Andy Warhol: Film Factory.* Ed. Michael O'Prey. London: BFI, 1989. 54–61.

Berman, Rusell A. "The Recipient as Spectator: West German Film and Poetry of the Seventies." *German Quarterly* 55 (1982): 499–511.

———. "Language and Image: Cinematic Aspects of Contemporary German Prose." In *Film und Literatur: Literarische Texte und der neue deutsche Film.* Ed. Sigrid Bauschinger, Susan L. Cocalis, and Henry A. Lea. Bern: Francke, 1984. 210–29.

———. "Konsumgesellschaft: Das Erbe der Avantgarde und die falsche Aufhebung der ästhetischen Autonomie." Trans. Birgit Diefenbach. In *Postmoderne: Alltag, Allegorie und Avantgarde.* Ed. Christa and Peter Bürger. Frankfurt am Main: Suhrkamp, 1987. 56–71.

Bloch, Ernst. "Non-Synchronism and the Obligation to Dialectics." Trans. Mark Ritter. *New German Critique* 11 (1977): 22–38.

Blum, Heiko. "Chronik der laufenden Ereignisse: Gespräch mit Peter Handke." In *Über Peter Handke.* Ed. Michael Scharang. Frankfurt am Main: Suhrkamp, 1972. 80–84.

Bohrer, Karl Heinz. "Die drei Kulturen." In *Stichworte zur 'Geistigen Situation der Zeit,* vol. 2: *Politik und Kultur.* Ed. Jürgen Habermas. Frankfurt am Main: Suhrkamp, 1979. 636–69.

———. "Die neue Kultfigur." *Frankfurter Allgemeine Zeitung,* 30 March 1981, 22.

Boujut, Michel. *Wim Wenders.* Paris: Edilig, 1983.

Brockmann, Stephen. "Syberberg's Germany." *German Quarterly* 69.1 (1996): 48–62.

Buchka, Peter. *Augen kann man nicht kaufen: Wim Wenders und seine Filme.* Frankfurt am Main: Fischer, 1985.

Bürger, Christa, and Peter Bürger, eds. *Postmoderne: Alltag, Allegorie und Avantgarde.* Frankfurt am Main: Suhrkamp, 1987.

Bürger, Peter. *Theory of the Avant-Grade.* Trans. Michael Shaw. Minneapolis: U of Minnesota P, 1984.

Bullivant, Keith, ed. *After the "Death" of Literature: West German Writing of the 1970s.* Oxford: Berg Publishers, 1989.

Burns, Rob, ed. *German Cultural Studies: An Introduction.* Oxford: Oxford UP, 1995.

Butler, Judith. *Gender Trouble: Feminism and the Subversion of Identity.* New York and London: Routledge, 1990.

———. "Performative Acts and Gender Constitution: An Essay in Phenomenology and Feminist Theory." In *Performing Feminisms: Feminist Critical Theory and Theatre.* Ed. Sue-Ellen Case. Baltimore: Johns Hopkins UP, 1990. 270–82.

———. "Imitation and Gender Insubordination." In *Inside/Out: Lesbian Theories, Gay Theories.* Ed. Diana Fuss. New York: Routledge, 1991. 13–31.

Brinkmann, Rolf Dieter. "Anmerkungen zu meinem Gedicht 'Vanille.'" *März Texte 1* (1969): 141–44.

———. *Westwärts 1 and 2.* Reinbek: Rowohlt, 1975.

———. *Rom, Blicke.* Reinbek: Rowohlt, 1979.

———. *Standphotos.* Reinbek: Rowohlt, 1980.

———. *Der Film in Worten.* Reinbek: Rowohlt, 1982.

———. *Eiswasser an der Guadelupe Str..* Reinbek: Rowohlt, 1985.

Buch, Hans Christoph. *Kritische Wälder: Essays, Kritiken, Glossen.* Reinbek: Rowohlt, 1972.

———. *Der Herbst des großen Kommunikators: Amerikanisches Journal.* Frankfurt am Main: Suhrkamp, 1986.

———. *Waldspaziergang: Unpolitische Betrachtungen zu Literatur und Politik.* Frankfurt am Main: Suhrkamp, 1987.

———. *Die Nähe und die Ferne: Frankfurter Vorlesungen.* Frankfurt am Main: Suhrkamp, 1991.

———. *An alle! Reden, Essays und Briefe zur Lage der Nation.* Frankfurt am Main: Suhrkamp, 1994.

Byars, Jackie. *All That Hollywood Allows: Re-reading Gender in 1950s Melodrama.* Chapel Hill: U of North Carolina P, 1991.

"Bye-Bye, USA." *Probleme des Klassenkampfs* (special U.S. issue) 19.1 (1989).

Calandra, Denis. "The Antitheater of Rainer Werner Fassbinder." In *Plays.* Ed. and trans. Denis Calandra. New York: PAJ Publications, 1992. 9–18.

Cobbs, Alfred L. *The Image of America in Postwar German Literature: Reflections and Perceptions.* Bern: Peter Lang, 1982.

Collins, Jim. *Uncommon Cultures: Popular Culture and Post-Modernism.* New York and London: Routledge, 1989.

Cook Roger, and Gerd Gemünden, eds. *The Cinema of Wim Wenders: Image, Narrative, and the Postmodern Condition.* Detroit: Wayne State UP, 1997.

Copjec, Joan, ed. *Shades of Noir.* New York: Verso, 1993.

Corrigan, Timothy. "The Realist Gesture in the Films of Wim Wenders: Hollywood and the New German Cinema." *Quarterly Review of Film Studies* 5.2 (1980): 205–16.

———. *New German Cinema: The Displaced Image.* Austin: Texas UP, 1983.

———. "Cinematic Snuff: German Friends and Narrative Murders." *Cinema Journal* 24.2 (1985): 9–18.

————. *A Cinema without Walls: Movies and Culture after Vietnam.* New Brunswick, NJ: Rutgers UP, 1991.

————. "The Temporality of Place, Postmodernism, and the Fassbinder Texts." *New German Critique* 63 (1994): 139–54.

————, ed. *The Films of Werner Herzog: Between Mirage and History.* New York: Methuen, 1986.

Covino, Michael. "Wim Wenders: A Worldwide Homesickness." *Film Quarterly* 31 (1977): 9–19.

Dawson, Jan. *Wim Wenders.* Trans. Carla Wartenberg. Toronto: Festival of Festivals, 1976.

De Certeau, Michel. *The Practice of Everyday Life.* Trans. Steven F. Rendall. Berkeley: U of California P, 1984.

Diner, Dan. *Verkehrte Welten: Antiamerikanismus in Deutschland.* Frankfurt am Main: Eichborn, 1993.

Doanne, Mary Ann. *The Desire to Desire: The Women's Film of the 1940s.* Bloomington: Indiana UP, 1987.

Doss, Erika L. "Edward Hopper, "Nighthawks", and Film Noir." *Post Script.* 2.2 (1983): 14–36.

Doty, Alexander. *Making Things Perfectly Queer: Interpreting Mass Culture.* Minneapolis: U of Minnesota P, 1993.

————. "There Is Something Queer Here." In *Out in Culture: Gay, Lesbian, and Queer Essays on Popular Culture.* Ed. Corey K. Creekmur and Alexander Doty. Durham: Duke UP, 1995. 71–90.

Drews, Jörg. "Welt ohne Fernsehen." *Merkur* 33.6 (1979): 593–97.

————, ed. *Herbert Achternbusch.* Frankfurt am Main: Suhrkamp, 1982.

Durançon, Jean. "Entretien avec Wim Wenders." *Camera/Stylo* (August 1987): 101–6.

Durzak, Manfred. *Das Amerikabild in der deutschen Gegenwartsliteratur: Historische Voraussetzungen und aktuelle Beispiele.* Stuttgart: Kohlhammer, 1979.

————. *Peter Handke und die deutsche Gegenwartsliteratur: Narziß auf Abwegen.* Stuttgart: Kohlhammer, 1982.

Dworkin, Andrea. "Against the Male Flood: Censorship, Pornography, and Equality." *Harvard Women's Law Journal* 8 (1985): 1–23.

Eco, Umberto. *Travels in Hyperreality: Essays.* Trans. William Weaver. San Diego, New York, and London: Harcourt, 1990.

Ellwood, David W., and Rob Kroes, eds. *Hollywood in Europe: Experiences of a Hegemony.* Amsterdam: VU UP, 1994.

Elm, Theo. "Die Fiktion eines Entwicklungsroman: Zur Erzählstrategie in Peter Handkes Roman *Der kurze Brief zum langen Abschied.*" *Poetica* 6 (1974): 353–77.

Elsaesser, Thomas. "Achternbusch and the German Avant-Garde." *Discourse* 6 (1983): 92–112.

————. "Germany's Imaginary America: Wim Wenders and Peter Handke." In *European Cinema Conference Papers.* Ed. Susan Hayward. Birmingham: Aston UP, 1984. 31–52.

————. "American Graffiti und Neuer Deutscher Film: Filmemacher zwischen Avantgarde und Postmoderne." In *Postmoderne: Zeichen eines kulturellen Wandels.* Ed. Andreas Huyssen and Klaus Scherpe. Reinbek: Rowohlt, 1986. 302–28.

————. "Primary Identification and the Historical Subject: Fassbinder and Germany." In *Narrative, Apparatus, Ideology: A Film Theory Reader.* Ed. Philip Rosen. New York: Columbia UP, 1986. 539–45.

———. *New German Cinema: A History.* New Brunswick: Rutgers UP, 1989.

———. "From Anti-Illusionism to Hyper-Reaslim: Bertolt Brecht and Contemporary Film." In *Re-interpreting Brecht: His Influence on Contemporary Drama and Film.* Ed. Pia Kleber and Colin Visser. Cambridge: Cambridge UP, 1990. 170–85.

———. "Historicizing the Subject: A Body of Work?" *New German Critique* 63 (1994): 11–33.

Enzensberger, Hans M. "On Leaving America." *New York Review of Books,* 29 February 1968, 31–32.

———. "Gemeinplätze, die Neueste Literatur betreffend." *Kursbuch* 15 (1968): 187–97.

———. "Baukasten zu einer Theorie der Medien." *Kursbuch* 20 (1970): 159–86.

———. "USA: Organisationsfrage und revolutionäres Subjekt. Ein Gespräch mit Herbert Marcuse." *Kursbuch* 22 (1971): 45–60.

———. "Die Aporien der Avantgarde." *Einzelheiten II: Poesie und Politik.* Frankfurt am Main: Suhrkamp, 1984. 50–80.

———. "Das Nullmedium oder Warum alle Klagen über das Fernsehen gegenstandslos sind." *Mittelmaß und Wahn: Gesammelte Zerstreuungen.* Frankfurt am Main: Suhrkamp, 1991. 89–103.

———. "Ausblick auf den Bürgerkrieg." *Der Spiegel* 25 (1993): 170–75.

Ermarth, Michael, ed. *America and the Shaping of German Society, 1945–1955.* Providence, RI: Berg, 1993.

———. "German Reunification as Self-Inflicted Americanization: Critical Views on the Course of Contemporary Development." Forthcoming.

Farell, Tom. "Nick Ray's German Friend Wim Wenders." *Wide Angle* 5.4 (1983): 60–67.

Fassbinder, Rainer Werner. *Filme befreien den Kopf: Essays und Arbeitsnotizen.* Ed. Michael Töteberg. Frankfurt am Main: Fischer, 1984.

———. *Die Anarchie der Phantasie: Gespräche und Interviews.* Ed. Michael Töteberg. Frankfurt am Main: Fischer, 1986.

———. *The Anarchy of the Imagination: Interviews, Essays, Notes.* Ed. Michael Töteberg and Leo A. Lensing. Trans. Krishna Winston. Baltimore: Johns Hopkins UP, 1992.

Fauser, Jörg. *Gedichte.* Ed. Carl Weissner. Hamburg: Rogner und Bernhard bei Zweitausendeins, 1990.

———. *Blues für Blondinen: Essays zur populären Kultur.* Ed. Carl Weissner. Hamburg: Rogner und Bernhard bei Zweitausendeins, 1990.

Fiddler, Allyson. "There Goes That Word Again, or Elfriede Jelinek and Postmodernism." In *Elfriede Jelinek: Framed by Language.* Ed. Jorum B. Johns and Katherine Arens. Riverside, CA: Ariadne P, 1995. 129–49.

Fiedl, Konstanze. "'Echt sind nur wir!' Realismus und Satire bei Elfriede Jelinek." In *Elfriede Jelinek.* Ed. Kurt Bartsch and Günter Höfler. Graz: Droschl, 1991. 57–77.

Fiedler, Leslie. "Cross the Border—Close the Gap." *Collected Essays.* 2 vols. New York: Stein, 1971. 2:461–85.

———. *What Was Literature: Class Culture and Mass Society.* New York: Simon and Schuster, 1984.

Fischer, Marc. *After the Wall: Germany, Germans, and the Burdens of History.* New York: Simon and Schuster, 1995.

Fiske, John. *Understanding Popular Culture.* Boston: Unwin Hyman, 1989.

Foster, Hal, ed. *The Anti-Aesthetic: Essays on Postmodern Culture.* Port Townsend, WA: Bay P, 1983.

Fox, Steve. "Coming to America: An Interview with Monika Treut." *Cineaste* 19.1 (1993): 63–64.

Friedberg, Anne. *Window Shopping: Cinema and the Postmodern.* Berkeley: U of California P, 1993.

Frieden, Sandra, Richard McCormick, Vibeke R. Petersen, and Laurie Melissa Vogelsang, eds. *Gender and German Cinema: Feminist Interventions.* 2 vols. Providence: Berg, 1993

Galinsky, Hans. *Amerikanisch-deutsche Sprach- und Literaturbeziehungen.* Frankfurt am Main: Athenäum, 1972.

Gedron, Bernard. "Theodor Adorno Meets the Cadillacs." In *Studies in Entertainment: Critical Approaches to Mass Culture.* Ed. Tania Modleski. Bloomington: Indiana UP, 1986. 18–36.

Geduldig, Gunter, and Marco Saguarno, eds. *Too Much: Das lange Leben des Rolf Dieter Brinkmann.* Aachen: Alano, 1994.

Geist, Kathe. "West Looks East: The Influence of Yasujiro Ozu on Wim Wenders and Peter Handke." *Art Journal* (Fall 1983): 234–39.

———. *The Cinema of Wim Wenders: From Paris, France to "Paris, Texas."* Ann Arbor: UMI Research P, 1988.

Gemünden, Gerd. "On the Way to Language: Wenders' *Kings of the Road,*" *Film Criticism* 15.2 (1991): 13–28.

———. "Remembering Fassbinder in a Year of Thirteen Moons." *New German Critique* 63 (1994): 3–9.

Gemünden, Gerd, and Michael Töteberg, eds. *Wim Wenders: Einstellungen.* Frankfurt am Main: Verlag der Autoren / Atlas, 1993.

Gemünden, Gerd, Alice Kuzniar, and Klaus Phillips. "From *Taboo Parlor* to Porn and Passing: An Interview with Monica Treut." *Film Quarterly* 50.3 (1997): 2–12.

Gersch, Wolfgang. *Film bei Brecht: Bertolt Brechts praktische und theoretische Auseinandersetzung mit dem Film.* Berlin: Henschel, 1975.

Gitlin, Todd. "Postmodernism Defined, at Last!" *Utne Reader* (July–August 1989): 52–61.

Glaser, Hermann. *Die Kulturgeschichte der Bundesrepublik Deutschland: Zwischen Protest und Anpassung, 1968–1989.* Frankfurt am Main: Fischer, 1990.

Goodrich, Lloyd. *Edward Hopper.* New York: Harry N. Abrams, 1971.

Grafe, Frieda, et al. *Wim Wenders.* Munich: Hanser, 1992.

Grant, Barry Keith, ed. *Film Genre Reader.* Austin: U of Texas P, 1988.

Grimm, Reinhold, and Jost Hermand. *High and Low Cultures: German Attempts at Mediation.* Madison: U of Wisconsin P, 1994.

Gross, Thomas. *Alltagserkundungen: Empirisches Schreiben in der Ästhetik und in den Materialbänden Rolf Dieter Brinkmanns.* Stuttgart: Metzler, 1993.

Gürtler, Christa, ed. *Gegen den schönen Schein: Texte zu Elfriede Jelinek.* Frankfurt am Main: Verlag Neue Kritik, 1990.

Habermas, Jürgen. *Die Neue Unübersichtlichkeit.* Frankfurt am Main: Suhrkamp, 1985.

Hachmeister, Lutz. "Der Gesamtschuldner: Das Fernsehen als Antipode intellektueller Orthodoxie." *Merkur* 534–35 (1993): 841–53.

Hall, Stuart. "Cultural Identity and Cinematic Representation." In *Black British Cultural Studies: A Reader,* ed. Houston A. Baker, Jr., Manthia Diawara, Ruth H. Lindeborg. Chicago: U of Chicago P, 1996. 210–22.

Handke, Peter. *Der kurze Brief zum langen Abschied.* Frankfurt am Main: Suhrkamp, 1972.

———. *Ich bin ein Bewohner des Elfenbeinturms.* Frankfurt am Main: Suhrkamp, 1972.

———. *Das Gewicht der Welt.* Frankfurt am Main: Suhrkamp, 1979.

———. *Die Lehre der Sainte-Victoire.* Frankfurt am Main: Suhrkamp, 1980.

———. *Der Chinese des Schmerzes.* Frankfurt am Main: Suhrkamp, 1983.

———. *Die Wiederholung.* Frankfurt am Main: Suhrkamp, 1989.

———. *Aber ich lebe nur von den Zwischenräumen: Ein Gespräch, geführt von Herbert Gamper.* Frankfurt am Main: Suhrkamp, 1990.

———. *Versuch über die Jukebox.* Frankfurt am Main: Suhrkamp, 1990.

Hansen, Miriam. "Introduction to Adorno's 'Transparencies on Film' (1966)." *New German Critique* 24–25 (1981–82): 186–98.

Hartung, Harald. "Lyrik der 'Postmoderne': Vier Beispiele zu einer Ästhetik der Oberfläche." In *Abhandlungen aus der Pädagogischen Hochschule Berlin.* Ed. Walter Heistermann. Berlin: Colloquium Verlag, 1974. 303–28.

Hassan, Ihab. *The Postmodern Turn: Essays in Postmodern Theory and Culture.* Columbus: Ohio State UP, 1987.

Hauser, Arnold. *The Social History of Art.* 4 vols. Trans. Stanley Godman. New York: Vintage, 1958.

Hebdige, Dick. *Subculture: The Meaning of Style.* London and New York: Routledge, 1979.

———. *Hiding in the Light: On Images and Things.* London and New York: Routledge, 1988.

Heimann, Bodo, and Angela Kandt. "Film und deutsche Gegenwartsliteratur." *Deutsche Gegenwartsliteratur: Ausgangspositionen und aktuelle Entwicklungen.* Stuttgart: Reclam, 1981. 424–43.

Hermand, Jost. "Pop oder die These vom Ende der Kunst." In *Die deutsche Literatur der Gegenwart: Aspekte und Tendenzen.* Ed. Manfred Durzak. Stuttgart: Reclam, 1971. 285–99.

———. *Pop International: Eine kritische Analyse.* Frankfurt am Main: Athenäum, 1971.

———. "Fortschritt im Rückschritt: Zur politischen Polarisierung der westdeutschen Literatur seit 1961." *Deutsche Gegenwartsliteratur: Ausgangspositionen und aktuelle Entwicklungen.* Stuttgart: Reclam, 1981. 299–313.

Hoesterey, Ingeborg. *Verschlungene Schriftzeichen: Intertextualität von Literatur und Kunst in der Moderne/ Postmoderne.* Frankfurt am Main: Athenäum, 1988.

———. "Postmoderner Blick auf österreichische Literatur: Bernhard, Glaser, Handke, Jelinek, Roth." *Modern Austrian Literature,* 23.3–4 (1990): 66–75.

———. "A Feminist 'Theater of Cruelty': Surrealist and Mannerist Strategies in *Krankheit oder Moderne Frauen* and *Lust.*" In *Elfriede Jelinek: Framed by Language.* Ed. Jorum B. Johns and Katherine Arens. Riverside, CA: Ariadne P, 1995. 151–65.

Hoffmeister, Werner. "On the Reception and Dismantling of American Myths in Contemporary German Literature." In *Amerika! New Images in German Literature.* Ed. Heinz D. Osterle. New York: Peter Lang, 1989. 83–101.

Holthoff, Marc. "Die Hopper-Methode: Vom 'narrativen' zum 'abstrakten' Realismus." *Edward Hopper, 1882–1967.* Frankfurt am Main: Schirn Kunsthalle, 1993. 19–27.

Hutcheon, Linda. *The Poetics of Postmodernism: History, Theory, Fiction.* New York: Routledge, 1988.

Huyssen, Andreas. *After the Great Divide: Modernism, Mass Culture, Postmodernism.* Bloomington: Indiana UP, 1987.

———. *Twilight Memories: Marking Time in a Culture of Amnesia.* New York: Routledge, 1995.

Huyssen, Andreas, and Klaus Scherpe, eds. *Postmoderne: Zeichen kulturellen Wandels.* Hamburg: Rowohlt, 1986.

Iden, Peter. "Der Eindrucksmacher: Rainer Werner Fassbinder und das Theater." In *Rainer Werner Fassbinder.* Peter Iden et al. Munich: Hanser, 1974. 17–28.

Jacobsen, Wolfgang, et al. *Herbert Achternbusch.* Munich: Hanser, 1984.

Jacobsen, Wolfgang, Anton Kaes, and Hans Helmut Prinzler, eds. *Geschichte des deutschen Films.* Stuttgart and Weimar: Metzler, 1993.

Jameson, Fredric. "Imaginary and Symbolic in Lacan: Marxism, Psychoanalytic Criticism, and the Problem of the Subject." *Yale French Studies* 55–56 (1978): 338–95.

———. "'In the Destructive Element Immerse': Hans-Jürgen Syberberg and Cultural Revolution." *October* 17 (1981): 99–118.

———. *Postmodernism, or, The Cultural Logic of Late Capitalism.* Durham: Duke UP, 1991.

Jelinek, Elfriede. "die endlose unschuldigkeit." In *Trivialmythen.* Ed. Renate Matthei. Frankfurt am Main: März, 1970. 40–66.

———. *wir sind lockvögel, baby.* Reinbek: Rowohlt, 1970.

———. *Michael: Ein Jugendbuch für die Infantilgesellschaft.* Reinbek: Rowohlt, 1972.

———. *Die Ausgesperrten.* Reinbek: Rowohlt, 1985.

———. *Die Klavierspielerin.* Reinbek: Rowohlt, 1986.

———. "Ich möchte seicht sein." In *Gegen den schönen Schein: Texte zu Elfriede Jelinek.* Ed. Christa Gürtler. Frankfurt am Main: Verlag Neue Kritik, 1990. 157–61.

Johnson, Uwe. *Jahrestage.* Frankfurt am Main: Suhrkamp, 1970ff.

Jung, Werner. "Vom Bedürfnis anders zu werden: Die USA in der deutschen Literatur der siebziger und achtziger Jahre." *Monatshefte* 81.3 (1989): 312–26.

Kaes, Anton. "Mass Culture and Modernity: Notes towards a Social History of Early American and German Cinema." In *America and the Germans: An Assessment of a Three-Hundred-Year History.* Ed. Frank Trommler and Joseph McVeigh. 2 vols. Philadelphia: U of Pennsylvania P, 1985. 2:317–31.

———. "Literary Intellectuals and the Cinema." *New German Critique* 40 (1987): 7–34.

———. *From "Hitler" to "Heimat": The Return of History as Film.* Cambridge, MA: Harvard UP, 1989.

———. "History and Film: Public Memory in the Age of Electronic Dissemination." In *Framing the Past: The Historiography of German Cinema and Television.* Ed.

Bruce A. Murray and Christopher J. Wickham. Carbondale: Southern Illinois UP, 1993. 308–23.

Kaplan, E. Ann, ed. *Postmodernism and its Discontents: Theories, Practices.* London and New York: Verso, 1988.

Karasek, Hellmuth. "Ohne zu verallgemeinern: Ein Gespräch mit Peter Handke." In *Über Peter Handke.* Ed. Michael Scharang. Frankfurt am Main: Suhrkamp, 1972. 85–90.

Karsunke, Yaak. *Kilroy und andere.* Berlin: Wagenbach, 1967.

Karsunke, Yaak. "anti-theatergeschichte: Die Anfänge." In *Rainer Werner Fassbinder.* Ed. Peter Iden et al. Munich: Hanser, 1974. 7–16.

Kater, Michael H. *Different Drummers: Jazz in the Culture of Nazi Germany.* New York: Oxfod UP, 1992.

Kearney, Richard. *The Wake of Imagination: Toward a Postmodern Culture* Minneapolis: U of Minnesota P, 1988.

Kellner, Douglas. "Critical Theory and the Culture Industries: A Reassessment." *Telos* 62 (1984–85): 196–205.

Kittler, Friedrich. "Das Alibi eines Schriftstellers: Peter Handkes *Die Angst des Tormanns beim Elfmeter.*" In *Das schnelle Altern der neuesten Literatur.* Ed. Jochen Hörisch and Hubert Winkels. Düsseldorf: Classen, 1985. 60–72.

———. *Grammophon, Film, Typewriter.* Berlin: Brinkmann and Bose, 1986.

Knight, Julia. "Female Misbehavior: The Cinema of Monika Treut." In *Women and Film: A Sight and Sound Reader.* Ed. Pam Cook and Philip Dodd. Philadelphia: Temple UP, 1993. 180–85.

Koch, Stephen. *Stargazer: The Life, World, and Films of Andy Warhol.* New York: Marion Boyars, 1991.

Koepnick, Lutz P. "Colonial Forestry: Sylvan Politics in Werner Herzog's *Aguirre* and *Fitzcarraldo.*" *New German Critique* 60 (1993): 133–59.

Kolker, Robert Philip. *The Altering Eye.* Oxford: Oxford UP, 1983.

Kosofsky Sedgwick, Eve. *Tendencies.* Durham: Duke UP, 1993.

Kracauer, Siegfried. *Theory of Film: The Redemption of Physical Reality.* New York: Oxford UP, 1965.

———. *Das Ornament der Masse.* Ed. Karsten Witte. Frankfurt am Main: Suhrkamp, 1977.

Kreuzer, Helmut. "Neue Subjektivität: Zur Literatur der siebziger Jahre in der Bundesrepublik Deutschland." In *Deutsche Gegenwartsliteratur: Ausgangspositionen und aktuelle Entwicklungen.* Ed. Manfred Durzak. Stuttgart: Klett, 1981. 77–106.

Kroes, Rob, and Maarten van Rossen, eds. *Anti-Americanism in Europe.* Amsterdam: Free UP, 1986.

Krutnik, Frank. *In a Lonely Street: Film Noir, Genre, Masculinity.* New York: Routledge, 1991.

Kuh, Katherine. *The Artist's Voice: Talks with Seventeen Artsits.* New York: Harper and Row, 1972.

Kuhn, Anna K. "Rainer Werner Fassbinder: The Alienated Vision." In *New German Filmmakers: From Oberhausen through the 1970s.* Ed. Klaus Phillips. New York: Ungar, 1984. 76–123.

Kurz, Paul Konrad. "Beat-Pop-Underground." *Über moderne Literatur: Standorte und Deutungen.* Frankfurt am Main: Knecht, 1971. 3:233–79.

Kuzniar, Alice. "Desiring Eyes." *Modern Fiction Studies* 36.3 (1990): 355–67.

———. "Comparative Gender: Rosa von Praunheim's and Monika Treut's Cross-Cultural Studies." *Spectator* 15 (1994): 51–59.

Laemmle, Peter. "Von der Außenwelt zur Innenwelt." In *Positionen im deutschen Roman der sechziger Jahre.* Ed. Heinz Ludwig Arnold et al. Munich: Text + Kritik, 1974. 147–70.

LaValley, Al. "The Gay Liberation of Rainer Werner Fassbinder: Male Subjectivity, Male Bodies, Male Lovers." *New German Critique* 63 (1994): 109–37.

———. "The Great Escape." In *Out in Culture: Gay, Lesbian, and Queer Essays on Popular Culture.* Ed. Corey K. Creekmur and Alexander Doty. Durham: Duke UP, 1995. 60–70.

Lehmann, Hans-Thies. "Lichtspiele: Die Angst der Kultur vor dem Kino." In *Das schnelle Altern der neuesten Literatur.* Ed. Jochen Hörisch and Hubert Winkels. Düsseldorf: Claase, 1985. 211–30.

———. "SCHRIFT/BILD/SCHNITT: Graphismus und die Erkundung der Sprachgrenzen bei Rolf Dieter Brinkmann." In *Rolf Dieter Brinkmann* (Literaturmagazin: Sonderheft 36). Ed. Maleen Brinkmann. Reinbek: Rowohlt, 1995. 182–97.

Lettau, Reinhard. *Täglicher Faschismus: Amerikanische Evidenz aus 6 Monaten.* Reinbek: Rowohlt, 1973.

Levin, Gail. "Edward Hopper: The Influence of Theater and Film." *Arts Magazine* 55 (1980): 123–27.

———. "Edward Hopper's 'Nighthawks.'" *Arts Magazine* 55.9 (1981): 154–65.

Levin, Kim. *Beyond Modernism: Essays on Art from the 70s and 80s.* New York: Harper and Row, 1988.

Linder, Christian. "Gespräch mit Peter Handke: Die Ausbeutung des Bewußtseins." *Schreiben und Leben.* Cologne: Kiepenheuer and Witsch, 1974. 33–45.

Lorenz, Dagmar C. G. "Humor bei zeitgenössischen Autorinnen." *Germanic Review* 62.1 (1987): 28–36.

Lüdke, W. Martin, ed. *Literatur und Studentenbewegung: Eine Zwischenbilanz.* Opladen: Westdeutscher Verlag, 1977.

Lützeler, Paul Michael, and Egon Schwarz, eds. *Deutsche Literaur in der Bundesrepublik seit 1965.* Königstein: Athenäum, 1980.

Lützeler, Paul Michael, ed. *Spätmoderne und Postmoderne: Beiträge zur deutschsprachigen Gegenwartsliteratur.* Frankfurt am Main: Fischer, 1991.

Maase, Kaspar. *BRAVO Amerika: Erkundungen zur Jugendkultur der Bundesrepublik in den fünfziger Jahren.* Hamburg: Junius, 1992.

———. *Grenzenloses Vergnügen: Der Aufstieg der Massenkultur, 1850–1970.* Frankfurt am Main: Fischer, 1997.

Mahoney, Dennis. "'What's Wrong with a Cowboy in Hamburg?': Narcissism as Cultural Imperialism in Wim Wenders' *The American Friend.*" *Journal of Evolutionary Psychology* 7 (1986): 106–16.

Mamaya, Christin J. *Pop Art and Consumer Culture: American Super Market.* Austin: U of Texas P, 1992.

Mauranges, Jean-Paul. "Peter Handke: Une écriture cinématographique? Une 'chronique' en trompe-l'oeil des événements courants." *Études Littéraires* 18.1 (1985): 35–52.

Mayer, Sigrid. "Im 'Western' nichts Neues? Zu den Modellen in *Der kurze Brief zum langen Abschied."* In *Handke: Ansätze, Analysen, Anmerkungen.* Ed. Manfred Jurgensen. Bern: Francke, 1979. 145–65.

Mayne, Judith. "Fassbinder and Spectatorship." *New German Critique* 12 (1974): 61–74.

McCormick, Richard. *Politics of the Self: Feminism and the Postmodern in West German Literature and Film.* Princeton: Princeton UP, 1991.

McGee, Celia. "Hopper, Hopper, Everywhere." *New York Times,* 24 July 1994, sec. 2:1+.

Mathy, Jean-Philippe. *Extrême-Occident: French Intellectuals and America.* Chicago: U of Chicago P, 1993.

Mekas, Jonas. "Notes after Reseeing the Movies of Andy Warhol." In *Andy Warhol: Film Factory.* Ed. Michael O'Prey. London: BFI, 1989. 28–41.

Melzer, Gerhard. "'Lebendigkeit: ein Blick genügt': Zur Phänomenologie des Schauens bei Peter Handke." In *Peter Handke: Die Arbeit am Glück.* Ed. Gerhard Melzer and Jale Tükel. Königstein: Athenäum, 1985. 126–54.

Metz, Christian. *The Imaginary Signifier: Psychoanalysis and the Cinema.* Bloomington: Indiana UP, 1982.

Modleski, Tania, ed. *Studies in Entertainment: Critical Approaches to Mass Culture.* Bloomington: Indiana UP, 1986.

———. "Femininity as Mas(s)querade: A Feminist Approach to Mass Culture." In *High Theory / Low Culture: Analyzing Popular Television and Film.* Ed. Colin MacCabe. New York: St. Martin's Press, 1986. 37–52.

Moeller, Hans-Bernhard. "Brecht and "Epic Film" Medium: The Cineast, Playwright, Film Theoretician and His Influence." *Wide Angle* 4.3 (1980): 3–11.

Morshäuser, Bodo. "Neulich, als das Hakenkreuz keine Bedeutung hatte: Der Achtzigerjahrespaß und der Ernst der Neunziger." *Kursbuch* 113 (1993): 41–53.

Müller, Heiner. "Reflections on Post-Modernism." Trans. Jack Zipes with Betty Nance Weber. *New German Critique* 16 (1979): 55–57.

———. "I Am Neither a Dope—Nor a Hope—Dealer." In *Hamletmachine and Other Texts for the Stage.* Ed. and trans. Carl Weber. New York: PAJ Publications, 1984. 137–140.

Mueller, Roswitha. *Bertolt Brecht and the Theory of Media.* Lincoln: U of Nebraska P, 1989.

Nägele, Rainer. "Die vermittelte Welt." *Jahrbuch der deutschen Schillergesellschaft* 19 (1975): 389–418.

———. "Amerika als Fiktion und Wirklichkeit in Peter Handkes Roman *Der kurze Brief zum langen Abschied."* In *Die USA und Deutschland: Wechselseitige Spiegelungen in der Literatur der Gegenwart.* Ed. Wolfgang Paulsen. Bern: Francke, 1979. 110–15.

———. "Geschichten und Geschichte: Reflexionen zum westdeutschen Roman seit 1965." In *Deutsche Gegenwartsliteratur: Ausgangspositionen und aktuelle Entwicklungen.* Ed. Manfred Durzak. Stuttgart: Reclam, 1981. 234–51.

Nägele, Rainer, and Renate Voris. *Peter Handke.* Munich: Beck, 1978.

O'Prey, Michael, ed. *Andy Warhol: Film Factory.* London: BFI, 1989.

Osterle, Heinz D. *Bilder von Amerika: Gespräche mit deutschen Schriftstellern.* Fulda: Fuldaer Verlagsanstalt, 1987.

———., ed. *Amerika! New Images in German Literature.* New York: Peter Lang, 1989.

Owens, Craig. "The Allegorical Impulse: Toward a Theory of Postmodernism (Part 2)." *October* 13 (1980): 59–80.

Paglia, Camille. *Vamps and Tramps: New Essays.* New York: Vintage, 1994.

Paulsen, Wolfgang, ed. *Die USA und Deutschland: Wechselseitige Spiegelungen in der Literatur der Gegenwart.* Bern: Francke, 1976.

Payne, Robert. "New German Cinema / Old Hollwood Genres." *Critical Studies* (School of Cinema-Television, USC) 5.1 (1985): 8–11.

Percy, Walker. *The Moviegoer.* New York: Avon, 1961.

Petit, Catherine, Philippe Dubois, and Claudine Delvaux. *Les voyages de Wim Wenders.* Crisnée: Edition Yellow Now, 1985.

Phillips, Klaus, ed. *New German Filmmakers: From Oberhausen through the 1970s.* New York, Ungar, 1984.

Piwitt, Herman Peter, and Peter Rühmkorf, eds. *Das Vergehen von Hören und Sehen: Aspekte der Kulturvernichtung (Literaturmagazin 5).* Reinbek: Rowohlt, 1976.

Petro, Patrice. "Mass Culture and the Feminine: The 'Place' of Television in Film Studies." *Cinema Journal* 25.3 (1986): 5–21.

———. *Joyless Streets: Women and Melodramatic Representation in Weimar Germany.* Princeton: Princeton UP, 1989.

Peucker, Brigitte. "Literature and Writing in the Films of Werner Herzog." In *The Films of Werner Herzog: Between Mirage and History.* Ed. Timothy Corrigan. New York and London: Methuen, 1986. 105–17.

———. "High Passion, Low Art: Fassbinder's Narrative Strategies." In *Ambiguities in Literature and Film.* Ed. Hans Braendlin. Tallahassee: Florida State UP, 1988. 65–75.

———. *Incorporating Images: Film and the Rival Arts.* Princeton: Princeton UP, 1995.

Pizer, John. "Modern vs. Postmodern Satires: Karl Kraus and Elfriede Jelinek." *Monatshefte* 86.4 (1994): 500–513.

Platschek, Hans. "Schüsse in Hornberg oder Der Streit um die Avantgarde." In *Stichworte zur "Geistigen Situation der Zeit,"* vol. 2: *Politik und Kultur.* Ed. Jürgen Habermas. Frankfurt am Main: Suhrkamp, 1979. 615–35.

Polster, Bernd. *"Swing Heil": Jazz im Nationalsozialismus.* Berlin: Transit, 1984.

Pommerin, Reiner, ed. *The American Impact of Postwar Germany.* Providence and Oxford: Berghahn, 1995.

Radcliff-Umstead, Douglas. "Wenders: The Filmic Language of Loss." In *National Traditions in Motion Picture.* Ed. Douglas Radcliff-Umstead. Kent: Kent State UP, 1985. 92–100.

Rainer, Ulrike. "The Grand Fraud 'Made in Austria': Economic Miracle, Existentialism, and Private Fascism in Elfriede Jelinek's *Die Ausgesperrten."* In *Elfriede Jelinek: Framed by Language.* Ed. Jorum B. Johns and Katherine Arens. Riverside, CA: Ariadne P, 1995. 176–93.

Rauh, Reinhold. *Wim Wenders und seine Filme.* Munich: Heyne, 1990.

Reitz, Edgar. *Liebe zum Kino: Utopien und Gedanken zum Autorenfilm, 1962–1983.* Cologne: Verlag Köln, 1985.

Renner, Rolf Günter. *Die postmoderne Konstellation: Theorie, Text und Kunst im Ausgang der Moderne.* Freiburg: Rombach, 1988.

Rentschler, Eric. *West German Film in the Course of Time: Reflections on the Twenty Years since Oberhausen.* Bedford Hills, NY: Redgrave, 1984.

———. "Herbert Achternbusch: Celebrating the Power of Creation." In *New German*

Filmmakers: From Oberhausen through the 1970s. Ed. Klaus Phillips. New York: Ungar, 1984. 1–19.

———. "How American Is It? The U.S. as Image and Imaginary in German Film." *Persistence of Vision* 2 (Fall 1985): 5–18.

———, ed. *West German Filmmakers on Film: Visions and Voices.* New York: Holmes and Meier, 1988.

———. "Film der achtziger Jahre." In *Geschichte des deutschen Films.* Ed. Wolfgang Jacobsen, Anton Kaes and Hans Helmut Prinzler. Stuttgart and Weimar: Metzler, 1993. 285–322.

———. *The Ministry of Illusion: Nazi Cinema and Its Afterlife.* Cambridge: Harvard UP, 1996.

Rich, B. Ruby. "Homo Pomo: The New Queer Cinema." In *Women and Film: A Sight and Sound Reader.* Ed. Pam Cook and Philip Dodd. Philadelphia: Temple UP, 1993. 164–74.

Rick, Karin, and Sylvia Treudl, eds. *Frauen-Gewalt-Pornographie.* Vienna: Wiener Frauenverlag, 1989.

Ritter, Alexander, ed. *Deutschlands literarisches Amerikabild.* Hildesheim: Olms, 1977.

Ritter, Roman. "Die 'Neue Innerlichkeit'—von innen und außen betrachtet." *Kontext* 1 (1976): 238–57.

Roscher, Achim. "Gespräch mit Elfriede Jelinek." *Neue deutsche Literatur* 39.3 (1991): 41–56.

Ross, Andrew. *No Respect: Intellectuals and Popular Culture.* London and New York: Routledge, 1989.

Rutschky, Michael. *Erfahrungshunger: Ein Essay über die siebziger Jahre.* Cologne: Kiepenheuer and Witsch, 1981.

Santner, Eric L. *Stranded Objects: Mourning, Memory, and Film in Postwar Germany.* Ithaca and London: Cornell UP, 1990.

———. "The Trouble with Hitler: Postwar German Aesthetics and the Legacy of Fascism." *New German Critique* 57 (1992): 5–24.

Scherpe, Klaus R., and Hans-Ulrich Treichel. "Vom Überdruß leben: Sensibilität und Intellektualität als Ereignis bei Handke, Born und Strauß." *Monatshefte* 73 (1981): 187–206.

Schjedahl, Peter. "Hopperesque." In *The Hydrogen Jukebox: Selected Writings of Peter Schjedahl 1978–1990.* Ed. Malin Wilson. Berkeley: U of California P, 1991. 293–99.

Schmidt-Borenschlager, Sigrid. "Gewalt zeugt Gewalt zeugt Literatur . . . *wir sind lockvögel, baby* und andere frühe Prosa." *Gegen den schönen Schein: Texte zu Elfriede Jelinek.* Frankfurt am Main: Verlag Neue Kritik, 1990. 30–43.

Schmiedt, Helmut. "Peter Handke, Franz Beckenbauer, John Lennon und andere Künstler: Zum Verhältnis von Popularkultur und Gegenwartsliteratur." *Text + Kritik* 24–24a (1978): 87–114.

———. "No satisfaction oder Keiner weiß mehr: Rockmusik und Gegenwartsliteratur." *LiLi (Zeitschrift für Literaturwissenschaft und Linguistik)* 34 (1979): 11–25.

Schneider, Michael. "Das Innenleben des 'Grünen Handke.'" In *Über Peter Handke.* Ed. Michael Scharang. Frankfurt am Main: Suhrkamp, 1972. 95–100.

———. "Von der alten Radikalität zur neuen Sensibilität." *Kursbuch* 49 (1977): 174–87.

———. *Den Kopf verkehrt aufgesetzt—oder die melancholische Linke: Aspekte des Kulturverfalls in den siebziger Jahren.* Darmstadt: Luchterhand, 1981.

Schultz, Karla Lydia. "A Conversation with Hans Magnus Enzensberger." *Northwest Review* 21.1 (1983): 145–46.

———. "'Think: You Could Become an American . . .': Three Contemporary German Poets Respond to America." *Yearbook of German-American Studies* 23 (1988): 153–63.

Schwarzer, Alice, ed. *PorNo: Opfer und Täter, Gegenwehr und Backlash, Verantwortung und Gesetz.* Cologne: Kiepenheuer and Witsch, 1994.

Sebald, W. G., ed. *A Radical Stage: Theatre in Germany in the 1970s and 1980s.* New York: Berg, 1988.

Seeba, Hinrich. "Persönliches Engagement: Zur Autorenpoetik der siebziger Jahre." *Monatshefte* 73 (1981): 281–98.

Shadoian, Jack. *Dreams and Dead Ends: The American Gangster / Crime Film.* Cambridge: MIT P, 1977.

Sieg, Katrin. "Ethnic Drag and National Identity: Multicultural Crises, Crossings, and Interventions." In *The Imperialist Imagination: German Colonialism and Its Legacy.* Ed. Sara Friedrichsmeyer, Sara Lennox, and Susanne Zantop. Ann Arbor: U of Michigan P, 1998. 295–319.

Sloterdijk, Peter. *Versprechen auf Deutsch: Rede über das eigene Land.* Frankfurt am Main: Suhrkamp, 1990.

Sontag, Susan. *Against Interpretation.* New York: Delta, 1961.

Späth, Sibylle. "Die Entmythologisierung des Alltags: Zu Rolf Dieter Brinkmanns lyrischer Konzeption einer befreiten Wahrnehmung." *Rolf Dieter Brinkmann.* Munich: Text + Kritik, 1981. 37–49.

———. *"Rettungsversuche aus dem Todesterritorium": Zur Aktualität der Lyrik Rolf Dieter Brinkmanns.* Frankfurt am Main: Peter Lang, 1986.

———. "Im Anfang war das Medium . . . : Medien- und Sprachkritik in Jelineks frühen Prosatexten." In *Elfriede Jelinek.* Ed. Kurt Bartsch and Günter Höfler. Graz: Droschl, 1991. 95–120.

Sparrow, Norbert. "'I Let the Audience Feel and Think': An Interview with Rainer Werner Fassbinder." *Cineaste* 8.2 (1977): 20–21.

Spitta, Silvia. *Between Two Waters: Narratives of Transculturation in Latin America.* Houston: Rice UP, 1995.

Stempel, Hans, and Martin Ripkens, eds. *Das Kino im Kopf.* Zurich: Arche, 1984.

Straayer, Chris. "Lesbian Narratives and Queer Characters in Monika Treut's *Virgin Machine.*" *Journal of Film and Video* 45.2–3 (1993): 24–39.

———. "The Seduction of Boundaries: Feminist Fluidity in Annie Sprinkle's Art/Education/Sex." In *Dirty Looks: Women, Pornography, Power.* Ed. Pamela Church Gibson and Roma Gibson. London: BFI, 1993. 156–75.

Strauß, Botho. *Die Widmung.* Munich: Deutscher Taschenbuch Verlag, 1980.

———. *Paare, Passanten.* Munich: Deutscher Taschenbuch Verlag, 1984.

———. "Anschwellender Bocksgesang." *Der Spiegel* 6 (1993): 202–7.

———. "Der eigentliche Skandal." *Der Spiegel* 16 (1994): 168–69.

Streese, Konstanze, and Kerry Shea. "Who's Looking? Who's Laughing? Of Multicultural Mothers and Men in Percy Adlon's *Bagdad Cafe.*" *Women in German Yearbook* 8 (1992): 179–97.

Struve, Ulrich. "'Denouncing the Pornographic Subject': The American and German Pornography Debate and Elfriede Jelinek's *Lust.*" In *Elfriede Jelinek: Framed by Language.* Ed. Jorun B. Johns and Katherine Arens. Riverside, CA: Ariadne P, 1995. 89–106.

Syberberg, Hans Jürgen. *Hitler, ein Film aus Deutschland.* Reinbek: Rowohlt, 1978.

———. *Vom Unglück und Glück der Kunst in Deutschland nach dem letzten Kriege.* Munich: Matthes and Seitz, 1990.

———. "Wie man neuen Haß züchtet: Eine Stellungnahme von Hans Jürgen Syberberg zu den Angriffen in dieser Zeitung." *Frankfurter Allgemeine Zeitung,* 6 September 1990, 36.

Tavel, Ronald. "The Banana Diary: The Story of Andy Warhol's *Harlot.*" In *Andy Warhol: Film Factory.* Ed. Michael O'Prey. London: BFI, 1989. 66–93.

Taylor, Paul, ed. *Post-Pop Art.* Cambridge, MA: MIT P, 1989.

Telotte, J. P. *Voices in the Dark: The Narrative Patterns of Film Noir.* Urbana: U of Illinois P, 1989.

Theweleit, Klaus. *Das Land, das Ausland heißt: Essays, Reden, Interviews zu Politik und Kunst.* Munich: Deutscher Taschenbuch Verlag, 1995.

Töteberg, Michael. "Das Theater der Grausamkeit als Lehrstück: Zwischen Brecht und Artaud—Die experimentellen Theatertexte Fassbinders." *Rainer Werner Fassbinder.* Munich: Text + Kritik, 1989. 20–34.

Tomlinson, John. *Cultural Imperialism.* Baltimore: Johns Hopkins UP, 1991.

Torgovnick, Marianna. *Gone Primitive: Savage Intellects, Modern Lives.* Chicago:U of Chicago P, 1990.

Treut, Monika. *Die grausame Frau: Zum Frauenbild bei de Sade und Sacher-Masoch.* Frankfurt am Main: Stroemfeld / Roter Stern, 1984.

———. "Die Zeremonie der blutenden Rose: Vorüberlegungen zu einem Filmprojekt." *Frauen und Film* 36 (1984): 35–43.

Trommler, Frank, and Joseph McVeigh, eds. *America and the Germans: An Assessment of a Three-Hundred-Year History.* 2 vols. Philadelphia: U of Pennsylvania P, 1985.

Vaßen, Florian. "Die zerfallende Stadt—Der 'zerfällende' Blick: Zu Rolf Dieter Brinkmanns Großstadtprosa *Rom, Blicke.*" *Juni: Magazin für Kultur und Politik* 5 (1991): 189–97.

Von Dirke, Sabine. "New German Wave: An Analysis of the Development of German Rock Music." *German Politics and Society* 18 (1989): 64–81.

Von Moltke, Johannes. "Camping in the Art Closet: The Politics of Camp and Nation in German Film." *New German Critique* 63 (1994): 77–106.

———. "Trapped in America: The Americanization of the *Trapp-Familie,* or 'Papas Kino' Revisited." *German Studies Review* 19.3 (1996): 455–78.

Wagnleitner, Reinhold. *Coca-Colonization and the Cold War: The Cultural Mission of the United States in Austria after the Second World War.* Trans. Diana M. Wolf. Chapel Hill: U of North Carolina P, 1994.

Waits, Tom. *Nighthawks at the Diner.* Elektra/Asylum Records, 1975.

Walser, Martin. "Über die Neueste Stimmung im Westen." *Kursbuch* 20 (1970): 19–41.

———. *Über Deutschland reden.* Frankfurt am Main: Suhrkamp, 1988.

Walsh, Martin. *The Brechtian Aspect of Radical Cinema.* Ed. Keith M. Griffiths. London: BFI, 1981.

Ward, J. A. *American Silences: The Realism of James Agee, Walker Evans, and Edward Hopper.* Baton Rouge and London: Louisiana State UP, 1986.

Warhol, Andy. *The Philosophy of Andy Warhol: From A to B and Back Again.* San Diego: Harcourt, 1977.

Warhol, Andy, and Pat Hackett. *POPism: The Warhol '60s.* San Diego: Harcourt, 1990.

Weisstein, Ulrich. "Literature and the Visual Arts." In *Interrelations of Literature.* Ed. Jean-Pierre Barricelli and Joseph Gibaldi. New York: MLA, 1982. 251–77.

Wenders, Wim. *Emotion Pictures: Essays und Filmkritiken.* Frankfurt am Main: Verlag der Autoren, 1986.

———. *Written in the West: Photographien aus dem amerikanischen Westen.* Munich: Schirmer/Mosel, 1987.

———. *Die Logik der Bilder: Essays und Gespräche.* Ed. Michael Töteberg. Frankfurt am Main: Verlag der Autoren, 1988.

———. *The Act of Seeing: Texte und Gespräche.* Frankfurt am Main: Verlag der Autoren, 1992.

Wenders, Wim, and Sam Shepard. *Paris, Texas.* Ed. Chris Sievernich. Greno: Road Movies, 1984.

Wickham, Christopher. "Heart and Hole: Achternbusch, Herzog, and the Concept of *Heimat.*" *Germanic Review* 64.3 (1989): 112–20.

Williams, Linda. *Hard Core: Power, Pleasure, and the "Frenzy of the Visible."* Berkeley: U of California P, 1989.

Willemen, Paul. "An Avant Garde for the Eighties." *Framework* 24 (1984): 53–73.

Willett, John. *Brecht in Context.* New York: Methuen, 1983.

Willett, Ralph. *The Americanization of Germany, 1945–1949.* London and New York: Routledge, 1989.

Williams, Linda. "A Provoking Agent: The Pornography and Performance Art of Annie Sprinkle." In *Dirty Looks: Women, Pornography, Power.* Ed. Pamela Church Gibson and Roma Gibson. London: BFI, 1993. 176–91.

Willis, Hollis. "Bad Behavior: An Interview with Monika Treut." *Visions* 7 (1992): 11–13.

Wissmann, Jürgen. "Pop Art oder die Realität als Kunstwerk." In *Die nicht mehr schönen Künste: Grenzphänomene des Ästhetischen.* Ed. Hans Robert Jauß. Munich: Fink, 1968. 507–30.

Wollen, Peter. "Raiding the Icebox." In *Andy Warhol: Film Factory.* Ed. Michael O'Prey. London: BFI, 1989. 14–27.

Wondratschek, Wolf. *Früher begann der Tag mit einer Schußwunde/ Ein Bauer zeugt mit einer Bäuerin einen Bauernjungen, der unbedingt Knecht werden will.* Zurich: Diogenes, 1980.

———. *Menschen, Orte, Fäuste: Reportagen und Stories.* Zurich: Diogenes, 1987.

———. *Die Gedichte.* Zurich: Diogenes, 1992.

Wright, Elizabeth. *Postmodern Brecht: A Re-Presentation.* New York: Routledge, 1989.

Zeller, Michael. *Aufbrüche—Abschiede: Studien zur deutschen Literatur seit 1968.* Stuttgart: Klett, 1979.

————. *Gedichte haben Zeit: Aufriss einer zeitgenössischen Poetik.* Stuttgart: Klett, 1982.

Zeyringer, Klaus. "'Das Elend des Vergleichens': Peter Handkes Beschäftigung mit dem Film—Theorie und Praxis." *Österreich in Geschichte und Literatur* 27.3 (1983): 148–57.

Zipes, Jack. "Die Freiheit trägt Handschellen im Land der Freiheit: Das Bild der vereinigten Staaten von Amerika in der Literatur der DDR." In *Amerika in der deutschen Literatur : Neue Welt—Nordamerika—USA.* Ed. Bauschinger, Sigrid, Horst Denkler, and Wilfried Malsch. Stuttgart: Kohlhammer, 1975. 329–52.

Index